MEDIA DISCOURSES:
Analysing Media Texts

Donald Matheson

OPEN UNIVERSITY PRESS

Open University Press
McGraw-Hill Education
McGraw-Hill House
Shoppenhangers Road
Maidenhead
Berkshire
England
SL6 2QL

email: enquiries@openup.co.uk
world wide web: www.openup.co.uk

and Two Penn Plaza, New York, NY 10121–2289, USA

First published 2005

A catalogue record of this book is available from the British Library

ISBN 0 335 21469 X (pb) 0 335 21470 3 (hb)

Library of Congress Cataloging-in-Publication Data
CIP data applied for

Typeset by RefineCatch Limited, Bungay, Suffolk
Printed in the UK by Bell & Bain Ltd, Glasgow

CONTENTS

SERIES EDITOR'S FOREWORD

To declare that 'we live in a media-saturated world' is to acknowledge the seemingly all-encompassing array of media discourses that lend shape to so many of our everyday experiences. Our very sense of ourselves as people – our cultural values, beliefs, identities and the like – is actively fashioned anew by our daily engagement with these discourses in a manner at once banal and profound. And yet so intimately embedded are we in this process that we seldom pause to recognize its pull or purchase, let alone call into question the typically subtle ways it works to define the nature of the realities around us.

Donald Matheson's *Media Discourses* boldly addresses this challenge to deconstruct the discursive mediation of our social world. In focusing on the key issues demanding our attention, two primary objectives inform the ensuing critique. The first is to clarify what can be understood by the elusive term 'discourse' by exploring the common ground among a variety of theoretical approaches to examining media language, images and symbolic forms. The second is to introduce readers to the extensive range of ideas, concepts and frameworks available to conduct specific investigations in practical ways. Accordingly, with these objectives in mind, Matheson proceeds to interrogate a diverse selection of media forms and practices, including advertisements, newspaper accounts, crime drama, television interviews, radio phone-in shows, sports reporting, popular magazines, and weblogs. In the course of the discussion, *Media Discourses* opens up discourse analysis as a methodology to readers new to the field, as well as to those seeking further depth or updates on recent developments. In so doing, it demonstrates how discourse analysis can further our understanding of the media in relation to debates about consumerism, the construction of celebrity, ethnic prejudice and participatory journalism, among other topical concerns.

The *Issues in Cultural and Media Studies* series aims to facilitate a diverse range of critical investigations into pressing questions considered to be central to current thinking and research. In light of the remarkable speed at which the conceptual agendas of cultural and media studies are changing, the series is committed to contributing to what is an ongoing process of re-evaluation and critique. Each of the books is intended to provide a lively, innovative and comprehensive introduction to a specific topical issue from a fresh perspective. The reader is offered a thorough grounding in the most salient debates indicative of the book's subject, as well as important insights into how new modes of enquiry may be established for future explorations. Taken as a whole, then, the series is designed to cover the core components of cultural and media studies courses in an imaginatively distinctive and engaging manner.

Stuart Allan

ACKNOWLEDGEMENTS

This book would have still been a vague plan in my mind without Stuart Allan, the *Issues in Cultural and Media Studies* series editor, who invited me to write for the series, and who gave me probably more encouragement and helpful criticism than he was hoping to have to give along the way. So my first and biggest thanks are to him. I've also been conscious as I wrote of the many conversations I had over the years with Debbie Cameron and Martin Montgomery at Strathclyde University, Glasgow. They sowed the seeds in my mind of most of the ideas worked through here. Thanks also to Sue Tait for helping excise some dodgy bits of Chapter 2 and to the members of the Christchurch Discourse Research Group who gave helpful feedback on a draft of Chapter 1. Finally, thanks to Tordis Flath for an excellent index.

With the publisher, I wish to thank the following publishers and individuals for permission to use copyright material in the book: Cambridge University Press for the corpus analysis image from http://www.cambridge.org/elt/; the *News of the World*, London, for the text, 'Fears on Sex Crime Boom'; Sony Computer Entertainment Australia for the image from the PlayStation® 2 'Mountain' ad; Tif Hunter for the Boddingtons ad image (and to Sue Allatt and Bartle Bogle Hegarty for their help); Lowe Worldwide and The Coca-Cola Company for images from the 'Must be a Diet Coke® thing' ad; Continuum International Publishing for the transitivity wheel illustration from Martin, J. R. and Rose, D. (2003) *Working with Discourse: Meaning beyond the Clause*; ACP for text and image from the *Cosmopolitan* Australia article on Jessica Simpson; Alison Jackson for the image from her book *Private*; Television New Zealand for the image from http://flipside.tvnz.co.nz; and Christopher Allbritton for image and text from http://www.back-to-iraq.com.

INTRODUCTION: THE BIG IDEAS ABOUT LANGUAGE, SOCIETY AND THE MEDIA

Since our way of seeing things is literally our way of living, the process of communication is in fact the process of community: the sharing of common meanings, and thence common activities and purposes; the offering, reception and comparison of new meanings, leading to tensions and achievements of growth and change.

(Williams 1961: 55)

We study the media – indeed, call that study 'media studies' or 'communication studies' – because of an assumption that television, newspapers, texting and other widely available communication forms play an important role in mediating society to itself. We assume that the shared world of a culture – what its members think is real, interesting, beautiful, moral and all the other meanings they attach to the world – is partly constructed by each member and partly by institutions such as newspapers or radio stations, and prevailing ideas. To use Raymond Williams' words quoted above, the ways of seeing each other which people find in a soap opera such as *EastEnders* are part of their ways of living, part of the shared meanings and purposes that make a particular culture.

Discourse analysis of the media allows us to describe and assess this sharing of meaning in close detail. It analyses which representations of the social world predominate. It analyses what kinds of interactions media texts set up between people and the world and between the powerful and the rest. And it analyses how meaning is made differently in different media texts, and therefore what different ways of seeing and thinking tend to be found there.

At the heart of the book is a concern with the power of media institutions that is established through their ways of using language. Bourdieu (1991) calls this the oracular power of dominant institutions in society:

> If I, Pierre Bourdieu, a single and isolated individual, speak only for myself, say 'you must do this or that, overthrow the government or refuse Pershing missiles', who will follow me? But if I am placed in statutory conditions such that I may appear as speaking 'in the name of the masses' . . . that changes everything.
>
> (cited in Webb et al. 2002: 14)

Thus, while on one level the meanings that are found in the media are shared, the power to make those shared meanings is not shared. The British Broadcasting Corporation (BBC), for example, has in 80 years established itself in the role of addressing the British as a nation together, something newspapers with their narrower demographics could never do. It is through that discursive power that the BBC is a site of national culture (Scannell 1992). Media professionals in general are able to write or speak in authoritative ways about the world, making claims to know what other people feel or what is really happening which few others in society could get away with. They do so to the extent that they draw on the authoritative discourses of journalism and other media practices.

Discourse analysts also propose that these kinds of powerful ideas do not precede particular media texts, but are made and renewed through each instance of language use. Each text is potentially important and valuable to study.

Media discourse analysis is not alone in making claims about the centrality of language in social life. There is a large and rapidly expanding body of research on discourse across the academic disciplines, which is drawn upon throughout the book. Discourse analysis is often an interdisciplinary activity, so that we find important analyses of media language tucked inside arguments about quite different problems. For example, van Dijk's (1988a) persuasive model of how the news works by calling up mental models arises partly out of a project on racism in society. This is both discourse analysis's strength – it allows us to study media discourse in ways that show the media's connection to other parts of social and cultural life – but it also makes discourse analysis sometimes appear a 'large and rather messy' hotchpotch (Cook 1992: 2). It's a common complaint from students that there isn't a straightforward and definitive textbook on media discourse that tells them what to do. Because of the diversity of approaches to discourse, such a book would be very hard to write, but this book does set out to guide media students and academics through some of those approaches, bringing together key arguments on different kinds of media text and showing how each is valuable in different ways in unpicking the workings of media discourse.

The structure of the rest of the book will be discussed in more detail at the end of this chapter, but let us look briefly at what discourse analysts have established as their theoretical common ground, by way of an introduction to this kind of study. The chapter will discuss in turn:

- how language is interconnected with thought and action
- the importance of studying language as something people do rather than as deep, immanent structure.

Language and social life

Uniting the diverse studies of discourse is the conviction that analysts cannot separate out people's thoughts and actions from the communicative means that they use to perform them. Language and human society are inextricable. The violence of war, the discursive psychologist, Michael Billig (2001) argues, is not what happens when talk has been exhausted, but is the direct result of language: 'It is no coincidence that the only species which possesses the ability of language (or what Pinker 1994, has called "the language instinct") is a species which engages in organized warfare. Utterance is necessary to kill and die for the honour of the group' (Billig 2001: 217). Almost all, if not all, discourse analysts would agree that there is no war without talk about war. Organized violence depends on language to organize it at every level, from conceiving of state-sanctioned violence to planning to giving orders, and it depends on language to justify it through philosophy, heroic stories and the construction of notions such as national honour and the dishonourable enemy.

This interest in language's central role in social life is what sets discourse analysis apart from formal linguistics. Once we've described the rules of phonology, grammar, syntax and the other systems that form the nuts and bolts of a language, we are still a long way from analysing it. As pioneers of **sociolinguistics** found when they began tape-recording people's conversations, these only rarely formed complete grammatical sentences but they could not be dismissed as disorganized. Language use is surrounded by many more rules or conventions and does much more than simply denote objects and actions. Once we extend language analysis beyond simple sentences, we are in a realm that linguistics is not well equipped to explain, and which involves sociology, anthropology, psychology, philosophy and further disciplines besides. The term 'discourse analysis' is used by researchers in this tradition rather than terms such as 'linguistic analysis' or 'textual analysis' to signal that language is being situated within these wider frameworks on the nature of thought, experience and society.

But how language fits into the human world, and therefore how we theorize discourse analysis, are the subject of a fair amount of dispute among these scholars. To take Billig's example, some discourse analysts would want to argue that much of our shared lives happens *through* language, and discourse analysis can therefore help us understand social practice – including anti-social practice such as war. Language for these scholars is part of social practice. Others argue that war can only happen because it is surrounded by and *structured* by statements of justification and glorification. Language, in this view, is a store of values and ideas about war, the site therefore of ideology. It has been studied by structuralist and poststructuralists not so much as part of everyday lived activity but more as a structure which shapes the way people can experience the world. The idea of language as a structure has tended to lead to an interest in how far language determines what they can think and experience, and we turn to that next, as it has been a key issue in media discourse analysis.

Does language determine thought?

There are many questions here, such as whether it is possible to think outside the bounds of language, or how babies think before they come into language, or how people can ever know what is outside of language when their knowledge happens inside language which, while fascinating, are beyond the book's scope. What is important here is that we acknowledge the range of theories about how far languages shape people and where these theories take us in thinking about the media. The strongest versions of 'linguistic determinism' are often structuralist, that is, they seek to map structures of language onto the structures by which our experiences are organized.

If French has one word, *mouton*, for the two English words *mutton* and *sheep*, if its system of language divides up the world differently to that of English, what does that mean for the two languages' speakers? This is often called the Sapir–Whorf hypothesis, after two linguistic anthropologists. They observed differences in the basic structures of North American languages, such as Hopi, to European languages and postulated that grammar, syntax, vocabulary and other structural features of a language might cause us to think in certain ways. They argued that Hopi speakers, for example, might see the world differently because their language does not have the distinction of past and present that a language such as English has. Fitch (2001) gives the example of the Japanese word, *amae*, which she translates roughly as 'the bittersweet love between a mother and her child': 'The fact that there is no direct translation into English would suggest, from the strong version of the Sapir/Whorf Hypothesis, that conceptions of relationships between mothers and their children are vastly different in Japan than in English-speaking countries' (Fitch 2001: 59). It's a fascinating scenario that people might live within different worlds, literally talking past each other. However, the theory in its strong form does not hold much water. We can, for instance, translate *amae* using more than one word, so it is not an idea unavailable to English speakers just because we don't have a single word for it. Moreover, as is discussed shortly, a language is not a simple, homogenous structure: it contains many ways of talking and many competing meanings; it borrows words from other languages or invents them; and it is always changing. **Ideology** – in the sense of fixed patterns of thought – isn't hard-wired into language.

But it's harder to refute the notion that certain patterns that we find in a language *shape* rather than determine what speakers can experience or think. Montgomery (1995: 223) suggests speakers can think outside conventional ways of using language but, when not consciously doing so, they tend to follow them. They will use gendered vocabulary such as 'waiter' and 'waitress', 'actor' and 'actress', unless they stop to think about the gender hierarchies that this vocabu-lary or **lexis** implies – that the male version is somehow the standard from which the female version differs. So analysis of structures of language such as its vocabulary is often used to gather evidence about relations of power or ideologies at the heart of the culture to which the language belongs. This thinking leads, in the influential **critical linguistics** school of analysis (Chapter 1), to the argument that journalists and other media workers can never evade the power structures which shape the vocabulary and other aspects of the way the language makes sense. Particularly in relation to the news, it has sought to show that there is a systematic ideological bias to the media that is traceable to the kind of language we find there. This is not analysis of the basic building blocks of language, but of the 'ruts in the road' that have been formed over time in language use because of the dominance of certain social interests.

So language is ideological, in this view, to the extent that it causes us to think in ways that support the interests of powerful groups. This tradition centres on Marx and Engel's statement in *The German Ideology* (1997–8; first published 1846) that, 'The ideas of the ruling class are in every epoch the ruling ideas, i.e. the class which is the ruling material force of society is at the same time its ruling intellectual force.' So language can be analysed in order to identify the limited set of representations of the world which surround members of a soci-ety, and thereby show the limits placed on consciousness by the unequal society they live in. Thus, it may cause women to speak in patriarchal terms or DJs to define good music as the latest releases from the big labels.

But how do dominant groups such as patriarchal males and capitalists pull this off, in order to maintain their unequal share of resources in society? And what happens when different dominant power structures, such as the patriarchy and capitalism just mentioned, collide? Debate over such questions has tended to lead to a more complex view of ideology, which takes us away from seeing culture as a product of social power structures, from which we can 'read off' an image of the power of the ruling classes, and towards seeing culture as a place where power is struggled over and a place with many corners, in each of which different groups are dominant. Thus, Gramsci talks of 'hegemonic' power as the ability of various groups to convince the rest of us in society that ways of thinking that are in their interests – that keep their unequal share of resources in a particular part of society – are right and proper.

Hegemony is about meaning, about struggles over whose ways of making sense of things dominate within an area of social life. Therefore language and other **symbolic systems** are central to power. As Fiske (1991: 347) puts it, 'the textual struggle for meaning is the precise equivalent of the social struggle for power'. When people speak, they want to be understood and want to understand when they produce or consume language. People therefore draw upon ways of making sense which they know are shared and have some force within the community in which they are talking. People align ourselves, then, with dominant structures of meaning, often with those which have become so firmly established that they have the status of common sense. This is a common observation about the media. Journalists, talkshow hosts, soap opera scriptwriters, among others, all seek to construe the world in ways that will make sense to the wider public, mixing together specialist voices and translating them into common knowledge. This is what gives the media their power as 'cultural workers' (Ericson et al. 1987: 17–18), but it is also what draws them into ideological structures. The seemingly apolitical, no-nonsense, common-sense view of 'everyone' (Brunsdon and Morley 1978) is more often than not the view of those with most power in society to impose their perspectives, and to make them appear natural and beyond dispute. Thus, things make most sense – they fit together most easily in language – if we tap into well-established ideological structures. It is thus important to think of ideologically loaded language not just as words spoken by dominant groups but as words we all use if we want to get on in society.

Take the example of a criminal court case about an alleged theft. We see the power of property holders in the language used – in the accusation that someone stole something, the defence to that charge and the sentencing – and in other symbols of power such as the judge's raised bench and the flag or coat of arms behind the bench, much more than in the physical force of the police or guards around the accused. The real power lies in the power to decide what makes sense here, what is normal, what is right. And when justice is *seen and heard* to be done it reminds not just the accused of its power to enforce certain ideas of right and wrong but also everyone else who is present at that use of language as well. It works to reassure those threatened by those who commit crime and it works to convince those who were unsure. This, as we will see in Chapter 1, is a form of power in which news media reporting of crime plays a major role.

Language speaks us

But where do these ideological structures come from, and precisely how is that power to define how things make sense reinforced in each court case or news story? The structuralist or semiotic tradition within media and cultural studies has been effective in critiquing the ideological work done in a culture's shared texts, but has been less successful in identifying the processes by which this happens. Barker and Galasiński argue that this is where contemporary critical discourse analysis is particularly useful:

> Though cultural studies has convincingly argued the philosophical case for the significance of language and has produced a large body of textual analysis, it is rarely able to show how, in a small-scale technical sense, the discursive construction of cultural forms is actually achieved . . . [C]ritical discourse analysis (CDA) is able to provide the understanding, skills and tools by which we can demonstrate the place of language in the construction, constitution and regulation of the social world.
>
> (2001: 1)

The point here is two-fold. Close analysis of language seeks to show precisely how a group of words carries a particular meaning, which we can then identify as performing a political role in reinforcing or challenging power. This is the analysis of representations. But it also seeks to show how language is located in human relationships, and therefore how it places us in relationship to hegemonic meanings. This is the analysis of language as social action. Hodge and Kress write:

> In order to sustain these structures of domination the dominant groups attempt to represent the world in forms that reflect their own interests, the interests of their power. But they also need to sustain the bonds of solidarity that are the condition of their dominance.
>
> (1988: 3)

Discourse analysis thus builds most successfully on the tradition of textual analysis when it draws upon its sociological, anthropological and philosophical heritage by looking at how people use language to make sense of things and get things done in daily interaction. These fields' emphases on language as the process rather than the product of society and culture take them beyond the question of whether language determines thought and experience. For in this **phenomenological** view, language doesn't determine experience: it is a kind of experience. In the philosopher Martin Heidegger's terms (1971: 192), we take shape as people living in a particular world when we use language: 'it is language that first brings man about, brings him into existence' (cited in Robinson 1997). When we speak, language speaks, and when it speaks us, we become who we are. What does this mean, and how does it take us in a different direction to the structuralist thinking discussed above?

The first point to make is that consciousness and human experience are better regarded not as attributes of individuals, but as socially shared. We think of ourselves as individuals, because we live within an individualistic culture which values how we differ from each other. But as the sociologist Karl Mannheim (1936) has said, 'strictly speaking, it is incorrect to say that the single individual thinks. Rather it is more correct to insist that the individual participates in thinking further what others have thought before' (cited in Shoemaker and Reese 1996: 105). If this is true of thought, it is most certainly true of language. We participate in language sometimes as individuals and sometimes as representatives of groups, but we participate in historically evolved and sedimented processes of communication through language.

There are two important ideas here. The first is that language depends on people actively doing something, that is, actively participating in it. **Ethnomethodologists** and other sociologists of everyday activity regard people as agents in their own destiny, and hence see the world, particularly today's information-rich environment, as 'vastly meaningful, providing seemingly endless resources and sites for constructing agency' (Gubrium and Holstein 1995: 565). But at the same time, language isn't ours in a personal sense, but belongs on the same level as our identities, relationships and activities in the outside world. We enter the social world by drawing on the resources of language. This is partly what Heidegger means. Wittgenstein (1953: #257) makes a similar point: a private language would make no sense, because naming something is an act we need a listener for, who accepts the act, in order for us to accomplish it.

Bakhtin and Vološinov[1] describe this participation in social life through language as a 'dialogic' process. That is, by talking, people enter into dialogue with past writers or speakers, whose words they are borrowing or disagreeing with, into dialogue with potential readers and into dialogue with many others who have some claim to the kind of ideas and language they are drawing on. That makes a word a crowded space, and Bakhtin (1981) speaks of the struggle people engage in to make their own meanings out of these already spoken and spoken-for words and styles and intonations:

The word in language is always half someone else's. It becomes one's own only when the speaker populates it with their own intentions, their own accent, when they appropriate the word, adapting it to their own semantic and expressive intention. Prior to this moment of appropriation the word does not exist in a neutral and impersonal language (it is not, after all, out of a dictionary, that the speaker gets their words), but rather it exists in other people's mouths, in other people's concrete contexts, serving other people's intentions: it is from there that one must take the word, and make it one's own.

(Bakhtin 1981: 293; cited in Maybin 2001: 67)

To put it another way, as Maybin quotes Dennis Potter, 'The trouble with words is that you don't know whose mouth they've been in' (Maybin 2001: 68). This approach to analysing language use immediately provides us with an image of the ideological struggle over meaning at work in and between individual texts. The individual text gets its meaning not from something else that structures it but from its **intertextual** references to all the other texts which precede or surround it. Becker (1983: 8) writes that, 'The real *a prioris* of language are not underlying structures, but prior language, prior texts' (cited in Swales 1990: 86; see also Vološinov 1986: 85). Ericson et al.'s point, quoted above, that the media translate specialist knowledge into common knowledge and thereby reproduce ideologies, can be seen afresh: news discourse's ideological power lies in the way it 'weaves together representations of the speech and writing of complex ranges of voices into a web which imposes order and interpretation upon them' (Fairclough 1995: 77).

Ideology and discourse

This brings us to Michel Foucault's understanding of **discourse**. Foucault (e.g. 1989; 1991) has influentially argued that we should not study texts as documents that are *about* something else but as discourse that is *part* of a network of relations of power and identity. Texts aren't to be interpreted, to be puzzled over like crosswords or Bible passages, within which some deep meaning is hidden, but should be studied as part of the ongoing oppression, prejudice, struggle to gain power by knowledge and so on in society, all the things that people engage in through these texts.

These two approaches may seem similar but lead to different analyses. Take a racist headline:

CUBANS IN A LINK WITH RIOT ESTATE

which 'exposes' the visit of some Cuban women to a London housing estate some time before street violence by young black people in Tottenham (*Daily Mail*, 15 October 1985, analysed further in van Dijk 1991). We can perceive a deep structure of prejudice at work here, a structure in which linking Cubans and subsequent riots makes perfect and immediate sense. This structure is what Barthes would call a 'mythology' (see Chandler 1995a) about Cubans, which makes sense of them as decidedly foreign to the British way of life and as therefore likely causes of disturbances. That structure obscures other explanatory structures for the subsequent violence such as poverty, unemployment and racism. Such an approach is an avowedly interpretative exercise, in which we look for traces of an invisible structure in the surface text.

Alternatively, as this book does, we might study how, over a number of texts, those written about in a certain way – for example, those labelled as Cubans – tend to be made sense of in similar ways – in this case, associated with violence – each text reinforcing and thus making the others more meaningful. This is an exercise in tracing prejudice in action in the patterns and linkages between texts. The two approaches are quite different in method: one presumes the prejudiced ideology exists and the other that discourse acts in prejudicial ways. Foucault's argument is that the deeper level of codes and ideologies is an abstraction, sometimes a valuable one, invented by analysts to make sense of how people gain power over each other by prejudging them in negative ways. He directs us away from what we might call 'ideology hunting', using our critical interpretative resources to look for the hidden messages in texts. Instead, he directs us towards finding patterns, series, hierarchies in language that position people within certain roles and ways of thinking.

Does this, however, imply that we should abandon the term ideology in favour of discourse? Some scholars, like Foucault, find ideology an unwieldy term that tends to direct us to broad and already given categories of ideas such as patriarchy and capitalism. McKee writes:

> using the concept of 'ideology' as our articulation between culture and politics tends to flatten out culture so that every text is 'political' in the same way. I don't think that *Doctor Who* and *The West Wing are* political in the same way; *Xena* and *The Panel* aren't 'political' in the same, structural sense.
>
> (McKee 2003)

Potter (2001) draws on Wittgenstein to make a similar point. When we use language we are using a 'toolkit' of lots of different kinds of ways of talking and writing and participating in lots of different 'language games':

The picture is of language being composed of multitudes of different 'games' each with their own aims and rules – some big, some small. Wittgenstein lists things such as giving orders and obeying them; describing the appearance of an object; reporting an event; speculating about an event; making up a story and guessing riddles (1953: #23) . . . This metaphor can be used to support the widespread discourse analytic assumption that people's practices are organized around the use of particular discourses or interpretative repertoires. It cautions against the goal of providing an overall coherent account of language as an abstract system and focuses instead on specific practices tied to occasions and settings.

(Potter 2001: 41)

Discourse analysis is a more fine-grained tool that allows us to see how ideas emerge differently in different contexts. You will find the term 'discourse' used much more than 'ideology' in this book for that reason. MacDonald (2003) calls her analysis of the contemporary media *Exploring Media Discourse* because 'discourse' helps her to focus both on how ways of thinking intersect and accumulate to form media and other cultural practices and on how individuals inhabit different sets of ideas or versions of reality at different times (so that women may be readers of *Cosmopolitan* at the same time as they reject the male gaze at work). However, she still finds ideology a necessary term precisely because it brings us back to the political, to the struggles between political movements and 'isms' in which critics are participating by critiquing the media. If we recognize and respond to *EastEnders* in our daily viewing as a middle-class view of the working classes always shouting at each other, then it makes sense still to talk of a bourgeois ideology.

It is not helpful to get bogged down in arguments about whether social life can be explained in whole by discourse, or by some other category. Harvey (1996) argues that any 'moment' of critique, whether it is power, discourse, social relations, material practices, institutions/rituals or beliefs/values/desires, 'internalizes in some sense everything that occurs in other moments' (cited in Chouliaraki and Fairclough 1999: 28). We are only able to see what the tools of our analysis let us see, and these fill our horizon. However, it is useful to recognize that terms such as ideology and discourse are not easy to mix in the same argument. Ideological critique tends to assume a stable structure of ideological meanings, while discourse does not.

The discourse of this book

This book sets out to introduce a range of viewpoints. As Harvey's notion of different moments of critique suggests, analysis is probably best when it recognizes that there are multiple valid ways to approach the study of social and cultural life, and that any one approach we choose gives just one set of answers. Many discourse analysts have taken such an approach, arguing that academic knowledge is itself discursive, constructing just one – though hopefully an insightful – knowledge of its material, and that it therefore makes sense to try to draw on more than one perspective. I use the pronoun 'we' throughout the book in an intertwined sense of 'we' researchers and 'we' participants in the media version of culture for this reason. The responses to the media of a discourse analyst are both those of someone trying to observe patterns and systems beyond a personal response and interest and those of someone who lives within the same culture and draws on the same language resources. When I write 'we' or 'us', then, I mean something of both senses of the pronoun. The book does, however, emphasize the value of critical knowledge. I would agree with Coupland and Jaworski (2001b: 134) that, 'The most incisive approaches to discourse are those that combine the detailed analysis of language, in particular instances of its use, with the analysis of social structure and cultural practice.' These approaches, certainly in the analysis of media texts, often come under the heading of **critical discourse analysis**, because it is the work of scholars who seek not just to understand how language works in society, but in whose interests and with what effects on the world that is constructed in language.

That thinking informs this book's structure. Each chapter looks at one of the major critical approaches to media discourse, and then uses it to address key questions on one particular media **genre**. That should not be taken as directing readers to think about the approach as only applicable to that genre. Intertextual analysis, for example, is well suited to specifying how advertisements draw upon and help shape life in a consumerist world, but it is equally well suited to analysing the power of newspaper headlines or the construction of identity in lifestyle magazines. The further reading at the end of each chapter includes further reading on the approach, but also flags up important discursive analyses of the chapter's genre which draw on other ways of thinking about discourse. Key terms and concepts, which are gathered together in the glossary, are marked in bold on their first mention in the text.

Overview of the book

Chapter 1 begins with the analysis of vocabulary or lexis and how it builds up meaning which operates in particular political and cultural interests. It looks at news language in order to do this, and in particular at crime news. It ends with a case study of a *News of the World* article on sexual abuse, which suggests the conventional nature of the news vocabulary but also the rhetorical power of media texts to deploy those conventions in ways which sell papers.

Chapter 2 is about intertextual analysis, using advertising as its object of study to explore the way texts draw on prior texts. It is particularly concerned with the way media forms insert themselves into culture through their intertexts as they struggle for competitive advantage, using a Diet Coke® ad to explore some of the ways that ads textually position themselves in this case as the drink of young women who are in control of their lives.

Chapter 3 analyses the discourse of consumer magazines for both men and women using **transitivity** analysis. It shows how, in the detail of who is represented in the processes of individual clauses, consumerist and rigidly gendered identity positions are mapped out for men and women readers. The analysis is applied in a case study comparing interviews from *FHM* and *Cosmopolitan*.

Chapter 4 discusses the role of narrative in discourse, showing how this powerful way of making sense of the world inter-relates with other forms of **coherence**. It uses an excerpt from the TV police show, *The Bill*, to explore the political implications of how texts do or do not hang together as stories.

Chapter 5 explores the discourse analysis of the visual through a discussion of the visual dimension of reality television. Starting from an argument that reality television is much more about watching people being watched than about watching stories, it then uses visual discourse analysis to unravel aspects of the **hyper-reality** of contemporary television. The reality TV satire, *Double Take*, a satire almost without words, is used as a case study.

Chapter 6 discusses **conversation analysis**, the study of the minutiae of unfolding talk, in order to explore the distribution of power in broadcast interviews, both television and radio. It uses an excerpt from a 'shock-jock' radio show to argue that such shows both depend on a myth to embody real people's talk and enact the exercise of power over those people.

Chapter 7, drawing largely on broadcast sports commentary, uses a theory of **social cognition** to show that, despite years of campaigning, ethnic prejudice is still deeply embedded in sports talk. The analysis is deployed in a case study of commentary on the 1998 World Cup Spain v. Nigeria football match.

Chapter 8 analyses discourse found on the Internet in terms of its **interactivity**. The chapter uses discourse analytic thinking on how language sets up relationships between people to explore the question of just how different these so-called 'new media' are. It argues in particular that the relationships between the reporter and the public of print and broadcast journalism are being renegotiated online. The discussion is focused on weblogs, and the chapter's case study is the 'blog' of a freelance American journalist in Iraq.

Further reading

There are a number of good readers on discourse analysis. These include Jaworski and Coupland (1999) and Wetherell et al. (2001). Cameron's textbook (2001) is a good introduction to analysis of spoken discourse, particularly on how to do such analysis, while the second chapter of Barker and Galasiński (2001) gives a clear overview of the relationship between the study of language and cultural theory. MacDonald (2003) gives a clear discussion of Foucault's theory of discourse in relation to media discourse. Gumperz and Levinson (1996) have gathered together a range of perspectives on the Sapir–Whorf hypothesis.

1 | NEWS AND THE SOCIAL LIFE OF WORDS

Quite simply, the vocabulary of a language, or a variety of a language, amounts to a map of the objects, concepts, processes and relationships about which the culture needs to communicate.

(Fowler 1991: 80)

Introduction

This chapter argues that the news does not simply reflect the world as if it were a mirror, as journalists often claim. But it also argues that the news does not simply construct a picture of the real either, as critics since Lippmann (1922) have suggested. Instead, the discourse analytic perspective introduced in the Introduction proposes that news makes sense within a social context: if it acts at all as a mirror, it reflects preoccupations within that society, and when it constructs a picture of the world, that picture is often very close to what members of that society already know. The key point, which the chapter will develop, is that the meaning of the news is about the act of deploying shared interpretative resources, and the job of close analysis of news texts is to analyse how those resources are being deployed.

So when an inquest was held into the death of a woman and her adult son in a rich neighbourhood of Christchurch, New Zealand, the local paper wrote:

STARVING MOTHER SHUNNED HELP

Man was dead for two months in mum's bed

> An elderly Christchurch woman who starved to death in her Fendalton home shunned offers of help even as her son lay dead in her bed.
>
> For two months, [JR], 75, lived with the decomposing body of her 43-year-old son, [TR], in her bedroom.
>
> [story continues]

> (*Christchurch Press* 23 July 2004: 1)

The prominence given to the story (on page 1) and the dramatic language (the juxtaposition of 'man' and 'mum's bed', the phrase 'decomposing body') are producing a version of the event that is much more than a mirror. This is a mirror with an interest in certain kinds of death. Yet, on the other hand, the newspaper did not invent the idea of elderly women as helpless or of the intensity of mothers' love for their sons, nor did it create the fear of dying alone or of the loneliness of life in suburban western society. Instead the reporters and sub-editors responsible for the text drew upon a social reality and shared ways of expressing that shared lifeworld, in the process giving further life to what it reproduced – re-emphasizing social roles, feeding fears. Indeed, the news can only appear as a reflection of society, and can only make sense, if it adheres to a set of social norms and principles of discourse. If the *Press*'s sub-editors, whose job it is to devise the headlines, had written something like

ONLY GOD KNEW GRIEF OF LONELY MOTHER

the story would have appeared to a contemporary secular society as overly pious, sententious and therefore non-factual. It would, in other words, have risked undermining the news story's claim to be factual information.

The journalist sitting down at the computer to write a news story does not therefore simply face a blank screen on which to construct a world or record a faithful record, but a space that we can imagine as already filled with conventions. There are two types of convention that are discussed below. There are journalistic conventions about such things as how a text should begin and end, what readers are thought to be interested in, what they should know and when a news story can claim something is true. And there are wider social conventions, which the news depends on and which it sometimes helps shape, about such things as what people are like, what words mean, what is natural and common-sensical, who gets to speak in society and what is real. News discourse is therefore the result of the coming together of a variety of norms and principles and unstated assumptions. It is, as one newspaper editor puts it, a daily rhetorical achievement (Fuller 1996: 117). By analysing news language within the approach sketched above, this chapter proposes we can do a number of things at once: to uncover the social basis of the news, to explore the role of the news in perpetuating or challenging that social base, and to describe the power of the news to convince and even manipulate.

The chapter will focus upon just two aspects of news language, where these points can be made particularly clearly, although similar critiques could be made by applying many of the approaches to language explored in later chapters in relation to other forms of media discourse. The two aspects are both about the individual words used: the use of labels and the vocabulary of the news. Both have been well studied, and have been the basis for important findings on the social life of the news. They are also elements of news language which can be analysed without having first to introduce theories of language. But studying individual words also begins the book's movement towards such theories, and towards more complex discourse analysis, for both, as is discussed below, have been re-examined as new theories emerge on how language works. The chapter will make particular reference to crime news, again a well-studied aspect of news discourse, but there too the points made can be extended to other forms of news.

The strengths and weaknesses of a critical approach

News discourse analysis is often explicitly critical, and many of its techniques have developed with the aim of showing 'how [news] language contributes to inequality' (Fowler 1991). This has been a significant strength, providing the motivation to undermine simplistic statements within journalism about its impartiality, and linking description of language with critical theories of ideology and power. As van Dijk notes, American scholarship, operating with less deliberately critical agendas than European or Australian research, has historically tended to be anecdotal or to focus on examples of distortion and corporate control, often falling short of systemic critique (1985: 73). European critical media scholars, starting from Marxist theories of the nature of meaning, have argued since the 1970s that news language not only makes sense within conventions but within conventions that are in dominant groups' interests. Following Althusser, Hall (1980) talked of culture being 'structured in dominance', that is, of constructing meaning in ways which reinforced or propagated ideologies. The news, particularly crime news, was an important example for the argument because of its clearly conventional nature. Hall and colleagues at the Birmingham Centre for Contemporary Cultural Studies argued, on the back of a study of the rise of fear of mugging in the 1970s, that journalism is an essentially conservative practice, supporting the status quo, in the way it makes sense of the world (Hall et al. 1978).

A report on the conviction of a violent killer, for example, reminds us of our community's standards and society's power to prosecute such breaches, as in the following 'intro', or opening sentence, of a news article:

> A fairground worker obsessed with the violent cult film *A Clockwork Orange* who battered two of his girlfriends to death 13 years apart was sentenced to life in prison yesterday.
>
> (*Birmingham Post*, 11 December 2003: 9)

The news text becomes part of the legal process, enabling justice to be seen to be done, and therefore re-emphasizing both the legitimacy of the legal process and the illegitimacy of murder and physical abuse. In the process, critics have suggested, it performs a kind of ritual role for society in reminding us of what our values are and of the normal and well-adjusted lives that the rest of us lead (Katz 1987). Even when the initial crime is being reported, the labelling of it as a transgression against society's rules and the implied shock at that transgression bring the unsocial under the naming power of civil society.

Hall and his colleagues extend the point to the news in general. The news, concerned as it is with what is new or unexpected, is all about making sense of a problematic reality within a conservative consensus. At the heart of this theory of the news' position in society is the notion of 'cultural maps'. The argument is worth quoting at some length because it was influential in the way discourse analysts have also interpreted the news:

> An event only 'makes sense' if it can be located within a range of known social and cultural identifications. If newsmen [*sic*] did not have available – in a routine way – such cultural 'maps' of the social world, they could not 'make sense' for their audiences of the unusual, unexpected and unpredicted events which form the basic content of what is 'newsworthy'. Things are newsworthy because they represent the changefulness, the unpredictability and the conflictual nature of the world. But such events cannot be allowed to remain in the limbo of the 'random' – they must be brought within the horizon of the 'meaningful'. This bringing of events within the realm of meaning means, in essence, referring unusual and unexpected events to the 'maps of meaning' which already form the basis of cultural knowledge, into which the social world is *already* 'mapped'.
>
> (Hall et al. 1978: 54)

Thus, the news is not telling us something new, but reminding us of the resilience of already known structures of knowledge. Sociological analysis of newsrooms has also shown that the news is closely aligned to institutions such as the police or courts, waiting for them to turn a happening into a bureaucratic event (such as an arrest), before turning it into a story, and following their perspectives closely (Fishman 1980). This argument is perhaps a little overstated. Hallin (1987: 308) points out that cultural institutions do not always develop in ways which are functional for the dominant order, so media theory needs to be able to account for news reporting which helps destabilize the powerful, such as the American news media's belated attention to photographs of abuse of prisoners in occupied Iraq in May 2004 or German newspapers' investigations of corruption at the top of the governing Christian Democratic Union (CDU) in 2000. But critical theory is effective in accounting for much reporting.

Discourse analytic work has dovetailed with these arguments about the ideological effects of news conventions, as is discussed shortly. However, despite its strengths in linking analysis into systemic analysis of society and culture, analysis within this position is at risk of becoming blinkered. It can spend too much time hunting for ideological structures and miss some of the complexity of the news text. The critical linguistics approach introduced below often, in fact, has no other way of accounting for textual choices than ideology, because it studies texts in isolation. The *Birmingham Post* story above, for example, describes the convicted man as a 'fairground worker'. We might want to ask why he was labelled like this, rather than as mechanic, retail worker, father of two, or however else he might have been reasonably labelled. However, before we concluded that the newspaper chose a term that placed the man in the itinerant world of circuses and fairground workers, and therefore labelled him as not inhabiting a normal lifestyle, we would want to know, for example, whether the newspaper was able to print any further information about the man, or whether a court order or simply the limited information on the court papers forced it to use this term. As the chapter argues, it is important to see texts within their contexts, and particularly as language in action as part of social practice, rather than as stand-alone texts.

Choosing words

However, before we critique critical linguistics, the influential school of thought that emerged from the work of Fowler, Hodge, Kress, and Trew (see Further reading), the rich findings of that approach must be acknowledged. The approach was called critical linguistics because it drew on new forms of linguistics in the 1960s and 1970s that analysed language and grammar as they are used by people to achieve communicative purposes, rather than as an abstract system. In broad terms, they followed Halliday's (1994) **systemic functional linguistics** rather than Chomsky's **transformative generative grammar**. In particular, they applied a number of Halliday's insights, including the notion that language users choose from the limited range of options that a language provides to make and combine words. Hodge and Kress argued that close attention to the various choices made in a specific text ('freedom fighter' over 'guerrilla', in a classic example) could show how social forces were pushing the text one way or another. As Kress describes the method: 'At each point in the text choices are available to the speaker/writer . . . Why was this form chosen, rather than one of the other available ones? Why was this linguistic process applied and not these other possible ones?' (Kress 1983: 125; see also Hodge and Kress 1993). This becomes a methodological principle in a number of critiques: the choice of one form over another is always potentially meaningful in language use, as it marks the decision (whether consciously made or merely conventional) not to use a number of potential alternatives.

Lexical choice: fields and maps

One way to apply this principle is by looking at the range of possible vocabulary items that a reporter could have chosen, in order to critique the ones we find used – and particularly those used repeatedly – in the news. Linguists divide words and phrases into lexical items (that is, meaning words and phrases, such as 'eat', 'house', 'big business') and grammatical items (the little words, such as 'and', 'of' and 'as if'). The lexical choices will be particularly important in building the meaning of a text, as in the following example:[1]

CONSTABLE'S CAREER RUINED AFTER £10 THEFT

A policeman's career lies in ruins after he was convicted of stealing £10 from his sergeant's office at their Londonderry police station.
 It took a Belfast Crown Court jury just over two hours to unanimously convict 37-year-old Constable [RW] of stealing the money and to reject his claim that he was only 'borrowing' the cash.
 [story continues]
(*Belfast News Letter*, 13 May 2004: 5)

The headline writer chose 'ruined' from a range of possible terms in the 'lexical field' of words to describe the ending of the policeman's career: ended, finished, over, in tatters, ruined, wrecked, and so on. The reporter who wrote the rest of the text chose the very similar 'lies in ruins'. 'Ruined' lies at the strong end of the field of words, and it stands in stark contrast to the small size of the theft ('£10'). It also carries with it an implication that it was not the officer himself who ruined his career, an implication that would not have been available if the more unmotivated 'career ends' had been used. It is clearly language that indicates an attitude of sympathy towards the man, and indeed the text goes on to quote the man's defence lawyer using the same word. Following the analytical approach of Hodge and Kress (1993), we could see this choice of lexis as organized by a sympathy towards the police force in general, and in turn interpret that sympathy in terms of the ideological commitment of this historically Unionist newspaper to Protestant institutions in Northern Ireland more generally (the Northern Ireland police force has traditionally been strongly associated with Unionist, as opposed to Catholic, interests). The choice of 'office' rather than 'wallet' works in similar terms, reducing the scale of the theft and the culpability of the police officer. In that analysis, the article is a mundane restatement of sectarian ideology.

To be fair, this ideological lexis might better be called rhetoric at times. The choice of words may draw attention to itself – 'ruined' stands out from the text, contrasts with '£10' and asks us to consciously share a position of sympathy – rather than commonsensically draw on unexamined ideological assumptions about the topic (in this case, the police).

Yet, this is still about a power to shape perception. Take the lexis deployed by the military in wartime press briefings, language which is clearly jargon and euphemism, which is also often consciously rhetorical. During the 2003 invasion of Iraq, British and American military spokespeople talked of 'mouseholing' (the practice of blowing holes in the walls of houses during house-to-house searches instead of entering through the door and risking booby traps), of 'embedding' journalists with troops, of 'blue on blue' attacks (killing one's own side) and of course the ever useful 'collateral damage' (killing civilians by accident). This and similar language is clearly propaganda and has been subject to wide criticism (e.g. Chilton 1985), criticism which has found its way into newspaper commentary (Norton-Taylor and Watt 2003). However, although we might scoff when we first hear a press officer speak of a 'blue on blue', discourse analysts would point to a cumulative effect of such language in drawing our attention away from the messy effects of war and towards a discourse celebrating military precision and control.

This is the sense-making apparatus of the military, and to understand them and to share patriotically in their fighting, audience members must come to share, if only tangentially, that language. The lexis inserts the listener into the 'horizon of the meaningful', in Hall's terms, of the military, and so causes that listener to find that the propagandist jargon begins to make sense. As this chapter's epigraph from Fowler suggests (1991: 80), we can think of the words available to language users as appropriate for a situation as a kind of 'map of the objects, concepts, processes and relationships about which the culture needs to communicate'. The military language constructs a coherent system for the military to get on with their violent job without having to confront or defend that violence in their daily language use, and that becomes the unremarkable language that audiences expect from the military. It comes to belong to the military **register** and to the social competence of those who listen to the military.

Lexical analysis is therefore at its strongest when it finds something more than choices between words, but consistent patterns which suggest preoccupations within the particular discursive context, and which therefore add up to a representation of the world for a culture or for a group which holds status within a culture – 'the world as perceived according to the ideological needs of a culture' (Fowler 1991: 82). Sometimes these consistent patterns may be identified within a single piece of text (called **collocations**) and sometimes they are across different texts. In the following excerpt, for example, the news reflects the interest of legal discourse in the specifics of action and intention – who did what, when and with what intent – and it is much less interested in the emotional and social dimensions of that action. The ideological needs of the justice system dictate a particular 'lexical map':

LIFE SENTENCE FOR MURDER

An environmental campaigner has been sentenced to life for murdering his friend following a row at his flat in Glastonbury.

[JM], a former advertising worker with Mid-Somerset Newspapers, was found dead in his Bere Lane home 19 days after he was repeatedly stabbed.

At Bristol Crown Court on Friday, traveller [KN], aged 41, was told by Judge Neil Butterfield that he must serve at least 12 years of a life sentence.

[story continues]

(*Wells Journal*, 12 March 2004: 3)

To uncover the text's persistent interest in certain aspects of the story, and the lexical map it taps into, Fowler lists all the lexical items of a certain kind. The resulting list shows the preoccupations of the text. I have listed below all the words in the excerpt above expressing action (which I will call 'actives') and all the words expressing states of being or mind ('statives').[2]

active words: murder, sentenced, murdering, row, found, stabbed, told
stative words: following, dead, serve

(A note on how this list is put together: some of these words are nouns and some are verbs or adjectives. Within functional grammar, as is discussed further in Chapter 3, the emphasis is on what words do rather than on the traditional grammatical descriptors.)

The text is clearly full of active words. Even the words about states of mind are close to the border of the active. The article tells us next to nothing about what it means for a person to commit such an act, but more importantly it cumulatively emphasizes that this story is about a set of physical actions. There are two complementary reasons for this. First, news texts favour factual information, and actions are more verifiable as facts than emotions. This is reinforced by the legal constraints on court reporting, called 'qualified privilege', under which news organizations are only protected from prosecution for reproducing any defamatory statements made in court if they restrict themselves to an account that is fair, accurate and without malice. But, second, there is no room for anything other than facts in the legal activities being described. For many reasons, the news is constrained to follow a lexical map in which the complexity of life is reduced to a particular vocabulary of crime and punishment.

The newspaper is not simply drawing on legal jargon in doing this, for in fact it will have translated the legal jargon used into a more generally acceptable lexicon, but its meanings operate within a legal system that defines actions and constructs hierarchies and relations between them. It is a map in the sense of defining where each concept sits in relation to another and defining what each concept symbolizes, just as a topographical map does to a landscape. The verbal action here ('told') is carried out by the judge and it leads to the convicted man 'serving'. 'Stabbed' describes how 'murdering' was carried out, while 'murdering' describes the act of killing in a way that communicates a powerful social judgement. This mapping becomes clear when the words used are compared with others from the same lexical field. 'Murder' is a partial synonym of 'kill', 'execute', 'do away with', 'slaughter', 'stab to death', 'massacre', 'eliminate'. It sits in marked contrast, in the discourse of the legal system, to the terms 'manslaughter' and 'self-defence'. Each lexical item brings with it different assumptions about the legitimacy of the killing, the social context in which it happened, the responsibility of the person involved, and much else, and thus tells us about the attitude of the user of those words towards the event. The lexis, as is discussed shortly, labels the action, placing it within a particular social institution and helping to do that institution's work: [KN] is cast out of society by his actions being called 'murdering', and the story helps carry out that sentence by announcing it to the Somerset community. Active and stative **processes** have been analysed here, but similar maps could have been found in the text for the people and things involved in those processes. The lexis sorts the event into categories which depend upon social structures and institutions. The accumulation of words which draw on the same lexical map work together to reinforce those structures and give them verbal form.

Chibnall (1977: 12) similarly finds news stories about crime drawing on language which belongs to 'the dominant meaning system of the political elite'. He argues that the vocabulary of the news in particular reflects the framework of concepts and values of a dominant conservative consensus. This ideology:

> underlies and gives meaning to such well-worn phrases as 'the rule of law', 'the national interest', 'the politically motivated strike', 'holding the country to ransom', 'extremist agitators', 'fair-minded moderates', 'wage inflation', 'the silent majority', 'lowering moral and educational standards', and so on. With constant use these phrases become ideological cues, eliciting more-or-less predictable responses.
>
> (Chibnall 1977: 12)

These phrases come to dominate any discussion of law and order in the news, he argues, making any other perspective difficult to articulate in news language. Ericson et al. (1987: 31) follow this thinking too: 'The news media report on and enact the meaning systems of legal, scientific, religious, family, and other institutional spheres.' The media consistently rely on such institutions' ideas 'to construct cohesion out of the fragmented "facts" of life' (Hartley 1990: 104), and thus allow them to set the terms and limits of public culture (Ericson et al. 1987: 31).

Labels

Labels are a specific case of such lexis and a particularly powerful one in sorting people into often quite rigid social categories, as well as being useful in the tight space of a news text because they compress so much meaning into a few words. The act of labelling a person (or group or thing) defines how members of the society can understand and judge any action done by that person and allows them to generalize about them. As Ericson et al. (1987) point out, people interpret each other's behaviour and words in relation to what they expect of that kind of person. So people's organizational positions, their status, their personal biography, all shape the way the text makes sense (Ericson et al. 1987: 55). It is significant, then, that the convicted man in the *Wells Journal* story is referred to just by his last name, while the dead man is called 'Mr [M]' and the judge 'Judge Neil Butterfield'. The man in the dock loses his social rights to an honorific, and is thus discursively constructed as a criminal, rather than a full member of society who has done a terrible act. In fact, it is standard British news practice that people in the dock, even before conviction, lose their social rights to honorifics (although professionals such as doctors often get to keep theirs, even when convicted), suggesting that such labels are doing considerable work in signifying accused people's social marginalization.

[KN] is further labelled as an 'environmental campaigner' and then in paragraph three as 'traveller [KN]'. Both these labels are also significant in the social work they perform. The introduction, which after the headline, is the key place where our sense of the story is constructed, chooses to describe the violence as done by someone who campaigns for the environment, and chooses not to label him at first as someone from already outside the mainstream community, a Traveller or Gypsy. This is perhaps partly because the newspaper at first follows the British and Irish National Union of Journalists' guidance on reporting Travellers: 'Reference to an individual's ethnic origin should only be made where relevant and appropriate' (NUJ 2003). But the newspaper then slips in a reference to the person's ethnicity, and the prejudices which accompany that, in its second reference. The label 'environmental activist' also juxtaposes a group claiming the moral high ground with the act of murder, suggesting hypocrisy and making the story more dramatic. The newspaper also chooses not to label [KN] in the introduction by his occupation, by his origin (West Sussex) or his personality (his lawyer calls him a 'gentle giant'), and labels which would have made for a more complex and nuanced story by reminding readers of the killer's normalness. Through the labels used, a particular person comes into view, one who even before conviction is socially marginalized, marked as not of high status or deserving respect.

Labelling depends, therefore, on some of the most powerful social categories. As Clark (1992) showed in an analysis of representations of women in the British *Sun*'s reporting of crimes of sexual violence during the late 1980s, it can be a powerful expression of, and therefore in turn a support for, prejudice. She found, when analysing the labels used, that the *Sun*'s articles on violence against women fell into two categories.[3] On the one hand were stories on events where the violent man was constructed as sub-human. On the other were stories where the man was constructed as within the social fold. Clark found that the former category (the fiends) was almost invariably accompanied by women labelled as virtuous. The latter category (normal men) was accompanied by women labelled as fallen or sexually available. Table 1.1 shows her findings (the number in brackets signifies that the word occurred in multiple stories).

So one story is headlined: 'SEX-STARVED SQUADDIE STRANGLED BLONDE, 16', combining a label for the man which tends to explain and soften his violence with a label for the woman which portrays her as sexually attractive. The article goes on to note that the man's wife refused him sex, which Clark (1992: 218) argues works to cast the blame for the murder on her, and finds throughout that the 'non-fiend' men are often labelled at some point as suffering – in debt, sex-starved, and so on. Clark (1992: 211) sums these findings up as follows: ' "fiends" attack "unavailable" females (wives, mothers, and girls), while "non-fiends" attack "available" females (unmarried others, blondes, and sexually active girls)'. Husbands, even when their attacks on their wives were as serious as those by stranger-fiends, were almost never 'fiends'. Moreover, in

Table 1.1 Clark's typology of men and women

When men are fiends		When men are not fiends
man	*woman*	*woman*
fiend	wife (2)	blonde
monster	bride	unmarried mum
beast	housewife	Lolita (in *Sun* language a
or similar	mother (3)	sexually active under-age girl)
	young woman	blonde divorcee/mum
	girl, schoolgirl, girl guide (3)	woman/victim (no role)
	daughter	
	blonde	
	prostitute	
	woman/victim (no role)	
	individualized (no role)	

Source: Clark (1992)

almost all cases, Clark says, the women were not highly individualized, but referred to according to these types of either sexually available or sexually unavailable females, even in stories on non-sexual violence. She finds a consistent world-view expressed through such language use. First, responsibility consistently drifts from the violent men to women – either to women who were 'asking for it' by being sexually available or to women other than the abused woman who denied men their due. Second, fiends are outside society, usually strangers preying on virtuous women (and therefore society is not responsible for shaping their behaviour). Hence the *Sun* finds it difficult to call husbands 'fiends', because they hold a socially ratified position.

This reflects a straightforwardly patriarchal world-view. Bradby et al. (1995) find a similar pattern to the virtuous men–sexually available women collocation in their study of British tabloid coverage of professional misconduct cases against doctors in 1990–91, although Talbot (1997) finds the *Sun* less sexist, or at least more sensitive to social disapproval of sexism, by the mid-1990s. But in all these cases, the *Sun* taps into a highly conservative commonsensical frame through the labels it deploys, which the regular *Sun* reader can be expected to come to know: 'The newspaper and its readers share a common "discursive competence", know the permissible statements, permissions and prohibitions . . . (blondes are busty, work is a duty, play is a thrill, strikes are unpatriotic, and so on)' (Fowler 1991: 44). In the *Sun* and many other news media, social roles are rigidly mapped out for us.

From ideological structures to the social struggle over the sign

Critical linguistics has been able to show that the vocabulary of the news is strongly patterned. There is, however, a problem in jumping from this observation to the conclusion that such patterning is always driven by society's powerful. As linguists have shown in studying genres as diverse as Serbo-Croat oral heroic poetry (Lord 1960) and auctioneers' patter (Kuiper 1996), language users frequently draw on formulae, labels or set lexis to communicate effectively, because speakers and hearers share common sets of expectations about their relationship to the context. But that doesn't prevent creativity, for being creative (or radical or critical) involves not abandoning those conventions but tweaking and reorienting them slightly.

The point has emerged clearly in corpus linguistics, the computer-assisted analysis of millions of words of English from different contexts. It suggests that language users make meaning, not by drawing on individual words but by drawing on relatively set combinations of words. So critical linguistics' emphasis on choices available within the grammar and lexicon of a language is arguably too blunt an instrument. Corpus analysis shows that the verb 'worry' is followed by 'about' in by far the majority of cases, although other forms such as 'that' or 'because' are also correct (see Figure 1.1) (Cambridge International Corpus 2004). Words are not the basic units of meaning we might have thought, but mean different things when they sit alongside different words. Some words are also surprisingly limited in their use, contrary to dictionary definitions and even the intuition of speakers. Stubbs (2001) finds the word 'seeks', for example, occurs most often near the words 'female', 'black', 'male', 'attractive', 'similar', 'guy' and similar words. 'Seeks' seems to belong predominantly to lonely hearts ads. This is why it is easy to guess what the film, *Desperately Seeking Susan* (Seidelman 1985), will roughly be about. Words mean much more than dictionaries have tended to suggest, bringing with them quite specific cultural knowledge and expectations along with the conditions of their use. Such analysis has led to a new generation of dictionaries such as the Collins Cobuild English Dictionary (1995) which detail the usual use of words' usual phrasings.

But if such analysis shows that nearly all language use draws on predetermined collocations, it also offers fresh ways to think about the structures of news language. As discussed already in the Introduction we should perhaps think less of structures and systems of meaning than of conventions of use. Corpus analysis shows that a word's usual meaning is very closely tied to the contexts that language users are aware are conventionally invoked by it. Sometimes the use of such lexis will be formulaic, but we should also be alert to small changes to convention. The use of news language is therefore more of a rhetorical achievement than simply the reproduction of dominance, as newsworkers

```
             Opponents of the Bill worry it will mostly benefit affluent pare
       And of course, the more you worry about it the more it starts ex <$E>
carry one in the pickup, uh, and I worry about it being stolen.
n as the business needs it and not worry about the kinds of ups and downs on
               The thing I worry about-it isn't that I lose sleep ov
          However, you always worry this, you know, balance, - balance t
r is also an external agenda and I worry he might concentrate so much on the
          But some africans worry that A shift from aid to trade won't
ter of the United Nations that you worry about it.
ce worker dmitri zuckelov says, "I worry, but at the same time I see business
               They worry about health and safety issues or th
n member of Parliament people also worry about giving up a good thing.
       and not even worry about it.
       But many historians here worry that in all the excitement, evidence
day you celebrate, and inside you worry because you know the day before it w
and a growing number of Americans worry will be a time of widespread shor
the fat cat money managers that we worry about are managing the average perso
               Still, many worry about long-term consequences should
t didn't have to <$E> laughter<$E> worry about that before.
n ex tax inspector you go away and worry about your income tax over the weeke
          <$3>I really worry?
y defective, causing confusion and worry for the captains.
               What I worry about is this: the A.N.C.
               worry cos I 'll look
so I don't have to, you know, worry about it one way of the other and I
          Some however, worry the longer these unarmed internation
rograms which many young Americans worry will be bankrupt by the time they re
          parents worry it's not enough to stop millions of
          "Then you worry about spontaneous detonation," Smith
```

Figure 1.1 Computer corpuses of actual usage, such as these instances of the verb 'worry' from the Cambridge International Corpus, show that words tend to recur in relatively set combinations.

Source: Image courtesy of Cambridge University Press.

slot into expectations about the potential of a phrase such as 'environmental campaigner', and make new meanings by drawing on those expectations yet altering them slightly.

Such thinking is close to research on intertextuality (see Chapter 2). Language makes sense according to patterns of use – the struggle to reaccent signs which have already been in many people's mouths – more than in terms of the relatively rigid structures assumed in the ideological analysis of media texts above. If discourse is part of structures of dominance and power in society, it is through speakers' use of discourse and orientation to dominance. This model presumes an active role by the individual actor in meaning making, rather than the passivity presumed in structural theories. As Giddens (1984) points out, it may make more sense to talk of 'structuration', rather than the mutually exclusive terms, 'structure' and 'agency', in thinking about individuals and the systems they live according to. This approach has the benefit of not getting bogged down in accusations that journalists are biased or ideologically captured (there is a good discussion of journalists' response to such allegations in the preface to Schlesinger 1987), but focuses on how they try, in their writing, to negotiate their difficult tasks of making exciting copy that will attract audiences, staying on side with their sources, giving clear and authoritative accounts and avoiding accusations of bias or inaccuracy. Close analysis of what linguistic forms newsworkers draw on, among the wide array of ways of making meaning that are available in society, can perhaps tell us how they are picking their way through such pressures.

This is Fairclough's approach (1995: 68ff.) to an article from the *Sun*, CALL UP FORCES IN DRUGS BATTLE. He analyses what he calls the 'discourse practice' of the article, that is, the way it uses and transforms source texts such as statements by politicians and press releases in terms of how the paper imagines its readers' interests and ways of thinking and how it responds to commercial and political pressures. He shows how the article turns a parliamentary committee report's recommendation into a populist call to arms. The source text reads:

> The Government should consider the use of the Royal Navy and the Royal Air Force for radar, airborne or ship surveillance duties. We recommend, therefore that there should be intensified law enforcement against drug traffickers by H.M. Customs, the police, the security services and possibly the armed forces.
>
> (House of Commons Home Affairs Committee, cited in Fairclough 1995: 70)

This is transformed into:

CALL UP FORCES IN DRUGS BATTLE

> The armed forces should be called up to fight off a massive invasion by drug pushers, MPs demanded yesterday.
>   [story continues]

To Fairclough, the intertextual mix here of a populist lexis ('forces', 'drugs pushers') with a lexis reminiscent of the formal report ('armed forces') works to give populist force to official voices, as if the MPs spoke like *Sun* readers with their perspectives on the scourge of drugs pushers, at the same time as it preserves the legitimacy of official discourse (Fairclough 1995: 71). In Hodge and Kress's terms (1988: 40ff.), such a text expresses both solidarity, that is, a common bond between MPs, newspaper and its readership, and power, that is, the legitimacy of the MPs' position in the hierarchy of decision-making and social control. It can do this because it adopts a hybrid style, which Fairclough links to popular newspapers' tendency to mix the informative news genre with persuasive genres. He also sees the article's heavy use of war imagery ('call up', 'drugs battle', 'fight off', 'invasion') as intertextually invoking a common British heritage of defending the island, a potent mix of images from Sir Francis Drake defeating the Spanish Armada to contemporary politicians fighting European Union directives. The newspaper claims to share that popular memory and culture at the same time as it inserts drugs into this discursive heritage, immediately marginalizing other constructions of drugs (as a British social problem, as an enjoyable pastime, as a by-product of imbalanced global trade flows, and so on) in an ideologically potent way.

Fairclough theorizes the transformations he sees taking place here in two ways. First, he sees the news article as one communicative event in a chain of communicative events, which includes parliamentary committee meetings, press releases and the reading of the article by people over lunch or on the bus to work. This analysis looks at how the article adds to or changes the meanings passed along that communicative chain in order to see its role in reproducing or challenging power and dominance, rather than seeing simply one meaning, from dominant to dominated in society through the media, as critical linguists were at risk of doing (Fairclough 1995: 37). We could, then, analyse press releases or even people's lunchtime conversation over the *Sun* in order to look at different moments in that chain of meaning-making. Fairclough also thinks of each article in terms of how far it reproduces the news genre and how far it draws on other genres to produce something hybrid. So while he looks for similar language features to Clark and Fowler, he then interprets them not by looking for 'a number of well-defined, unitary and stable codes which dictate practice' (Fairclough 1995: 67), but instead by asking how the intertextual relations of its lexis – going both back in time and across to other contemporaneous texts – positions the text in relation to structures of power and meaning. Does it weave voices together in ways that support a conservative consensus or in ways that subvert it?

Guilty as charged? A brief example of crime news

The news story in Figure 1.2 will be used to apply the analyses of news lexis discussed above and to explore the question of how the news weaves voices and kinds of language together to intervene in the social life of words. The text, 'FEARS ON SEX CRIME BOOM', comes from the Scottish edition of the Sunday newspaper, *The News of the World*.

This short text contains, first, a high number of words communicating concern, including the very first word of the headline:

fears, warned, crisis, wave, strain, serious consequences

Fears on sex crime boom

Jacqueline McGhie
5 September 2004
The News of the World

MSPs and experts last night warned of a policing crisis after a new report revealed the number of sex offenders in Scotland has nearly doubled in three years.

Justice Minister Cathy Jamieson has revealed that over 2,200 perverts are now registered with Scots forces - compared to 1,480 in March 2001.

Scots police have received NO extra cash to monitor the growing wave of offenders.

Last night MSP Christine Grahame said: "We want these people to be registered but the strain on resources has to be met as a priority. Parents have to feel secure in the system."

Bill Whyte, director of Edinburgh University's Criminal Justice Centre said: "These figures have serious consequences for the resources required to administer the register."

But an Executive spokeswoman insisted last night: "We and the Home Office believe this has a relatively small impact on police and court resources."

(C) News of the World, 2004

Figure 1.2 Fears on Sex Crime Boom
Source: *News of the World* (Scottish edition), 5 September 2004

In the context of those words, other lexis such as 'revealed', 'feel secure', 'impact' takes on negative connotations as well. A parallel set of words suggests large numbers:

boom, number, doubled, 2,200, 1,480, growing wave, these people, figures

The 'growing wave of offenders' is literally represented in this wave of concerning words (see van Dijk 1988b, on the news rhetoric of numbers). The lexis calls up our background knowledge of widespread societal fears about growing sexual violence against children, fears already fed by the media and in particular by the *News of the World* which campaigned for 'Sarah's Law', legislation that would have made released sex offenders' addresses public. Indeed, it is only with difficulty that a reader would be able to deduce from the text that the concern of those quoted is not that there are more sex offenders in Scotland but that, because of increased powers of the legal system to require that people convicted of certain sex offences be monitored, the police are finding it difficult to effectively monitor those who have been released. The more obvious sense communicated by the accumulation of these words is to accentuate the existing fear.

Second, the text contains many words which are commonly found in bureaucratic contexts and which only secondarily belong in the news. These include:

policing, report, registered (twice), resources (thrice), priority, system, administer, register

The labels given to the story's actors contribute to the same lexical map, simply giving organizational titles (such as 'MSPs' [Members of the Scottish Parliament], 'Justice Minister', 'Home Office', 'director of Edinburgh University's Criminal Justice Centre'). On one level, then, this text associates itself with the bureaucratic rationality and objectivity of officialdom. Intertwined with this official language is a judgemental tabloid lexis ('perverts', 'forces', 'cash'), so that, for example, 'Justice Minister Cathy Jamieson has revealed that over 2,200 perverts are now registered with Scots forces'. The newspaper is weaving together the language of officialdom and the newspaper's demotic, and we could argue, following Fairclough, that it is working rhetorically to give official credence to its scare story, and to its long-running campaign. Rather than label the minister in a pejorative way, such as 'Minister of perverts', the newspaper represents her as presiding over a jump in the number of registered perverts. In Hodge and Kress's terms, the lexis chosen is both 'sex offenders' and 'perverts', both 'policing' and 'Scots forces', both 'resources' and 'cash', suggesting that the newspaper's campaigning discourse against perverts is paralleled by a government report.

Third, the text labels the news as a 'policing crisis'. This is, a scan of contemporary news articles shows, a crisis only reported on by the *News of the World* and by a brief in the following day's *Sun*, its sibling title. It is a common news technique. Ericson et al. write: 'The journalist uses the "crisis" frame to establish an event as newsworthy and to transform it into news discourse', with the effect that the reality and scale of the 'problem' become self-evident (1987: 62). In other words, it is labelled a crisis because the reporter needs to do considerable work to convince her news editor of the story's value, and the newspaper needs to do considerable work to convince readers. Were it self-evidently a crisis, the reporter could simply have written, 'A new report has revealed the number of sex offenders . . .' The 'policing crisis' label also makes sense of the text's language of fear and numbers: if there are growing fears about the sex crime boom, then there is logically a crisis brewing.

All these lexical features work in a similar way to emphasize fears of loss of social control over sexual perversion and over crime. At one level, they are part of the busy work of this particular newspaper in constructing a fearful readership which needs the newspaper's information and campaigning on its behalf. To return to the argument put forward at the start of the chapter, however, close analysis shows what the newspaper needs to do in order to add to that fear. While the *Sun*'s brief the next day, 'PERVS LIST UP 100%', was simply wrong, missing the difference between numbers of sex offenders and numbers registered with police, the *News of the World* text communicates much the same by the rhetorical techniques discussed above. It deploys the lexis of fear and growing sex crime in an article on police resources and deploys its campaigning lexis on 'perverts' in parallel to bureaucratic lexis. All of these displace responsibility for the language elsewhere than the news organization, onto the already existing fears it mobilizes, onto the ostensibly self-evident crisis and onto the official language which it quotes. The news text's power, as Fairclough points out, is the power to weave together existing conventions of language use. This analysis is important because it reveals the role of newswriting in meaning. The news is not simply reproducing dominance – indeed, the MSP and the expert quoted are concerned about a different issue to the newspaper – but it is a social action done by journalists upon the words of others. Uncovering the rhetoric of the reporter's word choice leads us towards critique of the way the news is written. The reporter may not have been conscious of raising fears and may have been shaped by little more than a desire to get the story published, but discourse analysis points a critical finger at newswriting and therefore asks reporters to abandon the pretence that their language reflects the real.

The analysis of the details of word choice in the news – and the approach applies also to other forms of media discourse – is fundamental to understanding the meaning potential of media texts. This chapter has explored a number of aspects of lexical choice, including labelling, the way the words chosen gain meaning from their difference to other words that could have been chosen, and the way meaning emerges from the accumulation of similar words over a text. But it has also shown that lexical analysis on its own is not sufficient to under-stand the ideological force of media language. Words and phrases get their meaning from the ways they have been used over time and from the ways those accumulated meanings are reinflected in the current text – so the phrase 'drug pushers' is made to do something new when it appears in the *Sun*. There are often pragmatic reasons for a word – the court reporter might have had no other words available to describe the 'fairground worker'. The following chap-ter, which explores the intertextual dimension to media language, is therefore an important complement to analysis of lexis. Indeed, as Fairclough (1992) has argued, there is value in thinking of language use on a number of different levels, from details of vocabulary to analysis of the social activity happening through the language to consideration of the wider relations of power shaping everything else, in order to build up a rich analysis of media discourse.

Further reading

Many of the ideas discussed above are developed more systematically in Fairclough (1995). Although the book is theoretically a little out of date, Fowler (1991) gives a highly readable series of close analyses of news language, which builds on the analysis of Fowler, Hodge, Kress and Trew (1979) and Hodge and Kress (1993). For analysis of how news language is produced, Bell (1991) is a key text, although it is less critical than the others mentioned. Reah (2002) provides a quick overview of analysis of news language.

2 | ADVERTISING DISCOURSE: SELLING BETWEEN THE LINES

In the US, Tide's no longer a laundry detergent; it's not about getting clothes clean anymore. All detergents get your clothes clean. Tide's about a much deeper thing than that: It's an enabler; it's a liberator. I guess you could think about moving Tide from the heart of the laundry to the heart of the family, because if a lady today in her busy life can send her kids, her husband, the rest of her family out into the world wearing the right clothes, clothes that look good, that last for a long time, then Tide's played a role in family harmony, not just in washday.

(Kevin Roberts, Chief Executive of Saatchi and Saatchi Worldwide, PBS 2003)

Introduction

Communication works because it draws on shared cultural resources in familiar social situations – something which becomes apparent when people who speak the same language but live in different cultures manage to misunderstand each other (Gumperz 1982). So an advertisement for Churchill Insurance which uses a bulldog as its emblem is unlikely to be associated by North Americans with an ethos of loyal determination, whereas British consumers are likely to know immediately what qualities are being called up. But ads are much more than actualizations of existing 'codes' of meaning in order to associate their products with aspects of culture. Ads often seek to lead taste, to make people think in new ways, to mix cultural practices in distinctive ways in the constant struggle for marketing advantage.

This causes a problem for discourse analysis, because theories of meaning which look at how a text draws on a bank or dictionary of meanings don't allow much scope for meanings to change or to be contested. It is also a problem more general than just the analysis of advertising, although it is posed starkly there. For contemporary society is characterized by change. Fairclough (1995: 67) observes that, if the notion that genres, meanings and power structures are fixed and stable was a poor generalization when discourse analysis began in the 1960s, it is a highly inadequate one today.

This chapter studies one way of thinking about the problem, which is to propose that all meaning is intertextual. The meaning of a word arises in the way a text draws upon previous meanings for that word used in previous contexts and by previous speakers. By tracing the links a text invokes, we can trace the attempt by a speaker to communicate a particular meaning as well as the space for hearers to interpret that text. We thus have a method to analyse how a particular text seeks to make its own meanings, against the backdrop of the power of existing ways of making sense and therefore of existing discursive structures. Intertextual analysis is not about identifying sameness and regular patterning, as we saw in the previous chapter, but about the cultural work a text is doing in relation to wider structures.

Intertextuality is particularly useful in analysing advertisements. Ads are, as is discussed below, purposive texts – considerable money is spent with the objective of having specific effects on consumers. They are also often highly condensed, comprising sometimes no more than a logo, and are often suggestive rather than explicit. An approach that sees such texts simply as instances of wider cultural forces risks missing much of their particularity. Ads are therefore a very useful genre through which to explore the intertextual. On the way to exploring intertextuality, I will discuss the dominant mode of advertising analysis in media and cultural analysis of advertising, semiotics, in order to suggest what alternative insights into this media form discourse analysis is capable of. Following Cook's lead (1992: xiv), I will 'save space and effort (both yours and mine)' by calling advertisements 'ads'.

Climbing the Mountain

A good place to start is the short film/ad, the 'Mountain', PlayStation® 2 (Figure 2.1).[1] The ad is in grainy washed-out colour, 1-minute in length, and shows hip young people of an array of ethnicities running and leaping through an urban landscape and piling together into a human skyscraper, to a naïve 1936 Shirley Temple and gospel chorus soundtrack, 'Get on board, li'l children, get on board'. The last quarter of the ad shows different young adults making it

Figure 2.1 The final image of the 'Mountain' television and cinema ad for PlayStation® 2
Source: Image courtesy of Sony Computer Entertainment Australia

to the top of the pyramid, waving their arms in triumph, and then falling off again. No images of PlayStation® 2 games or hardware are given, and no information about the product. Only the endline, or slogan, of the ad

fun, anyone?
Playstation® 2

which is printed over the final scene of the human mountain for two seconds, gives us a clue to its purpose. How does such a text make sense, and how does it contribute to selling gaming consoles? I want to suggest it works primarily through the way it calls upon a particular knowledge among particular consumers, positioning them as at the cutting edge of cool. You clearly need to be positioned already as part of a particular youth culture to get anywhere with it. In Althusser's (1971) terms, the ad 'interpellates' viewers, addressing them as already on the inside of its modes of making meaning and its repertoire of shared texts. You need to know that a new version of PlayStation is out, and what the games are about. You need to be familiar with the filmic references of the ad, from its opening prototypical gritty urban scene of a shirtless, muscular black or Hispanic man sitting laconically on the edge of a high roof in a rundown area, with faint police sirens in the background, to the crowd panic scenes of people falling over each other and crushing a subway ticket barrier (as Shirley Temple sings of the gospel train, 'She's nearing now the station'). You need to be able to enjoy these images as pastiche, rather than as sometimes horrific scenes of people being crushed[2] and to be able to enjoy the computer-generated artifice of the final skyscraper-height human pyramid. You also need to be familiar with the re-use, in a new context, of naïve singalongs from the youth of people born before 1930 as ironic, signalling subversion of conventional meanings and conventional society (you might, for example, be familiar with this from *South Park*). It adds up, in my reading after repeated viewings, to a reminder to viewers who understand it that they are already on board, on the inside of a culture PlayStation® claims to be part of too, and an invitation to them to identify themselves as those who make it to highest score level for a moment (when they reach the top of the pyramid).

There is a vast collection of other references and complexity to the ad's images and action. The man on the rooftop and aspects of the action suggest to me the underground urban youth sport, parkour or free running, which involves jumping between and around high buildings, often to the shock and non-understanding of their residents. There are further references which I lack the knowledge for (there is a fleeting image of a dog in a canine wheelchair which may not puzzle other viewers). But what a brief attempt to analyse the ad shows is that making sense of it requires background knowledge, a certain position within culture, a knowledge of a wide range of other texts, and an ability to relate the meanings from these different genres and verbal, visual and musical modes together. Through such meaning-making, certain viewers are being sold an attitude to the games console, through an attitude to society and culture.

The crucial dimension of meaning here is not so much about how the separate elements of text make sense, as discussed in Chapter 1, but much more how they inter-relate. In **hermeneutic** terms, our task as consumers of the ad and also much more consciously as critics, is to understand how the elements here display **coherence**, how they hang together as something larger, through their networks of references. As critics, we also want to use such texts to explore contemporary culture. By tracing the text's intertexts, we can identify some key aspects of contemporary advertising. Perhaps the most powerful texts in contemporary advertising are the ones which address us as already on board, in Shirley Temple's words, which ask us to inhabit certain positions of making sense, and therefore particular identities. As is discussed in more depth towards the chapter's end, ads such as this one work by appropriating meanings already circulating in culture for the purposes of selling – in a colleague of mine's words, this ad is 'commodifying the resistance' of *South Park*, parkour and critical youth culture, drawing yet more of people's lives and cultural references into the realm of the pursuit of happiness through purchasing.[3] Finally, the ad also reflects a society where, in order to sell their culture back to young people, ad agencies must recognize and negotiate their critical attitude. As one graphic designer comments on the 'Mountain' ad: 'PlayStation® commercials are always fresh, quirky, weird and different. It seems that by bombarding the audience with the unknown and strange we can actually wake the sleepy minds that have been trained to filter out all forms of advertisement' (Petrovic 2004). Selling toilet paper may still work by invoking stable codes of cute puppies and little girls, but many ads involve much more complex processes of meaning-making.

Coded messages

The dominant approach in cultural studies to analysing ads has without doubt been **semiotics**. Many key arguments about the way ads perpetuate and feed dominant ideologies, about the way they construct audiences as consumers, and about the impact they have on culture more generally, are grounded in semiotic analysis (see Further reading). The problem is that the theoretical base for those analyses has been chipped away at (e.g. Corner 1986; Pateman 1990), and if we are to rescue a strongly critical, textually informed approach to ads, we need to supplement semiotics with theories of the social.

Semiotic analysis – in stark contrast to discourse analysis – begins by theoretically separating out the realm of the symbolic, including language and other sign systems such as the meaning of images, from the realm of the social. Meaning is produced through an arbitrary system of difference. There is no good reason why people say 'horse' and not 'houynhnm' – it's just an arbitrary convention they all follow. Although people's acts of recognizing such convention by following it are the ground of the system, analysts drawing on semiotics traditionally place much more emphasis on the system than the people inhabiting it, the people doing the recognizing. Meaning arises in the difference between items in a sign system's physical notations (signifiers), so that 'cat' and 'hat' mean different things but a Glaswegian leaving off the 't' and a **Received Pronunciation** speaker drawing out the 'a' mean the same thing. Meaning arises also in the difference between the ideas those signifiers relate to, so that 'cat' and 'kitten' are different. This theory has the obvious advantage of allowing us to focus on the sign system and not the messy social world.

Texts make sense by the ways they instantiate structures of meaning. Although semiotic theorists recognize signs as 'polysemous', capable of many different shades of meaning, they see that meaning as restricted by 'myths', by the dominant patterns of association within a culture which naturalize one set of meanings as the significance which doesn't need stating because it is self-evident. People doing things for particular purposes in particular contexts do not appear in such terminology. So Thwaites et al. (2002) distinguish absolutely between the 'addresser' and 'addressee' constructed in a text, which they analyse, and the actual 'sender' and 'receiver' of any text, which they leave to social scientists:

> Though these may seem fine distinctions, they are crucial. They suggest that we may be able to talk about what happens in texts in specifically *textual* ways, without having recourse to hypotheses about what their sender may have intended them to mean, or without having to guess about what their effects on a single given receiver might be. In short, the separation of addresser from sender and addressee from receiver is what lets us do semiotics rather than psychology (Thwaites et al. 2002: 18).

This kind of analysis has worked well with ads partly because they appear pure semiosis with few traces of actual social and communicative activity. Ads often have no obvious senders (who is the voice saying 'fun anyone?'?). They are designed for large audiences to make sense of rather than specific groups, providing positions for us to locate ourselves within consumer culture. They are also divorced from their **co-texts** – an ad on a bus has nothing to do with the bus – and thus require consumers to invoke the semiotic system needed to interpret them by themselves.

This sophisticated theory is well described elsewhere (see Further reading), but it has its weaknesses as well as its strengths. These can be illustrated in analysis of the Boddingtons 'Cream of Manchester' ad campaign, launched in the early 1990s. In the early ads of the campaign, images such as Figure 2.2, an ice cream cone made of glass and filled with froth, were used with phenomenal success to promote the brew from a regional product to Britain's number one take-home bitter. To a semiotician, the combination of the signifier for the beer brand and the signifier for an ice cream cone suggests that the ad's consumers are being asked to recognize that the signifieds for both share a fundamental characteristic. That is, the beer is so creamy that it is like ice cream. The endline, 'BODDINGTONS. THE CREAM OF MANCHESTER', emphasizes (or anchors) this reading: the beer can be mistaken for something creamy. This is of course just the beginning of how people decode the ad. At the connotative level, the two meanings clash. In British culture, beer will often be associated with such codes as:

manliness
old Englishness
Friday nights at the pub

Figure 2.2 The Boddingtons Draught campaign from the 1990s featured verbal puns linking beer and cream

Source: Image courtesy of Tif Hunter, www.tifhunter.com

Consumers are used to it being marketed in these terms. Ice cream belongs to codes of:

    the summery outdoors
    children
    the exotic
    indulgence

Think of almost any ice cream ad. Different cultural codes of the desirable are thus being called up, and consumers must make sense of the contrast. In doing so, they are therefore able to see that the ad is making fun of advertising's usual strategy of associating its products **metaphorically** with objects of desire. The ad is mocking its own marketing strategy, and mocking too the constructed person who inhabits those codes – perhaps a young male who sees nothing wrong with being down at the pub with his mates on a summer's afternoon. The ad therefore appeals to the pleasure of the sophisticated viewer who can see through these meanings, and enjoy the hyperbole.

Cook accuses semioticians of not having either a sense of humour or an interest in seeing the complexity of the meaning of such ads and the skill of their producers and consumers. In particular, he criticizes the 'air of finality once these similarities are observed, which blinds the approach to what is unique' in ads' processes of making meaning (1992: 70). Hagart (2003), for example, in an analysis of just these Boddingtons ads, argues that the ice cream/beer ad in Figure 2.2 is really an in-joke by advertising executives at the expense of Manchester men whose idea of a good time is a pint of bitter. The ad was part of a series of similar semiotic jokes, where frothy beer was blended with various creamy substances, from cake to shaving foam and Brylcream, as well as some more complex ads that involved verbal puns, such as beer with a whip wrapped round it (i.e. whipped cream). Hagart argues that such ads contain a subliminal mockery of the lack of sophistication of Boddingtons drinkers, and in particular of their sexual inadequacy (in later campaigns the joke was extended to include sex explicitly, so that in one a man tells his partner who's been drinking the beer, 'By 'eck, you smell luvverly tonight'). The only sex these men get is in creaming – slang for masturbation. 'Put crudely, the ad men reckon Boddington's male beer drinkers are a load of effeminate wankers who couldn't "pull" a woman if they tried' (Hagart 2003). In this analysis, the success of the campaign was due to men subconsciously identifying with its portrayal of their sexual inadequacy and so feeling Boddingtons was their kind of beer.

The analysis here depends upon the meaning being in the text, the intertextual reference of the text being clarified and simplified by cultural myths and still more powerful forces (for Hagart, Freudian) motivating those myths. The critical point I wish to make here is not that all semiotic analysis is as weak, but that it runs the risk of such weakness, because it omits the historical and social contexts in which people would make sense of the ad. For discourse theory, it is 'dangerously adrift from communicative purpose and discoursal content' (Swales 1990: 91). While many semioticians would agree that it is essential to reconnect analysis with the history of what people have done with language and other symbols and to the social contexts the symbols are operating within, discourse analysts see the meanings of the ad less as a *structure* than as social *acts* of interpretation. We should therefore not seek codes at work in the Boddingtons ads as much as ask how they fitted so well in 1990s England that they could boost beer sales so spectacularly.

The key theoretical point of difference, as Pateman (1990) puts it, is that semioticians are analysing utterances as if they were languages, rather than symbolic actions in specific social situations. The social contexts in which the Boddingtons ad is produced and consumed include a desire by brewers to change beer's image so as to appeal to those wanting a more sophisticated image, including the growing female beer market, and thus broaden sales. The context includes consumer awareness campaigns against the power of multi-national corporations, such as Naomi Klein's *No Logo* (2000) and a trend at the same time towards more sophisticated and ironic advertising, which assumes some scepticism among its consumers about advertising's linking of its products with desirableness. It includes the 'new lad' magazine culture of the 1990s, in which fairly ribald sexual innuendo became more acceptable in the media. Within these cultural and economic contexts, the Boddingtons ad seems much more of a well-designed strategy to position the beer brand. In fact, I would reverse Hagart's analysis: the ad constructs its drinkers as relaxed enough about their sexuality to be able to laugh about the flaw in the link between beer and sexual potency. As is typical among products of 'new lad' culture, the ad's appeal is that it has it both ways, appealing to a sexist culture while projecting an 'unrelenting gloss of knowingness and irony, a reflexivity about its own condition which arguably rendered it more immune from criticism' (Benwell 2003).

So rather than see such a text as a site of meaning, analysis is more likely to have purchase if the text is located in a 'circuit of culture' (Johnson 1986), seeing the moment of representation in the text as part of a circle which also includes the moment of production, the identities available in our culture for the text to draw on and contribute to, the regulation of those identities by social institutions from advertising agencies to laws on indecency and the consumption of those texts. Du Guy et al. (1997) argue that each of these moments affects the other (see their analysis of the circuits of culture around the Sony Walkman).

Stunts, car crashes and model-making: The intertextuality of an ad

In placing the beer ad within a circuit of culture, we are identifying some of the ways meaning moves between texts and people in actual culture. We can do this partly by empirical research, asking where the ad was placed, how many people saw it, what the marketing budget was, and so on. We can also trace the movement of meaning by identifying the links that can be made between the text and other aspects of culture, using intertextual analysis. The overview of intertextuality below starts with the concept of genre, which it argues lies at the heart of how people place a text in relation to others, and then introduces three key questions which intertextual analysis is concerned with: how intertextuality constructs identity, its role in social struggle and the cultural power of intertextuality in the media.

Semiotics teaches that signs are polysemous, capable of many meanings. The basic assumption here is essentially the same as in the intertextual theory explored in this chapter. But instead of looking for 'deep' structures of meaning at work ordaining which aspects of a sign's meaning will arise naturally in a text, discourse analysts place a text in the context of previous language events, previous uses of the word or image. 'The real *a prioris* of language are not underlying structures, but prior language, prior texts' (Becker 1983: 8; cited in Swales 1990: 86). This is not to deny that organization of ideas in our minds and in our languages can be seen as codes, but it *is* to deny that the social practices must be organized by those structures. Discourse analysts tend to see meaning as organized instead by genre and discourse. A genre can be described as the set of expectations about what a particular text does in practical terms (is it a piece of correspondence, a legal judgement, a piece of fiction?), and what kinds of meaning the reader can expect to find there. By assigning a genre to a text, readers or viewers or listeners immediately place it in relation to a certain group of other texts and therefore begin interpreting it in the light of its intertextual relations.

This becomes clear when we ask why a text belongs to the genre of ads. Advertising is a difficult genre to describe precisely, because it is very wide and merges with other genres. The label on a can of baked beans is a form of advertising for what's inside as well as a label; a junk mail letter from a credit card company or a free keyring from an insurer are similarly ads as well as something else. Pateman (1990) argues that people therefore decide if something is an ad on **pragmatic** grounds – does it meet certain conditions for an ad? – rather than formal criteria such as its layout or the use of features such as slogans. The key test they must apply is whether the text is trying to convince them of something (to buy baked beans, or not to drink and drive at

Christmas). People know that ads seek to convince them to buy something or perform a certain behaviour. If the baked bean label merely told us about its contents, it would be hard to describe as an ad. If a flyer discussed the pros and cons of driving while drunk without ending with a strong message, you would be hard pressed to see it as an ad. Similarly, a t-shirt with a small green crocodile embossed on it might be regarded as an ad for Lacoste, but might sometimes be understood better as a badge of identity by a label-conscious consumer. The test of whether it's trying to convince you of something requires a judgement about the intention of the t-shirt wearer. Pateman argues that people use other pragmatic criteria as well, such as whether it's in a place you would associate with ads, such as on the back of a magazine. A reader asks, then, 'What is the most relevant likely reason for this piece of communication that I should apply in interpreting it?'

This approach makes sense of the shock tactics of some ads. When ads are easy to recognize, such as a supermarket ad for cheap bread in a newspaper, readers can quickly move on to decisions about interpretation, including the decision to skip the text altogether. When a passerby sees a billboard at the side of the road with a new style Mini Cooper stuck vertically to it, accompanied by the words:

You'll need:
some glue
a ramp
and a bit of a run-up.

she or he needs to work out what the car is doing there. The only likely explanation is that it's trying to sell this model of car, but many discourse analysts would argue that viewers' minds very quickly apply other possible genres or 'activity types' first. Clearly, this is not the scene of an accident, nor is it likely to be a stunt, or a practical joke at the expense of a Mini owner, nor an example of how to make a model. The ad gets people's attention for a second as they drive past because they have to do a little more cognitive work than usual in recognizing the kind of meaning intended.

This act of recognition is not, however, simply an either–or decision of which social rule to apply, but places interpretation within a network of social meanings. When glancing at the Mini for the first time, I quickly rejected a whole range of possible interpretative contexts based on my knowledge of the world and of other kinds of message. I recognized the phrase, 'You'll need some glue', as like the start of a *Blue Peter* or other children's programme modelling session, but rejected it as the activity going on here. I recognized but rejected the stunt explanation – that this was a pointless but exciting challenge someone had taken on. But the meaning of the ad still clearly draws on those other contexts.

(Other people in Britain might also recall an Araldite ad from the 1980s which demonstrated the glue's strength by sticking cars to billboards.) Even once we've recognized this as an ad, it happens in the context of the genres of children's model-making, the kind of stunts we find in youth-oriented media (e.g. MTV's *Road Rules*) and of course the genre of jokes. The 'Mountain' ad works similarly, pulling in references to many other kinds of text and social activity in its highly compressed space of meaning.

Alluding to other texts is a valuable technique for advertisers. It requires a high degree of cognitive work from consumers and, as is argued by rhetorical analysts, the more work people have to do to get a meaning, the further they follow a text down the particular path it is trying to lead them down and the more active their collaboration with the text's meaning is (Cronick 2002: 5). Intertextual references also compress meaning, in the 20–30 seconds of many television or radio ads, or the logo and a slogan of a print ad.

But, as argued in Chapter 1, all meaning, whether in advertisements or any other texts, can be seen to achieve things in the world by the way they draw intertextually on what others have said before them. We know what a word means because of its previous uses in particular contexts (as corpus linguistics traces in its databases). We know what genre categories to apply to a text when we recognize its echoing of previous instances of the genre. Thus, every text, as Barthes (1977a) argued in his later work, is a 'multidimensional space in which a variety of writings, none of them original, blend and clash.' It is 'a tissue of quotations' (Barthes 1977a: 146). So intertextual theory would have us ask three kinds of question not just of shock ads like the Mini on a billboard, but of all ads and, indeed, all texts:

1. *Identity*: If texts are always a tissue of quotation, then the creativity of writers must be seen as much more limited than Romantic literary theory has claimed. Instead, as Barthes noted, a writer's work is about positioning her or himself in relation to what has already been said. The point holds more generally. By using language with a particular history, we are placing ourselves, the meanings we construct and those we address in a particular relation to society and culture. So Chandler (1995b) argues that being able to spot the intertextual reference between a picture of the front door of the Prime Minister's residence, 10 Downing Street, in London and an Absolut vodka bottle rewards us with an identity of being members of an exclusive club.

2. *Social struggle*: Consequently, we can represent social struggle as partly a struggle to 're-accent' language that has been tied to particular interests before (Vološinov 1986: 103). We can then analyse the social life of the sign in order to trace the workings of power in society. We might analyse, for

example, what kinds of meanings about immigration predominate in talk-shows, and might find the topic regularly arises in laments about the decline of inner cities, rising unemployment and welfare cheats.

3. *Media culture*: This analysis leads us on, then, to ask about the role of communications media in shaping shared repertoires of intertexts in society. How do the media shape our repertoires on public issues such as immigration or private matters such as our bodies or our family life?

Intertextual analysis works by asking, first, what other texts are relevant to understanding a particular text, and then, second, what the social and cultural power of those texts is and how they are articulated with the text we are studying.

Discourse analysis's version of intertextuality has learnt much from post-structuralist thinking (particularly Barthes and Kristeva). However, it tends to differ from poststructuralist thinking in limiting itself to identifying a narrower range of intertexts, based on arguments about the social function of the text. I would suggest we look along three dimensions in identifying intertextual reference. The first is a pragmatic criterion. We should not extend our circle of intertexts to the most arcane references or possible 'codes' of meaning, but, as we saw when discussing the genre of the car ad above, ask what possible meanings are *relevant*. **Relevance theory** argues that hearers look for the most relevant likely routes of meaning (Sperber and Wilson 1986). This is a judgement they make in terms of their knowledge of how the genre works, what the set of cultural references being invoked in the rest of the text is and what is most likely to arise for the speaker and hearer of this text. It is a judgement that asks what references will add to the text's coherence as a meaningful whole, and what is likely not to be relevant to that. For example, we should think twice about invoking references to black emancipation to explain the PlayStation® 2 ad (the song, 'Get on board, l'il children', is thought to have had a double meaning as a gospel song, referring to both faith and to the Underground Railroad that smuggled slaves from the USA to Canada). We must come up with pretty good reasons about the context of the ad's consumption if we do claim that as relevant meaning.

The second dimension is the textual. Intertextual meaning will often arise directly from the text's echoing of previous texts – in aspects such as its words or structure or narrative progression or visual form. Thirdly, it need not be a direct reference such as 'You'll need some glue', but may be a more distant echo of something like (alleged) Mancunian male chauvinism, which we can nevertheless trace through references to the identity required to make sense of the beer ad. These more distant echoes are, paradoxically, the most powerful for they are the most pervasive. In every detail of a text, its receivers recognize previous ways of talking, particularly ways which have solidified over time and use into genres, and these alert them as to how they should fit the elements together into larger meaningful units. Fairclough (1995: 55) argues that it is through such generic heterogeneity that we can most strongly identify social change and challenges to social structures. A text may draw upon the language of another genre, it may perform some of the functions of another genre (a Nescafé ad may tell a romantic story), or it may draw upon the graphic form of another genre (Cook 1992, describes a Hamlet cigar ad that plays with the British Channel 4 station logo). What is important, however, is that we differentiate between intertext that is **accountable** meaning along some or all of the three dimensions sketched above (that is, a reference that we could have expected the text's producer to recognize as part of the way the receiver would make sense of the text) and intertext that is personal or otherwise marginal.

I will apply intertextual analysis in more detail shortly, but we can already see how intertextuality helps to understand and critique the Mini ad. The ad opens up a quite specific identity for its interpreters. The modelling reference is clearly ironic – no one would regard the invitation to make the model as actual, but as a reference to the false ease with which many model-making activities are portrayed in various media, from instruction booklets to television shows. The *Blue Peter* line, 'Here's one I made earlier', which has become a common wry intertextual reference in British popular culture, sprang to mind. We are being asked to be ironic readers of the ad and to take a critical attitude towards media, which so often give us the results of difficult activity but are a little mendacious in covering up the difficulties in the process. It is often pointed out that, before an advertisement can create a desire for a product, it must first create a sense of inadequacy which that desire will fill. In those terms, the Mini ad is constructing a dissatisfied consumer, asking us to remember how unimpressed we are by images of car bonnets draped with sexy blonde women, and providing a new, ironic and more satisfying position from which to consume.

The ad therefore participates in social struggle over advertising, seeking to re-accent the smooth sales pitches of car advertising and to disarm our scepticism about the usual claims to make us sexy, powerful, glamorous, invincible and skilful in our driving. So too, if we spot the reference to the 1980s' Araldite ad, in which a car was stuck to a billboard, the newer ad is seeking to disarm a critical attitude to the improbability of advertising messages in general. The ad is also participating in social struggle over the meaning of the Mini. The expensive ad campaigns for this car have clearly been designed to re-accent the meanings around a car that's tightly interwoven with the stolidness and decline of 1970s British society. The intertexts of the Mini on the billboard do considerable work to place the car within the enjoyable, anti-Establishment mode of MTV-type media (only partly, because it is clearly still an ad). They thus also call viewers to position themselves within that youth culture, with its interest in retro-culture. In doing all this, it is positioning the car, and the way viewers make sense of the car when they see it on the road, as fun, as a sophisticated cultural product and as part of young people's lives. At the same time, it is asking them to consume their way out of their cynicism with consumer advertising.

The power of advertising in culture: Must Be a Diet Coke® thing

Such intertextual advertising does not just draw in meanings, it sends the ad's associations back out into the discursive contexts it has invoked. This is part of the purpose of ad slogans (often called 'endlines' in marketing). One industry report argues that the use of endlines: 'not only keeps a particular brand name top-of-mind, but bolsters the consumer relationship with advertising, keeping it as salient a part of their lives as are some of their favourite films and TV programme' (Wateridge and Donaghey 1999). Advertisers use a range of techniques as well as endlines to embed the ad in consumers' lives. Interbrew, the owner of Boddingtons, ran a media campaign in the late 1990s after the main actor of the current 'Cream of Manchester' ads passed her driving test. She appeared on ITV's *Big Breakfast* and was photographed for the red-top tabloids (e.g. 'A Lovely Bit of Boddie-work!', *Scottish Daily Record*, 18 April 1998: 17). The publicity stunt both built on and helped construct the idea that the ad's star was part of contemporary culture. The 'Cream of Manchester' ads can lay claim, therefore, to have forged a lasting intertextual relationship with a wider cultural space, partly through the collusion of the editors and producers who accepted her construction as a minor celebrity. Similarly, a number of news stories on the 2002 Manchester Commonwealth Games talked of British athletes as the 'cream of Manchester' (e.g. *Mirror*, 24 July 2002: 43), a link the brewer emphasized by becoming a sponsor of the games. An *Independent on Sunday* article on a designer linked to Manchester bands called him 'the cream of Manchester' (11 May 2003: 13). And when the brewer sought to move production to Wales, the Boddingtons' slogan was used against it. 'Boddingtons, Cream of . . . Wales?' asked one newspaper headline (*Mail on Sunday*, 13 Oct. 2003). The Boddingtons' slogan has become part of Britain's shared textual repertoire – or at least part of a repertoire shared in media discourse.

The intertextual links both to and from an ad help us place it in contemporary culture. We might want to argue further that we can identify a considerable

power that advertising discourse accrues through its positioning of itself intertextually. Advertising works not just when people notice an ad, but when they
change their behaviour and in particular their habits in line with the ad. Thus,
the colonization of people's lifeworlds – their everyday activities and their
understanding of themselves and the world around them – is a goal of advertising campaigns. If we think of a particular bank when we hear Vivaldi's 'Four
Seasons', then the ad which had excerpts of the piece as its soundtrack has
managed to associate itself with our existing knowledge, attitudes towards and
responses to the music. The ad's success, therefore, is to become part of our
intertextual repertoire for that piece of music. Ads which can draw upon central
texts or genres in a culture or subculture are going to, by this logic, become
particularly successful in inveigling themselves into that culture. The 'Mountain' ad's reference to parkour, the underground urban sport, and more generally its adoption of discourses of cutting-edge youth culture, can be interpreted
as a strategy of placing PlayStation® 2 within that culture. Ads for laundry detergent are not just about getting your clothes clean, but about placing
the product, in Saatchi and Saatchi Worldwide Chief Executive Kevin Roberts'
words, at 'the heart of the family'.

This argument is not, however, straightforward. All the examples of ads
drawn upon above are strongly reflexive, monitoring their promotional display
in terms of an awareness that advertising constantly fights against audience
scepticism and a reduction in its power to convince. That is, ads such as the
'Mountain' and the Mini billboard take into account a reading position that
expects ads to be corny or even untrue, and which rewards that position with
additional dimensions of meaning. It is possible to find ads which are much less
reflexive, particularly those which rely simply upon psychological techniques
such as brand reinforcement, but I have chosen these particular ones because
they raise questions about the position of advertising in culture. Does the reflexivity displayed in many ads suggest that ads must do considerable work to
address alienated consumers in contemporary culture? Or does it suggest that
we live in a media culture (Kellner 1995) where self-reference or reference to
other ads are among the most powerful ways of appealing to consumers? These
questions are about the power of advertising to make meaning, and will be
explored in a brief case study of intertextuality, a 2003 Coca-Cola television
and cinema advertisement, 'Must Be a Diet Coke® Thing' (Figure 2.3).

This 40-second ad, featuring a young woman's commuter train journey while
drinking a bottle of Diet Coke®, ran during the second half of 2003 in the UK.
According to the advertising agency, it was expected to reach 83 per cent of
British adults at least eight times (Lowe and Partners Worldwide 2003). A string
of similar romantic-comic Diet Coke ads using the same slogan, 'Must be a
Diet Coke thing', followed that summer. The ad opens with a drab concrete

Figure 2.3 A young woman opens a fantasy with her Diet Coke® in these images from the 2003 Diet Coke® television and cinema ad, 'Must Be a Diet Coke® thing'

Source. 'Coca-Cola' and 'Diet Coke' are registered trade marks of The Coca-Cola Company and are reproduced with kind permission of The Coca-Cola Company.

landscape from a US city seen from a train window (this reading is anchored by the sound of the train's wheels). We switch to a pretty though not glamorous young woman, smiling slightly in a dreamy way, who opens a bottle of Diet Coke (close-up of the bottle). Music starts, the catchy bass line of a 1970s' funk-pop hit ('Strawberry Letter 23', by the Brothers Johnson), and she smiles a little more. She sees a truck going by on the freeway, with the start of its name 'Hey . . .' on its side. She then sees a shop sign, 'Sweet thing' flash past, followed by a large U, the word 'Turn' on road markings, 'Me' written by someone's finger on the dirty train window, and, as the train goes through a tunnel, an illuminated sign saying 'On'. Between each sign, she shows various expressions of surprise, perplexedness and finally wonderment as she puts together the sentence, 'Hey sweet thing you turn me on.' The music now develops a vocal track, 'Hello, my love, I heard a kiss from you,' as the city's signs spell out, 'let's get down 2' and the heading on the newspaper being read by the man opposite finishes the sentence, 'business'. She smiles winsomely at him. In these final 10 seconds of the ad, she puts the lid back on the bottle, the music stops, he appears from behind the paper, a young man in a tightly controlled ginger hair-do, no facial hair and a nasty buttoned-up shirt with orange car motifs. In the words of the agency's press release, 'the moment she enjoyed with her "Diet Coke" is over' (Lowe and Partners Worldwide 2003). She turns back to the window, rolls her eyes, and we see a Coke delivery truck with 'Must be a Diet Coke thing' on its back door.

To start the analysis, I will list some of the intertextual references here before investigating them in terms of the three issues discussed in the previous section. The signs are the most obvious. Seen through the train window, these are a cacophony of commercial messages and urban graffiti, and pull in references to the rush and noise of everyday life in a big city. This is direct textual inter-textuality. They are also specifically US signs, as are the cars and city buildings we see, and thus locate us at some distance from the UK viewer's context in a world associated a little more with their fantasies than their own daily lives. Through intertextual reference to various romantic genres, we can begin to link to fantasies of being special among the crowd, of the big city speaking directly to us, of finding love in the interstices of our daily grind. In particular, the US cityscape flashing by makes sense in terms of references to romantic film genres, where love could be the chance encounter around the next corner. *Notting Hill*, *Sleepless in Seattle*, *LA Story* (where a freeway sign inspires change in Steve Martin's love life) all depend on similar romantic scripts. There are no direct references to these films, but to a set of genre expectations. Nor is the filmic reference dominant, as the ad's clear colours and flashing, sometimes blurred, images out the train window belong to televisual and filmic conventions that suggest real life. The ad therefore connects also with our lifeworld genre of watching the world go by, slightly disconnected from us, out the train window. It also claims co-knowledge with us of real-world experiences of romantic thoughts for fellow passengers during commuter journeys as well as the wish not to get too close to some of them. The music is a funky Californian hit, perhaps linking the scene to the Afro hair-dos, soft drugs and laid-back image that we might associate with that era, but perhaps just to a funky mood (see Cook 1992: 37, on the difficulty of verbalizing how music works in ads).

The ad, not uncommonly among bigger budget campaigns, opens with filmic conventions – an orienting shot of the city, a close-up of the person through whose eyes we are seeing the scene – but within 5 seconds the focus on the drink locates us pragmatically in the ad genre (if we had not already picked this up from the context in which we were watching the ad). We are therefore being asked to locate ourselves in an ad that wants to be like a story. This filmic dimension and the specific genre links suggest that we are in an intertextual space not simply of fantasy but of fantasy-making, where we can play on the edge between the reality of drinking Coke and fantasy. The city flashing past sending us messages is a fanciful film running in our private mental movie theatre. The endline, 'Must be a Diet Coke thing', ironically recalls phrases about why people behave strangely (from 'Must be something in the water' to 'It must be love'). It also locates the ad alongside previous Coke endlines such as 'Coke is the real thing' – with perhaps an ironic twist.

The message of the ad is clear. Diet Coke can lead to little daily moments of feeling special, even a little bit dangerously sexy, as the near encounter with the man in the bad shirt shows. How does it work in terms of the questions about the intertextual discussed above? First, identity. Hodge and Kress (1988: 66) note that nearly every text is gendered in the way it addresses its audience.

The identity position constructed here is clearly female, a young woman familiar with the romantic scripts at work. The intertexts *not* called upon are also pertinent to the ad's construction of identity, and critical analysts often see their job as re-introducing suppressed or denied discourses to the text. We are asked to be satisfied with a story where the woman doesn't see anything sexy in the man in the shirt, where she doesn't have the sex promised in the signs, or fully enter a drug-world, but where she instead stays very safely in the real. She is someone in control of how she sees the world, in the way she puts signs together and in the way she shows ironic awareness of what she nearly let herself in for by smiling at the man. We are also asked to inhabit an ironic position, following the intertextual references to drug-induced hallucination without believing or wanting to believe that they apply to the drink. This sense of stepping back from the fantasy just as it is at risk of meeting reality, and stepping back from references to the urban jungle, drugs and the funky, is strongly signalled in the woman rolling her eyes. She doesn't need all that, just her Diet Coke. Like a good romantic comedy, the ad asks us to follow a route of meaning that presents a little danger but no disaster. As in many contemporary ads, it is the mode of making meaning offered to consumers which is important. Leiss et al. (1986) note that contemporary ads often offer not so much a particular use or satisfaction, but a way of being or living. In other words, Diet Coke© understands young women's lives, and offers to become part of a lifestyle that is replete with the imaginary pleasures of the settings and occasions the ad portrays.

Second, how does the ad seek to re-accent existing meanings? When it sits on the shop shelf, Diet Coke has none of the sexiness of the sugary and acidy excess of Coke. Choosing this brand is about restraint, about looking after your figure. The ad re-orients consumers towards the brand by constructing it as sexy and romantic, but at the same time it does not abandon its associations with control. The dietary appeal of the drink is, then, overlaid with cultural associations through intertextual references. However, simultaneously, the ad is seeking to place itself within our lifeworlds, particularly our negotiation of the commercial noise of everyday urban life, as a way of making sense of that noise and as a space of imagining. This, then, is partly how the drink sells itself. But by far the most powerful set of intertextual references is to discourses of control, of the bounded pleasure of day-dream fantasies. The ad's coherence is in terms of control over our lives (the woman firmly opens and shuts the Coke bottle). These are conservative discourses of contemporary femaleness, a long way from the celebrity endorsements of Kym Marsh and Mis-Teeq to market the full-sugar Coke to a younger female audience. In women's magazine terms, the Diet Coke ad is aimed at *Marie Claire* readers in their thirties rather than *Cosmopolitan* readers in their twenties, and there are perhaps echoes of women's consumer magazine discourses in the ad's version of romantic fantasy.

There is further irony to the ad. It shares a knowingness with the viewer not just about the pleasure in fantasies being their unrealness but also about how ads usually position themselves in relation to our desires in order to sell their products. As we have seen with other ads, the message, that drinking Diet Coke makes you see sexy messages everywhere, is not straightforwardly sustained. It is instead a joke we are asked to share, following the woman's enjoyment of and control over the illusion. What does this mean about the way the text inserts itself into a particular cultural space? Is it seeking to disarm critique, reflecting a loss of power of ads in a contemporary culture which is hyper-aware of the desire of mass media to call us into certain subject positions? The commonness of the strategy in ads, and its use by the biggest brands, suggest that advertising has lost a certain generic power. Threadgold and Kress (1998) argue that, 'Where power is strong, genres will be strictly policed and relatively rigid. Where power is less, generic form is liable to greater flux, fluidity.' Advertising is, then, a weak genre. It inhabits an intertextual space in which the banality and untrustworthiness of ads are a given.

Conversely, we might point to the ad's use of ironic reference to romantic comedy, the conventions of film, popular music and perhaps even consumer magazines. This wide range of references to popular culture suggests the dominance of popular culture as the site of the construction of our desires, self-understandings and ways of acting. In this view, the text is an example of the aestheticization of contemporary culture, in which the pleasure found in immersing oneself in consumer cultural texts is a key mode of identity formation (Lury 1996: 157). The irony here is not an apology by the ad, but a kind of intertextual reference in itself not to a text or genre but to a cultural mode, what Brecht called alienation, the technique of distancing ourselves from what we are consuming in order to begin to critique it. If Andy Warhol's pop art images of the mundane detritus of modern consumer culture were a radical strategy to confront us with our own consumerism, they are now a desirable mode of irony and knowing consumption. We are, then, asked to enjoy the ad as we enjoy a piece of 1960s pop art. Intertextual analysis can offer evidence for both analyses. However, the mode in which the ad coheres most richly is, I think, the latter. Pop art is a key, perhaps even central, intertext. The ad's designers were following – whether consciously or not is less important – the alienation, and therefore the fresh ways of seeing that pop art performed, when they gathered together the urban symbols in the Diet Coke ad. They thereby placed Diet Coke within the pleasure of being culturally literate. The detritus of modern life speaks to the sophisticated modern women not of alienation, but of Diet Coke's pleasures.

This chapter has sought to show how analysts can trace the intertextual linkages of an ad that allow it to have force in people's lives and in culture more widely. In contrast to classic semiotic analysis of ads, I've argued here for analysis that pays close attention to the processes involved in interpreting an ad, rather than focus on the text as a thing, underpinned by cultural codes. In this view, ads are a purposive form of communication whose purpose people recognize. They are moments in a circuit of culture, embedded in a wide range of social contexts. They are part of the continual change in the meaning of things, becoming part of people's interpretative resources as consumers and part of a variety of social struggles – over what they value, what they share, who they trust, and ultimately who they are.

Further reading

For more on what defines something as an ad, see Cook (1992: Chapter 1), and Goddard (1998: Unit 1). Cook also gives an excellent account of how words are used in ads, including logos and jingles, although not from a strongly critical perspective. Goddard gives a basic introduction to many aspects of print ads. There are many good accounts of the semiotic analysis of ads: the classic accounts are Barthes' 'Rhetoric of the Image' (1977a) and Williamson (1978), but Chandler's online text (1995) and Bignell (2002) give excellent introductions. Fairclough (2003: Chapter 3) clearly lays out his discourse analytic theory of intertextuality. Meinhof and Smith (2000) is recommended for intertextual analysis of a range of media genres.

3 | THE PERFORMANCE OF IDENTITY IN CONSUMER MAGAZINES

[T]he ideal individual [is] an owner, not only of accumulated property and goods, but also of his or her self.

(Lury 1996: 8)

Introduction

'The Gay Cannibal', shouts *FHM*'s headline about a man who made world news headlines in December 2002 after admitting killing and eating parts of his lover. Its standfirst (the opening line of a magazine article that is printed in larger type) continues: 'Keep the sickbag close at hand as *FHM* delves deep into the chilling kill-'im and grill-'im fantasies of German Armin Meiwes' (Bastick 2004). It is not hard to see why the magazine chose this story as a feature. It has everything a lads' magazine that thrives on sex, violence, gadgets and narcissism could ask for. Meiwes advertised over the Internet for a man to fulfil his sexual fantasies of killing and eating someone, and he and his victim cooked and ate the man's penis before the victim was killed. However, as this chapter discusses, *FHM* does much more than reproduce a juicy story. It selects, emphasizes and interprets the events through its choice of words – and, indeed, a story cannot exist outside of the words used to describe it. In doing so, it builds a shared space between itself and readers within which topics such as sex and violence can be discursively projected, and people like Meiwes made sense of within its terms. The headline, 'Gay Cannibal', for example, recalls nineteenth-century popular discourses in which cannibals represent the opposite of western civilization, 'savages' among whom male colonial heroes have dangerous adventures. That 'other' to the civilized man is labelled here as 'gay', intensifying the othering and sensationalizing it still further. The headline could perhaps address female readers participating in this popular discourse, and could perhaps address gay readers, but it makes much more sense to a reader who takes on a male and heterosexual position, particularly alongside the myriad of other clues the magazine gives of its readership. We can argue that the implied reader to whom all actual readers are asked to orient themselves is male and heterosexual.

However, such a magazine text produces a more complex space of identification than simply one of sensational horror at a gay man eating other men. As critics of women's consumption of lifestyle magazines have argued, such magazines perform on a number of levels – levels which need not make up a single coherent reading position. As readers, part of the pleasure is that we are not held accountable for the kinds of selves we take part in through reading a magazine we might recognize as trash. Thus, *FHM*'s cover line on Meiwes reads:

Cook a Friend! The joys of slaughtering *and* eating fellow humans

There are a number of layers to this. First, and literally, the text invites readers to participate in the discourse of cooking and eating friends. Second, it implicitly asks us to react in horror at the immoral and sensational invitation. Third, it asks us to understand the ironic intention of the magazine to 'wind us up', signalling the irony, if we aren't already attuned to the lack of seriousness of a lads' mag, through the exclamation mark, the overstatement of 'joys', the intertextual reference to 'bring a friend' and the reference to variants on the phrase, 'the joy of sex'.

From the first, then, we are asked to take pleasure in imagining the violence and the extreme sexual practice, yet also to recognize the behaviour as the opposite of our own (we are reminded throughout that the practices are 'shocking' and 'deranged'), and to find pleasure in that juxtaposition. We go 'deep into the chilling . . . fantasies' not to understand them, but to enjoy from a safe distance the sensational transgression. We are also invited to 'Keep the sickbag close to hand', placing the story in a discourse of how much horror we can stomach (the story's central two-spread is framed by images of bleeding meat) rather than the moralizing or psychologizing discourses preferred by most news reports on the events. It therefore offers similar pleasure to the same issue's 'Freakshow' section, full of images of deformed and severely injured bodies. Such images are a test of the reader's macho stamina, and thus the text positions its readers as (a certain version of) male. It is also highly individualistic to the point of being amoral, asking readers to respond with their stomachs rather than their moral sensibilities, and it is reactionary, assuming their participation in a stock response of horror (and a pleasure in being shocked). In all this there is no space for questions about Meiwes' state of mind, and of course the magazine has no interest in such questions.

All this is signalled in quite small details of language and in the story's first few lines. The argument proposed in this chapter is that the ideologies projected in media texts can be better understood through systematic analysis of such language features. It suggests that people's sense of who they are and of who others are is not only revealed in language but is constructed there. It also suggests that this identity is a performance rather than an essence – it is something people do rather than something deep within them. And it suggests that magazines are a key site within contemporary culture where identities come to be accorded legitimacy and power, and that they, as *FHM*'s account of Meiwes does, often position readers in strongly gendered ways and as consumers interested in pleasure more than anything else.

Identity construction

Critical theory is founded on the assumption that identity is a social and cultural phenomenon, something that emerges in relations with others and with social structures rather than an originary essence with which people are born. It is thus a political phenomenon. Marx argued that consciousness does not determine social being, but that quite the reverse is the case: our sense of self takes shape within the economic and political context of our society. Marx spoke of a 'false consciousness', that is, people learn to see themselves as those who dominate society want them to see themselves by consuming products that are structured in dominance. To take an example that was not available to Marx, the *Thomas the Tank Engine* stories are not just wholesome, if nostalgic, accounts of the merits of cooperation and hard work. They form a mass cultural product which serves the interests of the ruling classes by representing the relations of boss and worker as benign and consensual. The theory holds that my children, in watching the programme, are learning to place themselves in or alongside such ideologically loaded roles.

Identity is also a linguistic phenomenon, however, and here we see, as in previous chapters, that the notion of a single overarching structure to social life becomes difficult to sustain. Social actors take up different speaking positions when they speak in different contexts, and are thus, to an extent, different people. Gwyneth Paltrow's admission that her family knows she's just been talking to foreigners because her accent has changed is not the sign of a weak soul, but a sign of what goes on to differing degrees in every language event. Similarly, texts imply certain readers, providing spaces for actual readers to locate themselves with respect to the text and thus shaping the selves they bring to them. For Wolfgang Iser (1978: 34), this is not an imagined, ideal reader but 'a network of response-inviting structures, which impel the reader to grasp the text'. These details of a text set 'the conditions that bring about its various possible effects' on readers (Iser 1978: 18). In commercially motivated media texts, journalists and other media producers find themselves speaking for the desires of unknown readerships made up largely of people with whom they will have little in common. For their part, readers learn to set aside the values and experiences of their daily lives to engage with these desires. LeMahieu (1988: 21) writes of the emergence of this culture in early twentieth-century Britain: 'In commercial culture, it could be argued, the key relationship was often between the "communicator" and the "audience member", not between the two private individuals who happened to be filling those roles.' Both media producers and consumers, then, participate in a media culture that comes into being in their orientation towards media texts such as consumer magazines. All texts can be thought of as shaping the identity positions in terms of which they make sense, and commercial texts construct particularly institutionalized identities and relations, which may have little to do with the selves constructed by their participants in other aspects of their lives.

A key point to emphasize from Iser's and LeMahieu's analyses is that we need not look for a coherent ideal reader projected from the pages of a magazine such as *FHM*. What is coherent, instead, is the ways readers are asked to consume such identities. As critics of women's magazines have shown, such magazines instead invite readers to take up identity positions which may change from page to page, and which often conflict (this is one argument for close and careful discourse analysis of their texts). As is discussed later, *Cosmopolitan* constructs the singer and star of the reality show, *Newlyweds*, Jessica Simpson, as sharing readers' experiences at the same time as the glamour of her lifestyle is detailed and photographed. Ballaster et al. (1996) write of the 'instability and non-viability of the versions of female self-hood' on offer in women's lifestyle magazines. When the editor of the US edition of *Maxim*, Dave Itzkoff, quit in disgust in 2002, calling *Maxim* 'one of the most slickly cynical products you'll find on a newsstand', he wrote:

> What we specialized in were headlines whose promises weren't quite fulfilled by the accompanying articles, boxes of text cropped to the point where they couldn't possibly convey any information and, by design, gratuitous girlie pix everywhere, at the rate of one every five or six pages . . . Just one ploy after another, each one pleading with you, *Forget the page you just looked at – turn to the next one!* Like the women depicted in *Maxim*'s photographs, captured right at that boundary between an

R-rating and a PG–13, everything seems to be frozen right at the moment of revelation. It's all one big tease, except underneath those frilly under-garments there ain't nothing to show ... Is a magazine supposed to engage, enlighten and edify its readers, or is it only intended to distract them as they flip from one advertisement to the next?

(Itzkoff 2002)

Machin and van Leeuwen (2004) make a similar observation after analysing similarities in the discourse of the 44 international editions of *Cosmopolitan*. Such magazines do not offer stable identities or sets of ideas, but instead a mode of consumption. Each article provides solutions – sometimes conflicting – to the individual reader's problems. This constantly repeated format suggests:

a world in which there can be no solidarity with fellow human beings, no counsel from religious and cultural traditions, and no structural or political problems that can be addressed by means of collective political action. Instead it is all up to the individual.

(Machin and van Leeuwen 2004: 118)

What unites each issue of each of the 44 editions of *Cosmopolitan* is the motto of the 'fun, fearless female' who knows (partly because of her reading of the magazine) how to make the world work for her. This is the deeper, implicit structure by which the discourse and images of the text make sense.

Identity is dependent on language not just to construct social relations but also to shape what we might regard as internal psychological processes. Gergen (1991: 5) follows Wittgenstein (1922) in arguing that 'the limits of language ... mean the limits of my world'. Whether or not we extend such linguistic limits to all aspects of perception and thought, there are strong grounds for an argument that people act in relation to each other, judge each other and make sense of each other according to the resources for expressing self and attitudes to others provided in language. Gergen points out that we only have to try to imagine institutions such as the courts operating without their language of the 'inten-tion' to commit a crime to realize the power of such language items to shape the possibilities for the emergence of identities in those institutions. He writes: 'Without certain shared definitions of human selves, the institutions of justice, education and democracy could hardly be sustained' (Gergen 1991: 6). The same could be said of the language of consumer magazines. The shared mean-ings of key words such as 'girls', 'fun' and 'fearless' make up the parameters of the experience of being a *Cosmo* reader.

Foucault and power in discourse

We should talk of such language as 'shared' only with caution. While the discourse of a consumer magazine is shared in the sense of being something that its journalists can be confident that their readers will recognize, and therefore something they can deploy in the magazine, there is also considerable power bound up with its use. Few people have much power to challenge the legitimacy of such discourse. Foucault has argued that discourse forces us into subject positions when we talk or listen, not only providing modes of thought but the very senses of self from which those modes of thought are sayable. Barker and Galasiński write that, for Foucault:

> the speaking subject is dependent on the prior existence of discursive subject positions, that is, empty spaces or functions in discourse from which to comprehend the world. Living persons are required to 'take up' subject positions in discourse in order to make sense of the world and appear coherent to others. A subject position is that perspective or set of regulated discursive meanings from which discourse makes sense. To speak is to take up a subject position and be subjected to the regulatory power of that discourse.
>
> (2001: 13)

If we accept Foucault's position that subjectivities are produced by being talked and written about, then the constant talk and writing about us by others are a source of those others' power over us. Such theory, although it perhaps underestimates the power of the individual, can be applied quite immediately to lifestyle magazines, where commercial and cultural forces often lead to discourses of the self which neither editors nor readers feel they own.

Editors of magazines such as *Cleo* or *Men's Health* or *Good Housekeeping* are acutely aware that they must fill their pages with role models, values and problems which will appeal to their audiences, or risk losing their readers to one of the many other magazines on the newsagent's shelves aimed at that market. Editing a lifestyle magazine involves a claim to a 'special or sacred knowledge about the nature of their particular audiences' (Ferguson 1983: 128). This claim to be a cultural intermediary, a source of wisdom about what's new, what's right and what's beautiful is not just expressed through the text. Gough-Yates (2003: 121) argues that editors are increasingly in the public eye (talked about by others) and thus experience a pressure to project the ideals to which their magazines orient in their own lifestyles, in order to act as 'taste mappers and taste creators' for their market. In turn, these journalists are appealing to readers who, since the rise of consumer culture in the USA in the 1950s, have experienced both pleasure in consuming idealized lifestyles and a sense of failure and guilt at the impossibility of applying such representations to their own lives (Ferguson 1983). Neither magazine readers nor editors entirely own or are straightforwardly empowered by the lifestyles presented in their pages, although the discourses of self could not come about without both sets of actors seeking them out. Although we must also hold agents accountable, Foucault allows us to paint a picture of a somewhat agentless process of identity construction.

Sexualizing the self

Much of Foucault's later work focused on discourses on sexuality. He argued that, since the nineteenth century, sex has been the pre-eminent site by which identity has been controlled in western society. Sex became central, through medical, scientific, social scientific and moral discourses, in shaping both a sense of the inner psychological self and the self as a social being, relating to others. He writes: 'Sex was a means of access to the life of the body and the life of the species. It was employed as a standard for the disciplines and as a basis for regulations' (Foucault 1980: 145, cited in Schirato and Yell 2000: 94). Thus, Foucault takes issue with Freudian and Lacanian theories that argue that the production of gendered and sexualized selves happens early in life and produces the inner self. For Foucault, it is the psychoanalysts writing their case histories, and the many other institutions sexualizing our actions, which are forcing such subjectivities upon us. In doing so, they create a sense of the 'normal' person and a sense of those who are 'deviant'.

The power of consumer magazines can be reframed as not just that of sketching out lifestyles for us (on which more shortly), but more importantly of writing sexualizing discourses which define who we are. Like Foucault's doctors, and building on that scientific objective knowledge of the innermost psyches which they construct, magazines such as *Dolly* dole out advice to young people about how to behave in order to get and keep a sexual partner and construct 'narratives of normality' that offer relationship success and happiness through conformity (Schirato and Yell 2000: 95–100). Women in particular are bombarded with advice on how to achieve fulfilment in sexual relationships, to the extent that almost all pleasure, happiness, success and beauty are presented in relation to sexuality. Like the institutions of medicine and science, the institutions of magazines leave their mark on us, producing us, disciplining us in relation to the *Cosmopolitan* 'fun, fearless female' or the *loaded* lad 'who should know better'.

The *FHM* feature above is similarly doing sexualizing discursive work. It draws only rarely on scientific or legal discourses to understand Meiwes as news stories often did ('flesh fantasist' is one such borrowing which positions Meiwes scientifically outside 'normal' sexuality). Instead it makes him a spectacle of sexual deviance through its labelling ('The Gay Cannibal', 'bisexual', 'the cannibalistic orgy') and through its accumulation of statements of what Meiwes and his lover, Brandes, did and said to each other (in the terms introduced below, the text's transitivity is dominated by clauses of action and speaking in which these two men are the actors). This action, moreover, is expressed as ironic perversion of 'normal' actions, both those of eating ('his interest in becoming Meiwes's dinner') and of sex ('a victim willing to go all the way').

The postmodern self

One major qualification of Foucault's theory from within social and cultural theory is that the 'saturation' of contemporary life with so many discourses producing knowledge about us reduces the force of any one of them. Gergen (1991) argues that human experience in contemporary western society, in contrast to experience in the stable social worlds of less than a century ago, is so saturated with such talk that our sense of self has come under attack:

> [Society] furnishes us with a multiplicity of incoherent and unrelated languages of the self. For everything we 'know to be true' about ourselves, other voices within respond with doubt and even derision. This fragmentation of self-conceptions corresponds to a multiplicity of incoherent and disconnected relationships. These relationships pull us in myriad directions, inviting us to play such a variety of roles that the very concept of an 'authentic self' with knowable characteristics recedes from view. The fully saturated self becomes no self at all.
>
> (Gergen 1991: 7)

For Gergen, we exist instead in a state of continuous construction and reconstruction, always aware of possible alternative selves and able to play with being differently in different places. Thus, ironic positions open up. This is the knowingness that the ads looked at in Chapter 2 offer: why not try being the kind of person who drinks our beer? It is also the pleasure offered to the reader of the *FHM* article discussed above.

But we need not think of identity construction as always potentially layered and ironic. It is also, as Butler (1990) argues, a performance. People must find their ways through the different ways of being pushed upon them, and reaffirm their identities against those different constructions. We can understand children's play in these terms. I am relaxed about my children's videos because I know they consume many different media, and because they insert Thomas and friends into their own play in ways which cut across the discourse of the 'Fat

Controller' and the 'really useful engine'. From an early age, we inhabit multiple worlds and project multiple selves. This point has been well made in discourse analysis of everyday talk. Gee writes:

> When you speak or write anything, you use the resources of English to project yourself as a certain kind of person, a different kind in different circumstances. You also project yourself as engaged in a certain kind of activity, a different kind in different circumstances. If I have no idea who you are and what you are doing, then I cannot make sense of what you have said, written, or done.
>
> (Gee 1999: 13)

Thus, every use of language is a performance, a rhetorical achievement, and involves our orientation to certain identity positions available in discourse and genre. When we perform in discourse, we are signalling to listeners, viewers or readers which discourses are relevant, how we are mixing or juxtaposing discourses, where we fit within them and therefore what kind of self we are, for the moment, projecting. As Cameron (1999: 444) puts it, we might regard people not so much as talking the way they do because of who they are, but as 'who they are because of (among other things) the way they talk'. In this view, we should place more emphasis on the discursive resources – the ways of talking and ideas of what will be successful as talk in this situation – which a person is invoking and orienting towards in their language use. From this perspective, language does not speak us but it does provide us with a limited set of resources for getting on in life. The case Cameron discusses is gender. She quotes Butler's argument that 'feminine' and 'masculine' are not what people are but effects they produce by how they act and talk: 'Gender is the repeated stylization of the body, a set of repeated acts within a rigid regulatory frame which congeal over time to provide the appearance of substance, of a "natural" kind of being' (Butler 1990: 33). In speaking, people have to, therefore, continually restate identities, continually reposition themselves discursively and remind people of how to take them.

The political force of lads' magazines is clearly to restate and revise traditional interpretations of masculinity in reaction to discourses of the 'new man' (Jackson et al. 2001). Masculinity has become a complex category, one that is difficult to perform because of its competing definitions. The 'new lad' in *loaded* and its successors provides men with a set of performances of maleness through objectifying women, achieving sexual success and finding pleasure in violence, gadgets and fashion which negotiate traditional maleness's loss of status. Thus images of men grimacing as heavy weights hang off their penises provide a way to express traditional values around penis size and the traditional value placed on withstanding pain while making these concerns a game, a deliberate performance, and therefore not the same as the much-criticized traditional male culture.

Consuming identity

Such magazines are called lifestyle magazines because they offer identity as a style of living, and a style that can be performed primarily through consumption – the idea that to have is to be. They offer what Bauman (1992: 204) describes as the 'consumer attitude'. This attitude includes:

- individualism, that is, it is focused on the self rather than on a group identity;
- personal responsibility, so that we must solve our problems ourselves and should feel personal shame when we fail to do so;
- that there is a solution, prepared by experts, and that our job is to find it;
- that recipes of selfhood and ways of living can be bought;
- and therefore that the art of living becomes the skill of finding such recipes and objects, that is, the art of shopping.

(cited in Lury 1996: 50)

Theorists of consumer culture argue that members of society take on such ways of relating to the material world of things and to each other through reading lifestyle magazines, watching ads, going shopping and using products. Lury (1996) argues in particular that the consumer culture of texts such as magazines stylizes or aestheticizes everyday life, so that people try to achieve beautiful or harmonious selves by consuming the right products. In fact, identity itself becomes something that is seen as a possession, something to be owned. Consumer magazines provide one of the most important 'expert knowledges' through which this selfhood as a consumer durable is worked through, reflected upon, perfected.

Critical discourse analysis of the lifestyle magazine

A central concern of critical discourse analysis is to explore who has the power to speak or to set the terms of her/his own representation in language events, and who lacks that power, forced to perform a self or selves mapped out by others (Luke 2001). Fowler (1991: 129), for example, suggested that the language used in a feature article on waiting lists in a British hospital turned patients into the objects of doctors' management, even as it professed sympathy for their suffering. One key technique, used by Fowler and others, is transitivity analysis. This approach to texts, based on **Hallidayan linguistics**, focuses on each clause in a text, asking who are the actors, who are the acted upon, and what processes are involved in that action. Critical analysts have suggested that the accumulation of certain actors in relation to certain kinds of process across a text, and even more the accumulation of certain groups in the role of getting things done to them, indicates how the text represents the distribution of power in society, and the presence of ideological structures. The writer need not consciously shape the text according to such division of roles, but the text will make more sense, or feel right, or appear more straightforward in its account, if its syntax aligns with ideology.

Hallidayan linguistics contains an elaborate description of how aspects of language construct meaning, which this chapter can only touch on (see Further reading). A key element for Halliday is the distinction made between the **ideational** or representational function of a piece of text, the **interpersonal** function of that text and its **textual** function (that is, its role in holding the text together as a meaning-making unit). Transitivity is traditionally placed within the ideational function. However, if we follow Foucault's argument that discourses provide speakers and hearers with subject positions from which the text makes sense, thus shaping both bodies and minds, these distinctions will sometimes collapse. The representational function of a text – the way it renders the speaker's experiences of the world intelligible – positions us as much as the way the text addresses us or asks us to feel. A key criticism of Halliday's functional linguistics is that the functions of language are likely to differ from genre to genre and according to the discursive rules that are being invoked in the interaction. So in a teacher–student situation, the interpersonal dimension – such as the students' addition of modal verbs such as 'may' or 'can' or adverbs such as 'perhaps' in statements to express their uncertainty beside the teacher's certainty – is likely to be central to the way identities are constructed. But in a magazine text, which is performing identities for consumption by readers rather than speaking to them, the transitivity of the text can tell us much about the discursive construction of implied reading positions. The remainder of the chapter therefore focuses on an aspect of representation in magazines in order to understand the discursive construction of identity. Analyses of other sorts of text might require linguistic tools to be used in different ways.

The linguistic tools

Transitivity analysis allows the analyst to isolate the processes and participants of a piece of text. It thus depends upon the analyst's ability to do two things, before interpretation can take place. The first is to identify clauses in text, because each clause usually contains a single main process. The second is to identify the kinds of processes and participants in those clauses. But first, a brief note on terminology, which is often the most confusing aspect of this analysis. Transitivity, in Hallidayan grammar (1994), is more complex than traditional grammar's notion of transitivity as the distinction between verbs which take objects ('the theorist understood the idea') and those which don't ('the theorist celebrated'). For Halliday, transitivity is the basis of meaning-making in language. He thinks of six different types of process in English (material, mental, relational, behavioural, verbal and existential). He describes the subjects and objects of these processes as participants, whether it is a person or thing or abstract concept doing the participating, and uses different names for each process's participants, to indicate that they are participating in different ways. So material processes contain 'actors' doing things to the 'goals' of those actions, while verbal processes have 'sayers' and 'targets'.

A clause is generally recognizable by the presence of a verb. Sentences can be made up of many clauses, sometimes separated by commas or connectives such as 'and', 'as', and 'because' and sometimes embedded within other clauses in the same way as bracketed equations can be embedded inside each other in algebra. The sentence: 'Keep the sickbag close at hand as FHM delves deep into the chilling kill-'im and grill-'im fantasies of German Armin Meiwes' contains three clauses, organized around three verb units. The connective 'as' tells us that two clauses are being linked, and we can quickly identify the verbs belonging to these two clauses as 'keep' and 'delves'. Clauses are harder to identify by looking for the subject noun, as we can see here: the subject of 'keep' is logically 'you', the reader, but is absent because the verb is in the imperative mood (it is a command). So we will generally identify clauses by verbs. The third verbal unit, 'kill-'im and grill-'im' is embedded within the 'delves' clause. Grammatically, the whole clause is acting in the larger sentence as an adjective, qualifying 'fantasies', but within itself it has two imperative verbs, 'kill' and 'grill' (I treat them here as one because they're operating together). Once the clauses in a sentence have been identified, the processes going on there can be identified, usually performed by the verb, and the participants, as in Table 3.1. We will also often find an element describing when, where or how the action is occurring, called the circumstance or adjunct.

The analysis is already useful in pointing out the two textually absent but logically necessary actors, 'you' and the person doing the grilling and killing (ellipsis is indicated here by square brackets). Critical discourse analysts will often ask why a text omits such logically important information. In many university regulations, for example, passive clauses such as 'Students will be required to attend the lectures' are common. Although we must recognize the

Table 3.1 Analysis of the *FHM* sentence

Actors	Process	Acted upons	Circumstance
[you]	Keep	the sick bag	close at hand
FHM	delves into	the chilling . . . fantasies of German Armin Meiwes	deep
[imagined actor of the fantasy]	kill, grill	'im	

university's role in this clause, it is often argued such language gains power by omitting to say who it is that is requiring the student to do its bidding, thus putting its power beyond question and making it harder to identify individual officials wielding this power. It also places the student in the most prominent position in the clause, giving the (false) sense that he or she has some agency in the matter. The magazine text does not use a passive form, but an imperative, telling the reader to keep a sick-bag handy, a form which also omits the actor. (If we add a 'you' to make, 'You keep the sick bag handy', we have a different syntactical form.) Why it does this is less easy to analyse than in the university example. Magazine texts often begin by including the reader, positioning us alongside the magazine's voice (the *Cosmopolitan* text below on Jessica Simpson does this too). The imperative here doesn't carry much meaning of the story to come, but instead works to blur the line between the reader and the magazine – it speaks and we act – bringing us quickly into line with the *FHM*'s delving into fantasy in the next clause. The absence of an actor for the fantasy verbs, 'kill' and 'grill', works differently again: ellipsis of something that is syntactically required is a characteristic of causal speech and so makes the text less formal. Transitivity analysis therefore allows us to follow how language is put together to form meaningful clauses, opening up questions about why the text constructs a phenomenon within a particular 'semantic configuration', or structure of meaning, rather than another (Fowler 1991: 70, citing Halliday 1994: 101).

We can now ask what processes are being used in representing the phenomenon. Martin and Rose (2003) divide all processes into four categories:

1. *Doing processes*, which require an actor, and sometimes an acted upon.
2. *Saying processes*, in which an actor projects an object or another whole clause, as in 'she called his name' or 'she asked him what his parents called him'.
3. *Sensing processes*, which work in much the same way as saying processes,

except that they project feelings or thoughts or whole clauses, as in 'I can feel a pain' or 'I thought about writing the book'.

4. *Being processes*, which express the qualities of something, or that something is part of something else, or has identity with it; these usually involve the verb 'to be' or 'to have', as in 'they have plans' or 'they're together'.

These categories are simpler than those which other Hallidayan scholars use and I use them here for reasons of simplicity. Similarly, I refer to all participants in processes as 'actors', 'acted upons' and, in the case of 'being' processes, 'qualities'. Martin and Rose (2003) emphasize that these categories can blur into each other, so that 'we spoke about marriage' is in between doing something and saying something. They thus think of a continuum between different figures (i.e. clauses) that can be imaged as a wheel (Figure 3.1). If we apply this analysis, we immediately see that the processes in the *FHM* standfirst – 'keep', 'delves' and 'kill and grill' are all doing processes. They are action words, signalling to us that this story is not about how Meiwes felt or about commentators trying to make sense of it, but about what happened next, in graphic detail. The only feelings in that sentence are embedded within the word 'fantasies', a word from which the processes of Meiwes *fantasizing* that something *happens* is recoverable, but not emphasized in the text. The syntactical choice of a noun over a whole clause or even, as here, over a clause with its subordinate clause, is common in journalistic language for the simple reason that it saves

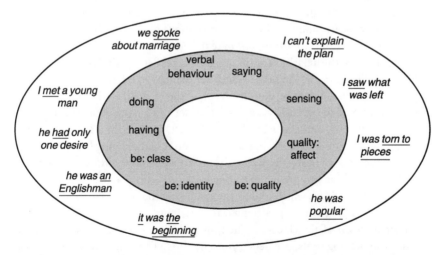

Figure 3.1 Martin and Rose (2003) argue that the process being represented in a clause can be defined in terms of one or more of these four overlapping categories
Source: Image courtesy of Martin and Rose (2003) and Continuum Press

space. Critical discourse analysts also argue **nominalizations** such as 'fantasies' are powerful ways of representing because they turn process into product and allow the people doing the action, as well as the circumstances (the time, place, manner, and so on) to be omitted. Thus, here, the word 'fantasies' not only saves space but takes readers' attention away from his mental state and the details of his homoeroticism, matters with which a lads' magazine is less comfortable than the categorizing of this person as 'deviant' and the physical details ('kill-'im and grill-'im') of what took place. It is through such details of syntactical choice that the text tells the reader what he or she should be interested in.

Cosmo and *FHM*: Writing on women

Transitivity analysis will be used in a comparative analysis below of the semantic configuration of two lifestyle magazine texts, and of the performance of gendered identities and the aestheticization of gendered selves within consumer culture. The first is the opening, descriptive paragraphs of an interview with Jessica Simpson, star of the reality TV show, *Newlyweds*, in *Cosmopolitan* (first published in the US edition of the magazine in May 2004, although I analyse here the version in the July 2004 Australian edition; see Figure 3.2). The second is the opening, descriptive paragraphs of an interview with Jamie-Lynn DiScala, an actor on the TV show *The Sopranos*, in *FHM* (first published in the US edition in April 2004, this version coming from the July 2004 Australian edition). The articles concern similar subjects, women made glamorous by the televisual.

The transitivity of the *Cosmopolitan* text (Figure 3.2) indicates that the focus of the article is the relationship of magazine readers with Jessica Simpson. Right from the start, the language places her identity in relation to 'us' (the 'us' being, as is discussed shortly, both readers and the magazine). The headline and the first clause of the standfirst act to define her in being processes: she is 'not dumb, just honest', and she is an 'It girl.' In fact, nine of the 58 clauses of the opening four paragraphs are being processes about her, defining her qualities or identity. She was a virgin, she was a drop-out, she is 'the girl of the moment' and she is 'anything but predictable'. She is placed within a grid of both intimate feminine attributes which allows the reader, as the text says, to 'feel you're meeting one of your closest girlfriends' and attributes of fame (see Table 3.2 for a full breakdown of the clauses). Then, in the second clause of the standfirst, she does something to us, she 'lets us into her life'. The magazine signals, then, that the article is also about her doing things either to us or more often implicitly in relation to us. Apart from such actions as spending money, farting, not being able to operate washing machines and fielding movie offers, she does many things that require us to be an audience for her, such as making no apologies, walking towards the *Cosmopolitan* reporter, playing a ditz, and making a fool of herself. Through these doing processes, the magazine text represents a performance of intimate feminine identity in our presence.

The category of 'us' is crucial to an understanding of Simpson. The text spends considerable time in its opening paragraphs establishing its relationship to the reader. The standfirst at first speaks for us, knowing what we earn in a month and stating that we love Simpson. Then, in the first substantive paragraph, the story describes the star's meeting with the reporter as if the reader was there: 'you can't help but feel you're meeting one of your closest friends'. Fourteen of the initial 58 clauses have 'you' as the actor, including seven sensing processes in which the magazine speaks for readers' responses to Simpson (she, by contrast, is the actor in only two sensing processes). The things 'you' sense are her idiosyncrasies, her domestic failings, intimate details of her marriage and her TV show and music. Readers are positioned, therefore, alongside the magazine as it constructs the star's identity, using 'we' and 'you' without discriminating between the two, and speaking for readers' responses. The knowledge here is highly gendered within a *Cosmopolitan* discourse. The Simpson that readers participate in constructing is known in terms of details such as her sexual history and her inadequacy in domestic terms, and all this is known through the consumer culture of television, music and film: 'you'd learn from listening to her recent album'. The article speaks for a shared power to discursively produce Simpson, position her with respect to an ideal *Cosmo* girl, and fill the rather unremarkable photograph of her that fills the story's first page with meaning. Of course, what is reinforced through this language is not some power of women to construct femininity, but the reader's knowledge of the already constructed *Cosmo* girl. Readers are being asked to consume what Bauman calls a recipe of selfhood. As Currie (2001: 260) writes, commercial culture 'fosters the production of women with both a need and a desire to "determine their identity" '. What the transitivity analysis allows us to see is how the woman reader is positioned with respect to Simpson's performance of that femininity and how she is in the process spoken for every bit as much as Simpson.

The *FHM* article, by contrast, does not invite us to know its subject's personality but to place her within a well-defined visual aesthetic. This objectification is performed by large air-brushed photographs of her in underwear smiling coyly at us, but is produced also in the text. The article opens:

CUBAN MISSILE
She's half-Greek and half-Cuban; as Meadow Soprano in *The Sopranos*, she's half-wiseguy; now in *FHM*, she's half-dressed. Gentlemen, meet the wholly desirable Jamie-Lynn DiScala . . .

Not dumb, just honest

When Jessica Simpson walks into the poolside lounge at the hip Avalon Hotel in LA, you can't help but feel like you're meeting one of your closest girlfriends (albeit the prettiest, richest, best-dressed one).

Like any friend, you already know many of her idiosyncrasies. In Jessica's case: her penchant for $US1400 Egyptian sheets, her inability to operate a washing machine or get across a room without tripping and the intimate details of her marriage to former 98 Degrees front man, Nick Lachey – all thanks to their mega-hit reality TV show, *Newlyweds*.

What details you didn't pick up from watching the show, you'd learn from listening to her recent album, *In This Skin*, which offers a blow-by-blow account of ▶

She's the It girl who lets us into her life, makes no apologies for farting and would spend more on underwear than we'd earn in a month, but the world is loving Jessica Simpson right now and so are we

Figure 3.2 The *Cosmopolitan* interview with TV star and singer Jessica Simpson positions female readers within a consumer discourse.

Source: Image and text from *Cosmopolitan* Australia, courtesy of ACP

Table 3.2 Clauses in Simpson text (*Cosmopolitan*)

Actor	Process	Acted upon/quality	Circumstance
[Simpson]	[is] (being)	not dumb, honest	
She	[i]s (being)	the It girl	
[she]	lets (doing)	us	into her life
[she]	makes (doing)	no apologies	
[she]	farting (doing)		on underwear
[she]	would spend more (doing)		in a month
we	[would] earn (doing)		
the world	is loving (doing)	Jessica Simpson	
we	are [loving] (doing)	her	
Jessica Simpson	walks (doing)		into the poolside lounge at the hip Avalon hotel in LA
you	can't help (doing)		
[you]	feel (sensing)		
you	[a]re meeting (doing)	one of your closest girlfriends (albeit, the prettiest, richest, best-dressed one)	
Like any friend, you	know (sensing)	many of her idiosyncrasies	already
[you]	[know] (sensing)	penchant for $US1400 Egyptian sheets, her inability . . . and the intimate details of her marriage to former 98 Degrees front man, Nick Lachey	In Jessica's case

[she]	[not able] to operate (doing)	a washing machine	
[she]	[not able] to get across (doing)	a room	
[she]	tripping (doing)		
[you]	[give] thanks to (doing/saying)	their mega-hit reality TV show, *Newlyweds*	
you	didn't pick up (doing)	What details	from watching the show
[you]	watching (doing)	the show	
you	[woul]d learn (doing/sensing)	her recent album, *In This Skin*	
[you]	listening to (doing/sensing)	a blow-by-blow account of her private life	
[the album]	offers (doing)	a ditty	about having sex
[account]	including (being)	sex	for the first time
[she]	having (being)	a virgin	until marriage
she	was (being)	all the other confessions	
there	[i]s (being)	everything from the shame	
[confessions]	keep tumbling (doing)		from the girl's mouth
[there]	[is] (being)	a drop-out of the *Mickey Mouse Club*	
[she]	being (being)	a brain surgeon	
[she]	wishing (sensing)	the passing of wind	
she	was (being)	the charm of Jessica Simpson	
[she]	finding (doing)	one of the reasons	so damn hilarious
that	[i]s (being)	'the girl of the moment'	
[that]	[is] (being)		
she	is (being)		

Continued

Table 3.2 continued

Actor	Process	Acted upon/quality	Circumstance
[she]	fielding (doing)	movie offers	
[she]	fending off (doing)		
other stars	wanting (sensing)		
[other stars]	to appear (being)		on her yet-to-be-titled sitcom
she	plays (doing)	a blonde ditz	
[the blonde ditz]	loves (sensing)		
[the blonde ditz]	to make (doing)	a fool of herself	
[this]	sound (doing/being)	familiar	
[this]	[is] not (being)	bad	
[her father?]	raised (doing)	a girl	on her father's Baptist bible camp
[you]	want (sensing)		
[you]	know more (sensing)		
what	makes (doing)		
her marriage	tick (doing)		
what	happens (doing)		
the cameras	stop rolling (doing)		
how real	is (being)	her show	
we	did [want] (sensing)		
[we]	discovered (sensing)		
this 23-year-old Texan beauty	is (being)	anything but predictable	

Jamie-Lynn DiScala sure does associate with some dicey characters. This season, she returned as the delectable Meadow on *The Sopranos*, where her lunch is paid for by blood and murder. And before long, the 22-year-old will go even further into the underworld, playing notorious Hollywood madam Heidi Fleiss in a new biopic called *Going Down*.

'I was able to get a taste of Heidi's personality by watching her *Sex Tips With Heidi Fleiss* video – and it's pretty darn good,' Jamie-Lynn says. 'The sex advice she gives is very explicit and dirty. Everyone thinks of her as a shrewd bitch, and she can be, but really she's a fine, nice girl.'

The text is clearly signalling that the reader should understand the star within a patriarchal discourse of women as sexual objects for men, rather than within, for example, discourses of acting or stardom or ethnic minority politics. How it does this is partly a matter of key adjectives ('half-dressed', 'delectable') but is to a considerable extent a matter of the transitivity of the text. Doing processes in which she is the acted upon start and finish the excerpt. Readers are invited, 'Gentlemen, meet the wholly desirable Jamie-Lynn DiScala'; the magazine 'has served up' the woman (see Table 3.3 for a full breakdown of the clauses). The text has only four being processes about her, and these are in the headline and standfirst, sketching in her identity – Cuban-Greek in ethnicity (and thus coded as exotic and sexually promiscuous), a television star and half-dressed – that go no further than constructing her an object for desirous viewing. They create no intimate knowledge, as the women's magazine did. Like *Cosmopolitan*, the men's magazine constructs a 'we' responding to DiScala and thus speaks for readers – it calls on us, 'Let us rejoice,' and states that 'we wait anxiously' for her to star in a film about prostitution. However, in comparison to the *Cosmopolitan* article, where there were 14 clauses with 'you' as the actor, this relationship is cursorily established in two clauses.

What is striking, then, is that the men's magazine does less textual work to establish its visual aesthetic and the viewer's position within it than the women's magazine does to establish its feminine lifestyle and its reader. The identity of the male watcher is quickly established, and the pleasure the text holds out lies not in the renegotiation of identity through the magazine but lies in the action performed for that gaze. For the dominant set of processes in the *FHM* text's 25 clauses are six doing processes associated with DiScala. The reader watches her 'associate with some dicey characters', return to television, 'go even further into the underworld', play a madam and then, in her own voice, 'get a taste of Heidi's personality' and watch a sex video. Transitivity analysis shows that the action in this text is predominantly that of DiScala performing for viewers a role of beautiful sex object. She is not a passive object, but actively fills the role of sexy woman by doing sexy things. These processes are followed

Table 3.3 Clauses in DiScala text (*FHM*)

Actor	Process	Acted upon/quality	Circumstance
[she]	[is] (being)	Cuban Missile	
She	[i]s (being)	half-Greek and half-Cuban	
she	[i]s (being)	half-wiseguy as Meadow Soprano in *The Sopranos*	
she	[i]s (being)	half-dressed	now in *FHM*
Gentlemen	meet (doing)	the wholly desirable Jamie-Lynn DiScala	
Jamie-Lynn DiScala	sure does associate with (doing)	some dicey characters	
she	returned (doing)		This season, as the delectable Meadow on *The Sopranos*
by blood and murder	is paid for (doing)	her lunch	
the 22-year-old	will go even further (doing)		Before long, into the underworld
[she]	playing (doing)	notorious Hollywood madam Heidi Fleiss	in a new biopic
[*unstated*]	called (saying)	*Going Down*	
I	was able to get (doing)	a taste of Heidi's personality	
[I]	watching (doing)	her *Sex Tips with Heidi Fleiss* video	
it	[i]s (being)	pretty darn good	

Jamie-Lynn	says (saying)		
She [Fleiss]	gives (doing)		
The sex advice	is (being)	very explicit and dirty	
Everyone	thinks of (sensing)		
her [Fleiss]	[is] (being)	a shrewd bitch	
she	can be (being)		
she	really . . . [i]s	a fun, nice girl	
we	wait anxiously for (sensing)		
the flick	to filter (doing)	Down Under	
[u]s	let . . . rejoice (sensing)		
FHM	has served up (doing)	young Jamie	on these very pages before you

by six being processes (clauses expressing qualities or identity). Again, though, these are not about DiScala, but are more active performance of the sexy woman. DiScala speaks these being processes in direct quotes as she talks about her role as the glamorous prostitute, Heidi Fleiss, in an upcoming film. She says that Fleiss's sex video is 'pretty darn good' and 'very explicit and dirty', while Fleiss is not 'a shrewd bitch' but 'a fun, nice girl'. The text gives voice to DiScala positioning herself within this aesthetic by describing the qualities of a sexy woman. The sexuality described is, moreover, one that is non-threatening (Fleiss is described as a 'nice, fun girl') and one that promises erotic pleasure for men (she describes the video as 'very explicit and dirty'). In common with much of lads' magazine discourse, the text foregrounds play and performance here. It positions itself against critique by showing the woman is not simply a sexual object but is playing at being alluring.

Both texts, then, spend a good deal of time discursively producing women in relation to men, and little producing male identities. As the literature would lead us to expect, transitivity analysis shows that women are heavily represented while men are left implicit in the act of representing. Berger (1972: 47) writes, 'Men act and women appear. Men look at women, women watch themselves being looked at.' *Cosmopolitan* offers the female reader a text in which to re-examine a saturated identity, only to become enmeshed in further discursive production of femininity. *FHM* offers a masculinity as consuming the images and actions of women, an identity belonging to a discourse which is so powerful in the magazine that it needs little reiteration through the text. Instead, the text performs femininity for the reader already positioned within this patriarchal identity. There is something curiously empty here about the masculinity performed which does not speak of a power to set the terms of men's selfhood. The male is simply sketched in and performs himself through the consumption of the women he sees. There is a parallel here with Baudrillard's comment on Disney's fantasy worlds:

> In both Disneyland and Disneyworld, it is clear that everything that can be derived from the imaginary has been caught, represented, made representable, put on display, made visual. Literally putting it on show for consumption without any metaphors is obviously a radical deterrent to the imaginary.
>
> (1983b: 246)

Men are not asked to imagine themselves in relation to women such as DiScala – that is, to place themselves in a discourse as the women readers of *Cosmopolitan* are – but simply to consume the 'simulacra', the images of these women. Male readers of *FHM* are not asked to invest themselves in the text in the same way as female readers of *Cosmopolitan* are. This is significant because it indicates the heavy discursive construction of social subjectivities for women, by which they can signal their membership of the social group.

While discourse analysis of media texts cannot offer firm conclusions about the implications for individual readers, because it provides analyses of the text and not of actual readers (see, for example, Frazer 1987), the analysis suggests that the social roles opened to men and women through such texts are well defined and limiting. Transitivity analysis can show how patterns build up in the details of how words are combined in clauses. Combined with Foucauldian analyses of how individuals' senses of self are performed in discourse, as this chapter has proposed, it provides close-grained analysis of the identity positions which emerge in the ways consumer magazines speak to and on behalf of their readers.

Further reading

The Hallidayan theories of social semiotics which underpin the transitivity analysis of this chapter can be explored further in Hodge and Kress (1988) and in Jensen (1995). A full account of the grammar is Halliday (1994), but readers may find Martin and Rose (2003) a good introduction. Transitivity analysis is applied in many analyses, particularly of news discourse, such as Trew (1979), Fowler (1991) and van Dijk (1988b). Good accounts of lifestyle magazine discourse include MacDonald (1995), Talbot (1992) and sections of Lury (1996). Winship (1987) is a classic account of the power of women's magazines.

THE STORIES THEY TELL US: STUDYING TELEVISION AS NARRATIVE

[T]he narrative form is maximumly meaningful. It provides a far greater context of understanding than is possible in life itself . . . By locating an experience in a narrative sequence with other experiences, experiences are given meaning.

(Wright 1995: 451)

Introduction

Narratology begins from the idea that all stories share the same fundamental structure. They all 'cohere' according to some basic rules. As a consequence, according to these theories, narratives all order experience and construct the identity of narrative actors in basically similar ways. This chapter explores such claims from a discourse analytic perspective, asking how far a theory of the basic structures of narrative takes us in understanding the ways that narrative is deployed in the media. A case study of the British police drama, *The Bill*, will be used to explore the political implications of the kinds of stories we are told.

The basic structure of the story is often identified by looking at simple stories, such as anecdotes. The US sociolinguist William Labov gathered a large number of these, including the following from a sailor in Columbus, Ohio, in 1970, from which he abstracted a set of basic functions that, he argued, the tellers and the audiences of stories would recognize. The claim of narrative theory, then, is that the following personal narrative differs little from the narratives in the news or televisual fiction or talk radio:

a Oh I w's settin' at a table drinkin'
b And – this Norwegian sailor come over
c an' kep' givin' me a bunch o' junk about I was sittin' with his woman.
d An' everybody sittin' at the table with me were my shipmates.
e So I jus' turn aroun'
f an' shoved 'im,
g an' told 'im, I said, "Go away,
h I don't even wanna fool with ya."
I An' nex' thing I know I'm layin' on the floor, blood all over me,
j an' a guy told me, says, "Don't move your head.
k Your throat's cut."

(Labov 1997)

As discussed later, the way this story develops, from a scene-setting clause (a) to sequences of action (such as (b), (c)) to evaluative comments that interrupt the action (such as (d)), can be seen as a universal characteristic of stories in all media.

Why is this? The key observation is that the sequential organization of events is a universal across cultures. This organization involves what Barthes (1977b: 94) called the 'fallacy of sequentiality'. Listeners to the anecdote above are simply given the words the narrator said to the Norwegian sailor followed by 'an' nex' thing I know I'm layin' on the floor, blood all over me.' But all listeners know to hear the clauses as a causative chain (his tough talk *leads* to him splayed out on the floor and bleeding). For this reason, Wright (1995) terms narrative a fundamental ordering of experience. This is partly a matter of the content of the stories that narratives provide as templates for thought. People can read their own lives according to templates of hero and villain, and so on. But, for Wright, narrative's fundamental ordering of experience is much more a matter of the ways it links elements together into episodes focused around characters and the ways it constructs cause and effect relationships. The details of the story become 'maximumly meaningful'. Readers know that, in the story world, each detail will make sense in terms of those links and causal relations. The act of telling a story thus transforms experience into something that can make sense (Labov 1999). Gergen and Gergen (1983: 255) argue that a sense of identity itself is constructed through narrative: 'The fact that people believe they possess identities fundamentally depends on their capacity to relate fragmentary occurrences across temporal boundaries' (cited in Young 1999: 430).

Narrative theory is not the only way to account for the ordering of experience in culture. As discussed in earlier chapters, the relationships between words and the intertextual relations between texts are also powerful ways of analysing discourse and are not reducible to narrative. But seeing texts as narratives is particularly powerful in exploring the ways elements link together into larger units of text. The discourse analytic perspective adopted in this book leads us also to see narrative not as something immanent, something that always already exists, but something that is achieved through texts and something that is therefore a rhetorical achievement of people in certain contexts. It is not a library of basic story types but a way of talking. This chapter therefore emphasizes narrative as what Wright calls 'models of social action', that is, the active dimension of the ordering, transforming and relating that take place through the stories we get in the media. The chapter focuses particularly on television fiction.

Coherence

Discourse analysis has shown that language users have a number of ways of making a text hang together as a meaningful whole, of which narrative is one way, if a powerful one. This has two implications for analysis. First, we will often find narrative embedded within other ways of ordering experience, with important effects. Second, we can also analyse narrative in the light of the other forms not chosen. Both these points suggest that we can analyse the extent to which texts draw on narrative as rhetorical acts. If making a text cohere involves aligning it with powerful ideas about the way the world coheres (or should cohere), these rhetorical acts are also potentially political acts. Consider the opening sentences from a BBC television news item on a hurricane: 'Winds of 130 miles an hour and driving rain are already battering the eastern coast of Cuba. Hurricane Michelle is approaching' (BBC News Online, 3 November 2001).[1] This piece of text, accompanied by shots of a wind-battered Caribbean coastline, describes part of a meteorological phenomenon. The two sentences therefore cohere as scientific observation: the second one gives scientific explanation for the observation in the first. But it can also be understood as a fragment of a story. The **deictic** 'already' signals to us that we are at a particular moment on a longer timeline and also cues us to expect the battering of the wind to get worse, while the second sentence similarly looks forward to the next event, the arrival of the hurricane. As part of a story, the two sentences ask us to look forward as viewers literate in the plots of storm narratives. This is signalled at the same time as we observe the unfolding phenomenon.

Why does this matter? The descriptive dimension asks us to think in terms of the phenomenon and its causes. The narrative dimension points us towards actors and a plot. Bad weather is not just approaching, but takes on anthropomorphic attributes. It has a name, 'Hurricane Michelle', but more importantly the story's action, 'battering the eastern coast', is done by this entity, requiring us to infer some intention, just as besiegers 'batter' the gates of city. This is of course meant metaphorically, and the BBC story is doing nothing new, as storms are often talked of in terms that echo the visitations of spirits or gods. But political sense-making work is nonetheless being done. Narratologists often argue that plots are about the disruption of an equilibrium. Here the equilibrium is left unclear, and we would have to infer some image of normal life before the storm. As a result, there is an almost mythic sense to the disruption, the entry of the anthropomorphized storm and the normal world which precedes the event, a vagueness that militates against asking questions such as whether the experiences of Cubans match this so briefly sketched story, whether preparations for such regular storms are sufficient, or whether human impacts on climate might be implicated. Thus, at the same time as these two **clauses** position the implied reader scientifically as aware of the cause of the disruption, they position the reader also narratively within a certain mode of understanding.

One way to pin down the sense-making work of narrative and other ways in which the parts of a text hang together is in terms of coherence. Coherence describes the qualities that distinguish a text from an incoherent or arbitrary jumble (van Dijk 1997: 9). Thus it accounts for what is happening between two or more clauses that add up to something larger. Narrative is a major and basic form of coherence, because it links elements together in a series of cause and effect. There are, though, other forms. **Syntax** is a local form of coherence: the nouns, verbs, qualifiers and other constituents belong together and add up to a larger sense-making unit, the clause. Groups of clauses also hang together by linguistic means, often through connectives such as 'and', 'although' or 'who' which string clauses together and through deixis – the use of words such as 'she', 'then' or 'here' which require a reader or hearer to refer back to previous moments to work out who the 'she' is or where 'here' is. A series of clauses may cohere sequentially – as a narrative, where one thing follows another in time, or as an argument, where one thing follows another in ways that make it more convincing – or it may cohere as matching pairs – such as questions and answers, contrasting pairs, an idea and example, and so on (see Hoey 2001: 30). We can test this by comparing a minimally coherent text, such as a shopping list (which hangs together only in the sense that all the linguistic elements describe things to be bought and which rarely displays any sense of one thing being ordered above another for a communicative reason) with a more coherent text such as an academic essay (which has an introduction and a conclusion, asides, amplifications, a developing argument and much else) (Stubbs 1983: 15). Reorder the elements of the shopping list and you should still be able to do your shopping, but reorder the elements of academic argument and you have a pretty garbled text.

Coherence is often thought of as a quality of a text, but can be thought of as

happening as much in readers' or listeners' minds. Much of what we are analysing here is constructed between clauses, literally between the lines, and must
therefore be interpreted. For this reason, Ochs (1997: 186) suggests that, while
we might from a cultural perspective identify the most basic narratives in culture as myths, we might from a discourse analytic perspective start instead with
conversational narratives, because these are interactive achievements, com-
pleted as much through the nods, shared evaluations and additions of those
who start the story as listeners. Narratives such as Labov's sailor story therefore
shape the expectations of narrative coherence we take to other texts.

As discussed below, we should also be aware that texts cohere to different
degrees, and we should not approach all texts expecting to find every element
strongly linked to every other. This is particularly the case with television,
where a number of critics argue that the context of viewing does not favour
highly structured texts, but instead favours what Raymond Williams (1974: 93)
called flow. This kind of discourse analysis therefore tries to make a more
complex point than the common argument that most forms of media text,
whether entertainment or journalistic, are structured around narratives. Casey
et al., for example, argue: 'It is narratives that draw us in, engage us and
encourage us to keep reading, viewing or listening. The unfolding of narratives
is one of the principal sources of pleasure in media' (Casey et al. 2002: 138).
Bell (1991) makes a similar point about news as narrative. But when we look
closely at texts, we can see that the media draw on other forms of structure as
well, and meaning arises often in the productive tensions and overlaps between
forms of coherence.

Story as structure

The analysis of narrative as a form of coherence draws on but differs in some
fundamental assumptions from the structural narratology made famous in film
theory. In particular, it sees narrative as a choice and as a rhetorical achievement more than as a deep structure underpinning culture. Following Propp,
Todorov, Lévi-Strauss and others, film theorists have been able to argue that film
narratives reiterate already given narratives, giving pleasure by allowing us to
recognize fundamental character types and plots, or by mixing or slightly changing these prototypes. The weather story above therefore gives us a fragment of
a story recognizable as much from myths or fairy tales as from previous weather
stories. This thinking begins from the observation that any specific telling of a
story – what is in variants of structural narratology called the plot, *syuzhet* or
discours – only makes sense in terms of an underlying story – the real story, the
fabula or *histoire*. It is possible to juggle the clauses or images in a story into

almost any order and, with a few changes of tense and pronouns, still make a readable story (for some extended examples, see Hoey 2001). The 'real story' has its own unalterable order: as Propp (1968: 21) puts it, 'Theft cannot take place before the door is forced'. So it might be argued that meaning is coded at a deeper level of the story, which is independent of the text. Rather than identify coherence between elements, then, these theorists identify a whole structure that shapes how a story can emerge. So the *histoire* must follow a temporal structure, while the *discours* can leap around, often starting in the middle and working first backwards and then forwards. Similarly, Propp used over 100 examples of traditional Russian 'heroic wondertales' to identify eight character roles which not only recurred in each story but structured all the characters possible. These are:

> the villain, the hero, the donor (who provides something which allows the hero to take the plot forward), the helper, the princess (the person the villain and hero fight over, or the person who is the hero's reward), the princess's father, the dispatcher (who sends the hero off) and the false hero.
> (cited in Branston and Stafford 2003: 34)

These roles may be filled by the same character at different points, as different storylines emerge. In 'The Cartridge Family' episode of *The Simpsons* (episode 183), the main plotline concerns how buying a gun changes the father, Homer (witness his comment at one point: 'I felt this incredible surge of power, like God must feel when he's holding a gun'). Part-way through, however, the mother, Marge, becomes the plot's protagonist. Now her fears, her determination to rid the house of the gun and her final appropriation of the gun drive the story.

Analysts can draw upon structural narratology without accepting that a small number of basic characters and plots structure the plot. It is useful to see that the hero role is shared, but probably not useful to attempt to define which of *The Simpsons* characters is the 'real' hero. Homer and Marge instead share aspects we could describe as heroic. As in many episodes (in a repeated parody of patriarchy), Homer loses power through the course of the plot to Marge, as she becomes the driver of the narrative, that is, the person who develops as a result of the action. This parody of patriarchal storylines can be seen as a kind of generic heterogeneity (Chapter 2).

Narratology: Principles of storytelling

Contemporary narratology tends towards describing narrative principles and conventions, rather than the rules of narratives – a notion that requires that all narrative texts must follow a set of rules in order to work.[2] As a result, proto-narratives (such as: hero faces danger and then triumphs) are less important than techniques of storytelling. The underlying story is emphasized less than the act of telling.

The basic logic of telling a story involves an arc from the initial complication of a situation to its final resolution (Fabb 1997: 165). So a story is worth telling to the extent that something out of the ordinary has happened. This disruption is what makes the story 'reportable' (Gülich and Quasthoff 1985: 171). The narrative driver of the text is to resolve the crisis and attempt to restore the equilibrium. Each episode within the story replicates the model on a smaller scale. This basic logic, which may be signalled in the text but depends on readers' or viewers' ordering of the text in their minds, is what provides a large dimension of the coherence of the text, placing each element on the arc from the first crisis to the final resolution. This becomes clear in the analysis of an event such as the US bombing of Baghdad which started the invasion of Iraq in March 2003. Official US and British publicity before the invasion placed the upcoming event within a narrative of 'shock and awe', that is, a very short arc where heavy bombing would lead to the Iraqi Government's quick capitulation (while critics of the war plans and the Iraqi Government put forward quite different narratives, from a long drawn-out war to a rapid defeat for the USA). The event, then, was surrounded by competing narrative arcs which sought to make sense of it. Then, on 20 March, as the world waited for the bombing to begin, a surprisingly small attack took place, requiring a fresh set of propaganda narratives, as the news agency, Reuters, reported:

UPDATE 1 – AIR WAR SCRIPT PRE-EMPTED BY
DECAPITATION BID

DOHA, March 20 (Reuters) – President George W. Bush threw away the script and timetable for war on Iraq on Thursday when U.S. intelligence came up with one of its most long-sought after and elusive prizes: the location of President Saddam Hussein.

It began a day, or maybe even two, ahead of schedule with narrow-focus cruise missile strikes at dawn Baghdad time, surprising analysts who expected a 'shock and awe' blitz using more than 3,000 precision-guided bombs and missiles.

Despite the abrupt change of plan, one can only imagine Iraq's shock and awe if Saddam had died. In Washington, it would have been greeted as victory.

The missiles fired by U.S. submarines and warships were meant to kill

Saddam and his aides. But the Iraqi leader was quickly shown on television reading a speech of defiance.

(Reuters news wire, 21 March 2003, 04:24 GMT)

The new narrative justifying the attack began with precision bombing, with the hope of a still quicker resolution in Saddam Hussein's death and US victory. When this story did not finish as planned, the 'shock and awe' narrative was returned to, and when Iraqi Government capitulation did not ensue, the elements were again organized for our reading by another official narrative, that of the capture of Baghdad. Indeed, the US political manoeuvring in Iraq since, up to the time of writing, can be interpreted as attempts to provide endings to the US occupation which cast the occupation in a positive light.

This is the power of narrative. As Wright suggests, once viewers recognize a narrative arc as relevant to making sense of some text, they can be expected to regard every detail as significant, as organized for maximum meaningfulness, in terms of that narrative. It becomes difficult to read the bombing as angering Iraqi citizens into rallying around their government or acts that destroyed lives and the social fabric or that further polarized Middle Eastern politics, as these very tidy narratives worked to resolve political problems through the spectacular cause and effect sequences of bombing.

We can see here both a problem and a strength of narrative analysis. The weakness is that so much takes place between the lines and with reference to unstated principles of storytelling. Readings have to be relevant (as discussed in Chapter 2), and it is sometimes difficult to pin down analyses. The strength is that we can then see how ideas are propagated without being stated. The problem is lessened if we are able to point to signals in the text which prefer certain readings. The Reuters text does this through key words, such as 'prizes' or 'victory', which direct us to a sense of ending, and 'after' or 'it would have been greeted,' which signal progression through the narrative. Fabb (1997) notes that perhaps still more important in signalling a story's arc is the assumption that listeners make, unless told otherwise, that a sequence of elements implies a relationship of cause and effect. As discussed above, listeners know to hear the clauses in the sailor's story told to Labov as a causative chain, where what happens later happens because of what happened earlier. Listening to a story is partly about listening for the teller's sense about why something happened that is woven in through the way moments are chained together.

Part of the politics of journalism is that it often resists the narratives of its sources, reorganizing the elements according to newsworthiness and therefore placing the source narrative as only one among a range of possible ones. The text above contains little of the sequential fallacy, making the US Government's changes to its planned narrative itself the reportable event and the existing war plan the equilibrium that is disrupted ('Bush threw away the script and time-table'). The headline and the first three sentences tell an interrupted narrative sequence. Each paragraph has two clauses, where one clause relates back to the original plan and one to the bombing. Although a story emerges in those latter half sentences – US intelligence finds Saddam Hussein, strikes are launched at dawn, the shocked and triumphant responses that would have resulted if Saddam had died – these are not allowed to flow one from the other and are framed within the journalist's focus on the change of plan. The news text does not put forward other possible narrative arcs for the events (some critics of the war plan, for example, started the story in the 1980s, when Western govern-ments fed arms and aid to Iraq to weaken neighbouring Iran) and it takes our focus away from the military event and onto the political event of Bush's think-ing. This brief narrative analysis suggests the text is political in the sense that it resists the propagandist narrative, raising questions about military planning. Yet, on another level, it is apolitical, in the sense that it allows readers to forget that bombs are also about fear, death and a violent display of western might.

Fabb describes narratives as divided into episodes, each of which is character-ized by internal continuity in location, time and participants, and separated by discontinuity in one or more of these factors. So the text marks the division of the story into moments – for example, in television, the camera cutting away to a new scene – but the story itself happens as much between these moments, in the gaps that are left for us. When watchers of satellite news channels saw bombers leaving the British RAF Brize Norton airfield and then six hours later saw flashes in the sky over Baghdad, they had to connect the two, imagining the continuity in between of the bomber aircraft crews crossing Europe and the Middle East. Each scene also sets up an entire narrative world around itself through its establishment of time, place and participants, a world dependent on listeners' knowledge but also coherent with what is going on. This is as true of non-fiction as it is of fictional narrative. The sailor story invokes a rough pub filled with sailors; the Reuters text above requires readers to think of Iraq as a government rather than as a landscape full of fragile human beings. If the text was read in the next day's newspaper, readers would have had to recognize it as happening in yesterday's world. Readers must suspend their own experiential worlds and enter the narrative's time and space coordinates and the experiences of the inhabitants of that text.

The social life of narrative

Literary studies, and the cultural studies which grew out of it, often involve an assumption that the critic's context of reading is universal. Discourse analysis, by contrast, requires analysts not just to look for a particular set of narrative meanings but for the ways that readers or viewers will draw on those meanings. As a result, discourse analysts emphasize the relationship between the viewing world and the narrative world. Gülich and Quasthoff (1985) discuss the findings of sociolinguists who have recorded oral stories in various settings, and argue that narratives have many functions in different contexts which listeners process unconsciously, from unburdening the narrator and self-aggrandisement to entertaining others, evaluating an event and presenting evidence in a convincing form (Gülich and Quasthoff 1985: 175–6). The sailor story is an extreme and sensational personal narrative, probably told to impress and shock listeners and perform the identity of a sailor who has sailed the world and seen it all. Some parts of the text become particularly important when we look for a story's functions in its social context. Narrative openings and closures perform important roles in cuing interpretative frames, through stock phrases such as, 'Once upon a time' or 'You'll never believe what just happened to me', or through the opening graphics and music of a television programme. The way the narrative text invites us into its world is key to the way meaning is made there. Most narratives also provide an orienting sentence or two (or sometimes deliberately leave them out, forcing listeners to do extra work in orienting themselves to the material). It is significant, then, as discussed below, that television viewing often involves viewers channel-hopping, and arriving at narratives midway through. The way meaning is made, according to narrative theory, must be quite different to those who watched the text from the beginning.

Labov laid the groundwork for this kind of work, arguing that the oral personal narratives he studied almost always had a number of other functional elements as well as the action and resolution (Labov and Waletzky 1967). The narrative is framed by an *abstract*, which takes us into the narrative world and sketches what is to come, and a *coda*, which takes us out of the narrative back to our time and place. Within the telling, we are next given an *orientation* to the narrative setting (in Labov's sailor story, 'Oh I w's settin' at a table drinkin''), and then scattered at climactic moments in the action, moments of *evaluation*, which justify or give the point of the story. These categories give us a checklist to compare narratives by. So the Reuters text is full of evaluation (i.e., Bush threw away the script, analysts were surprised), while the sailor story has almost none, suggesting perhaps that the journalist must do much more work to make his story interesting and keep our attention.

Stories on television

The social context of television is quite different again. Television, as Williams and Ellis have pointed out, has an intimate position in people's homes. It does not intrude, as a caller at the door does, and therefore viewers do not need to perform in formal ways towards it, but can relax: it is 'profoundly domestic' (Ellis 1992: 113). Television is continually on offer, as a kind of wallpaper, but only occasionally taken up by viewers, and only half attended to as they talk, eat or do other household activities. Ellis argues that this social context has pointed television writers and directors to distinctive narrative forms, character-ized by a sense of flow rather than narrative arc: 'According to Williams's model of flow, then, everything becomes rather like everything else, units are not organized into coherent single texts like cinema films, but form a kind of montage without overall meaning' (Ellis 1992: 117). As a result, we find narra-tives which concatenate small segments without any final ending. Soap operas operate in this way, weaving together multiple plotlines across time often with-out any obvious ending – even for their writers, who may have long-term narra-tives they are working through but who are often writing just weeks ahead of viewers. This open-ended structure, that may last literally for decades, would be deeply unsatisfying in a theatre play, but in the domestic setting of the home, critics such as Allen argue, it provides a rich experience:

> The long-term, loyal viewer of the soap opera is rewarded by the text in that her knowledge of the large and complex community of characters and their histories enables her to produce subtle and nuanced readings, whereas a single episode of any given soap opera, viewed out of context by a textually-naïve critic, appears to be so much pointless talk among undistinguishable characters about events of maddeningly indeterminable significance.
>
> (Allen 2004: 246)

He argues that the soap opera takes place at a similar pace to viewers' lives, often celebrating Christmas or Thanksgiving at the same time, so that viewers share a collective history with its characters. The most important sites of mean-ing in a soap are in the intimate spaces between each episode, and in the contrasts between plot strands, which viewers fill with speculation, imaginings and talk (Allen 2004: 251).

This point holds across much television. Although much television is organ-ized into self-contained episodes, whether it is a serial or a game show, Ellis and Allen suggest we should not think of the single episode of most shows as the coherent text, but see that text within the context of the season, the series as a whole, its repeats, its spin-offs and the domestic context of consumption. Ellis finds the structure of television instead at a much more local level: in short segments which explore a dilemma and then move on, so that shows resemble the 30-second ads which they share the televisual flow with. Linear, causal structures within episodes are present, but are weak. This has ideological implications, breaking down any barriers between the fictional world, advertising, and the viewing family (Feuer 1995: 495).

'The Cartridge Family' episode of *The Simpsons* already discussed makes sense in these terms. Marge refers explicitly at one point to the previous 'Who Shot Mr Burns?' episode: 'Homer! I don't want guns in my house. Don't you remember when Maggie shot Mr Burns?', constructing a sense of continuity across episodes, as a soap opera would (and indeed the storyline of the baby shooting the villainous nuclear power station owner is clear parody of the 1970s soap, *Dallas*). Yet, as a number of observers point out on a fansite, guns have featured in previous episodes, including one where Marge became a police officer to combat domestic boredom and showed no concerns about gun ownership.[3] The characters do not always cohere across episodes, a phenomenon common in the serial genre, where crises in one show are often completely forgotten in the next.

Olson (2004: 124) argues that the further a film or television narrative strays from proto-narratives such as the fairy tales described by Propp, 'the less familiar, less accessible, and less coherent these narratives become'. These mythic structures provide a powerful ground of truth for individual narratives and their abstract type-characters and settings are highly inclusive. Powerful narrative coherence of this sort may be drawn on, as in the hurricane story above, but it is questionable that television, with its casual, domestic gaze, always projects us into such mythic time. In fact, looking for unity of action and actor may be doomed to failure in satirical fiction such as *The Simpsons*, which parodies US politics and culture and thus makes much of its sense intertextually. *The Simpsons* episodes are probably more thematically organized. In this episode, for example, National Rifle Associations arguments that gun-owning is a defining and positive feature of (male) life in the United States are ridiculed.

Police problems: Case study of *The Bill*

This final section will explore the arguments discussed above in relation to one episode of the British police drama *The Bill*. This episode (broadcast in the UK on ITV1, 8 January 2003) comes from the nineteenth season of the serial, which began in 1984. It contains a number of storylines: the two major storylines concern, first, how the police deal with threats against a convicted paedophile priest by a vigilante mob and then deal with newly surfaced allegations against him and, second, how one uniformed officer, PC Gary Best, uses his power as a policeman to intervene in his sister's domestic situation. Surrounding these are fragments of a number of other stories of different duration which are flicked into for a few seconds or minutes at a time, including the cocaine addiction of PC Nick Klein (one of the repercussions for him and his colleagues of the death of another officer and his lover Cass Rickman), the former alcoholism of PC Jim Carver (who discovers Klein's habit), the suppressed affection of DC Danny Glaze for a nun who appears in a number of episodes, the corruption of one detective, Phil Hunter, who convinces his wife to sleep with a local crime boss, the emotional turmoil of gay Sergeant Craig Gilmore over a (straight) constable and wider storylines of police corruption, tensions between the police and the local community and tensions over government policing targets.

The overlapping and intertwined narratives of the characters, some of which continue for a whole season (Gilmore's crush) and some of which are years old (Carver's alcoholism) place us firmly within the soap genre, even before we consider the sensational and personal themes of these stories. The narrative world invoked is, as Allen puts it, one that viewers can share as part of their own lives, as the police station's personal lives unfold before them twice a week, year after year. These soap narratives were introduced into the formerly highly realistic programme (complete with hand-held cameras, topical social themes and rich references to its London setting) in 1995 to boost flagging ratings (Kibble-White 2002). The multiple, sensational storylines, each of which is treated in segments of a few minutes at a time, increase the pace and are seen by producers as better able to draw audiences into a viewing habit than self-contained stories.

But at the same time as the recourse to sensational soap opera narratives, *The Bill* episode also sticks to a 20-year-old formula of documenting a crime investigation through police officers' eyes, with the typical plot uncertainties of a British crime drama (is the old priest only pretending to be unwell, does the woman only now pursuing a complaint dating back to childhood have ulterior motives?). Here there is considerable narrative unity in Labov's terms. There is an initial orientation to a narrative world in the episode's opening scene, as Father Frank Keegan hides in a church from a vigilante mob. Key characters are introduced here, as are topical themes of mob hysteria over paedophiles and debate over the police's double role in protecting released paedophiles and protecting the public.

This is a fictional version of contemporary Britain, coming two years after riots on housing estates over sex offenders living there and only six months after a tabloid newspaper campaign for a 'Sarah's Law', making public the whereabouts of released paedophiles, had petered out. Keegan is rescued by the police, but the plot is then complicated by the introduction of Bridget

Thomas, who wishes to press charges for a sexual assault by Keegan when she was 10 but whose emotional turmoil may hamper a conviction, placing DC Glaze in a dilemma about how to meet his ideal of improving people's lives (the nun provides a dramatic counterpoint here). Investigative plots (such as in whodunnits, police dramas and personal quest dramas) provide classic cases of what Barthes (1974: 17) called the enigma code, new plot complications and puzzles that pleasurably delay the plot's resolution. Glaze seeks to resolve the case by making the old man face up to his past, whereupon Thomas' brother tries to kill the man, only to be restrained. Glaze is cast straightforwardly as the plot's hero ('Alright, but tread carefully, Danny,' warns his boss Jack Meadows) whose skills as a humane detective are put to the test. The occasional characters then disappear from view, and the narrative is quickly, if clumsily, wrapped up with Glaze being told by his boss that Keegan does not wish to lay charges against the brother. The **realist** drama conventions of *The Bill* resist a tidy ending for Thomas, but the police officers are returned to their initial equilibrium, if a little wiser ('It's never enough, though, is it,' Glaze reflects). The narrative thread concerning Gary Best and his sister follows a similar thematic and progression through crisis to resolution for the police officer.

This generic hybridity is typical of televisual fiction since the 1990s, including crime dramas (such as *Merseybeat* (2001–4) and *City Central* (1998–2000)). This is perhaps partly attributable to a loss of faith by producers in serial formats and what the scriptwriter Jimmy McGovern has called 'dramatic inflation', where writers and producers look less to actor-led plots and instead to increasingly dramatic storylines which must top the last one to carry narrative energy (cited in Kibble-White 2002). But it may also be attributed to the blurring of programme and genre boundaries in people's casual, domestic and channel-hopping viewing experience. If viewers are looking for even a moderate degree of coherence in *The Bill* episode, the two kinds of plot surely conflict, with an involved police investigation plot jostling for space in a half-hour episode with so many other strands, unable to pleasurably delay or satisfactorily reach resolution, and with a realist social setting of a police station clashing with hyperbolic plots in which at least two officers are killed each season. Feuer (1992: 158) argues that the advent of the remote control may lead to 'the end of genre' entirely (cited in Rose 2003) as a rapid flow across genres characterizes viewing. However, making meanings across genres requires that people recognize the genre boundaries to start with, so the end of genre is not quite so simple to theorize. Close analysis of a segment of *The Bill* episode suggests instead the coherence of its televisual segments is complex and multi-layered, but still a key component in how viewers make sense. The following 30-second segment occurs a minute and a half into the episode. PCs Gary Best and Tony

Stamp have been told to patrol the Underground as part of the station's bid to meet crime prevention targets.

(*Establishing shot of London Underground sign pans down to mid-shot of two men walking along pavement*)

1 GB: This is <u>stupid</u> (.) we're coppers not flipping bouncers
2 TS: Rather be here than nurse-maiding some <u>perverts</u>

(*camera closes in to two men's faces, shop frontages in background*)

3 GB: Yeah (0.5) must bring back some bad memories eh Tone?

(*camera swings round to back of GB's head and very close-up of TS*)

4 TS: I was [<u>innocent</u>
5 GB: [(I) didn't <u>mean</u> it like that
6 TS: It's scum like <u>Keegan</u> that bring suspicion down on [<u>all</u> of us

(*camera swings again so both men's faces in view, pedestrians in background*)

7 radio: [<u>All</u> <u>units</u>
                                                      Sierra Oscar
          48 Grattan Street reports of domestic informant is neighbour
9 GB: That's <u>your</u> gaff[4]
10 TS: T' I don't <u>believe</u> it (.) I'm doing your sister a <u>big</u> <u>favour</u> letting her stay there
11 GB: I know mate
12 TS: I've had <u>enough</u> trouble off the neighbours trying to <u>lynch</u> me
13 GB: Come on it might be something or nothing let's go and check it out

(*GB leaves to right, camera lingers on TS looking exasperated*)

See Appendix for transcription conventions.

The segment is a mini-narrative, analysable in Labov's terms as:

- *orientation*: the Underground sign and the two policemen grumbling on the beat, commenting on the paedophile priest plot begun in the preceding scene.
- *complicating action*: GB refers to a plot in the previous season where TS was accused of child abuse.
- *complicating action*: TS reminds GB of the resolution of that plot ('I was innocent') and so accuses his partner of being disloyal and doubting his integrity.

- *evaluation*: for TS, paedophiles create distrust of upright citizens like himself.
- *complicating action*: radio alerts them to a fight at TS's house, currently let to GB's sister, leading to one of the episode's major plots.
- *evaluation*: GB tells TS it's TS's house (thereby explaining this to the viewer).
- *complicating action*: TS complains that GB and his sister are letting him down.
- *evaluation*: TS explains his anger in terms of a previous plot where his house was used in a CID operation that went wrong.
- *resolution*: GB decides they will answer the call.

The narrative focuses on the personal relations of the two officers (hence the very close-up shots), exploring a dilemma and then moving on, much as Ellis predicts. Stamp's affront is not resolved, but is interrupted by the radio, opening a slightly different source of tension between the men. This is not resolved either, instead Best, who should be apologizing, exits stage right in a minimal kind of resolution. The segment shows, then, a minimal coherence: nothing much happens, just a lot of poorly resolved talk. As Ellis puts it, dilemmas are worked through, worried over for a while, then dropped.

There is narrative impetus of a sort, as other plot strands are woven through the scene. Already in the first two orienting lines, the segment is for a moment a telling instance of the political pressure police are put under to walk the streets, in the knowledge that few crimes are detected that way (line 1), and then in the next moment an instance of the pressure police feel in shielding paedophiles (line 2). Then the old child abuse allegation against Stamp is woven into the present (lines 3–6) before the radio interrupts with an incident that pulls in past plots concerning both officers. The scene thereby acts as an orientation of the story to come on PC Best and his sister, setting the scene and reminding us of the characters, in terms of previous *Bill* stories. At the same time, the viewer is asked to regard the action as a moment in a slowly moving tangle of narratives, building to the 'subtle and nuanced readings' of character which Allen describes in soap operas. Ellis (1999: 67) talks of the 'contingent and co-present quality' of such television narratives – 'they offer themselves as narratives that are evolving'.

However, the segment is much more coherent as a casual conversation, and this opens up fresh forms of interpretation. As will be described in more detail in Chapter 6, conversations are characterized by the participants taking turns to talk, making up pairs of statement and response, which often introduce a wide range of topics. As Ochs points out, narrative is often intertwined with other genres. If we regard viewers as watching a story unfold, we can interpret *The Bill* conversation above as produced for viewing as part of that narrative – as maximumly meaningful for the many plot strands it interacts with and which it is designed to draw viewers into – but if we regard viewers as looking upon a fictive world, in a much more detached mode of consumption, the conversation is simply part of that continuing world. As in the observation of characters that takes place in reality television (see Chapter 5), the interest is in much more **ontological** than **teleological** problems, questions such as: are these people sincere, true to their character, or performing to get some social benefit from the talk; rather than how will this end. The programme asks viewers to bring their expertise in human relationships in viewing slices of people's lives more than their expertise in televisual genres. The 'real person' isn't self-evident, but has to be discovered, and part of the pleasure seems to be in doing what we do whenever we meet others, the complex business of appraising them. As Ellis puts it (1999: 56–7), images of the world are given stability through framing and narrative, but they are also surrounded by forms of talk – justifications, explanations, appeals, speculation, complaints, and so on. The 'real' London scenes, complete with London slang, faithful details such as the uniforms, urban backdrop and the officers' tensions, is made enjoyable and understandable through both conversational and narrative coherence, but not too safe, so as to give a pleasurable sense of the disorder of real life.

Structural analysis of narrative often finds a politics in the oppositions constructed by the action and resolved by the plots (Bignell 2004: 91). There is thus a politics to the narrative's enacting of a police equilibrium that is disturbed by New Labour policing targets. A number of scholars argue that 1980s British drama often pursued highly politicized themes because of pressures from the Thatcher Government restricting news and documentary makers, and *The Bill* still pursues such social realist thematics. However, it also engages in a much more intimate politics through its depiction of the relationships and reflections of the working life of police in London. At work here is a moral claim to show us how it 'really is', a reality claim which *The Bill* has made since its beginning as a gritty police drama. Realist police dramas have been greatly criticized for legitimating and making comfortable the repressive nature of policing (Casey et al. 2002: 44–6). *The Bill* no longer enacts a unified story of solving crime – its heroes are busy solving their own rather than society's problems – and so perhaps is less open to such critique. Yet it instead inserts the programme more intimately into viewers' everyday lives, making police still more 'like us'. The political coherence – the ideology – of the fiction is perhaps not disturbed by its generic hybridity. But there is a cultural politics at work in the show's 'theatre of intimacy' (Dovey 2000), in its recourse to characters' subjective experiences of policing instead of a narrative coherence. The real is aestheticized as fragmented rather than as narratively unified.

The idea of coherence, of the way in which a text hangs together as a whole, has been at the heart of this chapter. Television, among other media, spends much of its time telling stories, and these stories are immensely powerful ways of ordering experience and providing meaning. But television language use also hangs together as argument, as description, as conversation, and as any of the other ways that language users link words together. Moreover, as scholars since Williams have explored, sometimes television is not maximumly meaningful, in Wright's (1995) phrase. This characteristic leads us on to reality television, in the next chapter, where showing the world 'as it is', in its incoherence as much as its coherence, takes prominence.

Further reading

Ochs (1997) gives an overview of discourse analytic approaches to narrative and Hoey (2001) puts narrative in the context of other forms of coherence. Fabb (1997) is a textbook with a clear and systematic account by a linguist of narratology, while Rimmon-Kenan (1983) will introduce readers to the wider narratological literature. Labov's narrative analysis is applied to news discourse in Bell (1991). The section on the 'Moving Image' in Boyd-Barrett and Newbold (1995) has excerpts of many key readings from film studies of narrative.

5 | MAKING SENSE OF IMAGES: THE VISUAL MEANINGS OF REALITY TELEVISION

On the one hand, there is the world of the printed word with its emphasis on logic, sequence, history, exposition, objectivity, detachment, and discipline. On the other there is the world of television with its emphasis on imagery, narrative, presentness, simultaneity, intimacy, immediate gratification, and quick emotional response.

(Postman 1993: 16)

Introduction

At 7.31 pm, on 27 November 2002, a dialogue was videoed between four people sprawled on couches in a house in Hertfordshire. It was broadcast the next day on British television.

1 voice-over: <u>seven</u> thirty-<u>one</u> (.) <u>pm</u>

(*long shot from above of four people on couches arranged in a square, looking around them*)

2 Les: (1.5) [*laugh*] I can't <u>believe</u> we're playing I spy

(*camera cuts to middle distance side view, over Mark's back*)

3 Mark: Shall I <u>tell</u>   [you
4 Sue/Les: [Yeah
5 Melinda: [Tell us
6 Mark: <u>Two</u> <u>way</u> mirrors

7 Sue: [Ohh
8 Melinda: [Ohh [laugh]

(*very close-up of Les*)

 9 Mark: (0.5) I'm enjoying myself [*over-loud and slow*]
10 Les: I am too (.) having (.)a (.) <u>great</u> time

(*very close-up of Sue*)

11 Mark: Luverly init? (0.5) (*very close-up from above of Mark*) I
             spy wiv my liddle eye <u>some</u>fing 'ginning wif (1) duh
12 Les: Death
13 Others: [*laugh*]

(*camera cuts to middle distance shot over Mark's back*)

14 Mark: Yeah
15 Melinda: [*laugh*]
16 Sue: Dullness dol[drums defeat [desperation (*very close-up of
             Les*) [despair
17 Mark: [Naa   [Naa
                 [Naa

This is an excerpt from day eight of the British show *Celebrity Big Brother II* (Channel 4 2002), a combination of competition, charity fundraiser, soap opera, documentary and social experiment, and one of the off-shoots of *Big Brother* (Veronica/Yorin (Netherlands) 1999–, Channel 4 (UK) 2000–). Six minor celebrities[1] were locked in a house, with microphones on their lapels and cameras in every room except the toilet, and over the course of a week's continuous filming were voted off one-by-one by viewers until a winner was left. The dialogue above should not, in classic accounts of television drama, documentary or quiz shows, make good television. It is banal and devoid of content, to the extent that it could be read as a parody of game show and talk show formats. The participants are bored (Mark, Les and Sue say as much). There is very little action (there is no narrative coherence), and no physical movement to keep the eye entertained. The quality of the directing is low, with the camera often focusing on a person who is not talking and sometimes looking over Mark's back as he talks. The setting is entirely manufactured, so viewers learn little about these people's lives – indeed, they learn little at all about anything. Yet *Big Brother* and its spin-offs have been spectacular successes in 20 television markets (Endemol 2004), with audiences of 7 to 10 million people recorded for some editions of *Big Brother* UK. *Big Brother* is also far from alone in drawing large audiences to images of the everyday. From grainy images of petty credit card fraud on *Crimewatch* (Jermyn 2004) to scenes where girlfriends meet the boyfriend's parents for the first time on *Bachelor*, television since the mid-1990s has been fascinated with capturing images of real people leading their lives in front of cameras. To explain this phenomenon, we must reach for generalizations such as that contemporary western culture – certainly as it is refracted through the media – appears deeply interested in what reality looks like on television. It appears interested also in exploring the inherent tensions between reality and what is produced for the camera, between authenticity and performance and between how people look and what they're 'really like'.

These are ontological tensions, that is, tensions about what it's like to be who we are, and particularly who we are in contemporary society – hence the interest in putting people on faraway islands to see how they respond (e.g. *Survivor, Castaway, I'm a Celebrity, Get Me Out of Here*) or in putting them in new roles (e.g. *Faking It, 1900 House, Jamie's Kitchen*) to see how people from our society respond to changes in their surroundings. This chapter is about one aspect of that interest, and moreover one which seems central to it: the visual. Reality television depends upon a response from the audience to visual modes – to the surveillance camera gaze, the intimacy of the video diary and to the portable camcorder following its subjects around. The verbal surrounds these visual representations, with reality being 'worked through', as Ellis puts it (see Chapter 4), in the discussion on chat shows, the dialogue between participants, in tabloid news stories, website comments and many other forms of talk. But always the specialness of reality television, whether of a mother and daughter in love with the same man on a daytime chat show or of the interior design plans carried out in a home renovation show, lies in the spectacle of seeing these real people performing in front of us on screen.

The rise of the visual spectacle has been theorized in a range of ways. For Kress and van Leeuwen (1996: 38), the western semiotic landscape is changing, giving new value to the visual and challenging the previous dominance of words. To them, cultural priorities are changing as a result: visual media do not inherit the verbal's distinctions between entertainment and information, and its privileging of the rational. To McLuhan (1964), we live in an 'electric age', in which the tyranny of the printed word, characterized by a one-after-the-next logic, that addresses us as individual rational subjects able to think in abstractions, is lessening. In its place comes a revaluing of simultaneous experiences of seeing, hearing and feeling through electronic media. To Baudrillard (1983a: 130), we live within a culture of 'obscenity', in which the distance between public and private spaces has collapsed, and in which 'to be someone' involves opening all aspects of the self to open view. With no interior and no exterior, everything becomes a spectacle and 'the most intimate processes of our life become the virtual feeding ground of the media' (cited in Dovey 2000: 88).

This book has so far emphasized texts as either talk or writing or as discursively shaped by talk, but there is clearly a case that media discourse analysis needs an expanded theory of meaning to include other modes, and particularly to engage with arguments about the changing status of the visual. Kress and van Leeuwen argue that the common-sense idea that: 'language is the central means of representing and communicating even though there are "extra-linguistic", "para-linguistic" things going on as well is simply no longer tenable . . . it never really was, and certainly is not now' (2001: 111). Their argument has two parts. First, they argue that every mode, from the visual to music to smell, can be thought of as having a grammar, just as language does. They quote, for example, perfume experts on how three different basic aspects of smell combine to make up further smells (Kress and van Leeuwen 2001: 114). Second, these modes then combine together in complex **multimodal** texts. In other words, Kress and van Leeuwen analyse the visual as if it was, first, language and, second, analyse it as it mixes with language. They have, however, their critics. Language-based philosophy from Wittgenstein to Foucault emphasizes that, although there is much to experience outside of language, understanding and knowledge happen predominantly through talk. In this view, language is used to make sense of images. The following chapter uses the explosion of reality television to explore how discourse analysis has been extended from language to the visual and at the same time to explore the debate over the relationship between images and words. The chapter's case study discusses a parody of reality genres which uses very few words, the BBC show *Double Take*.

Reality plus

News and entertainment media present us not with reality but with a selected, edited, polished version of the real. Just as fiction boils identity down into character types and lived experience into plots, media texts which purport to reflect the real always and necessarily reflect certain portions. The text, Barthes (1977a: 19) points out, 'is an object that has been worked on, chosen, composed, constructed, treated according to professional, aesthetic or ideological norms' (cited in Bignell 2002: 95). Its relation to any anterior real events is refracted through multiple judgements about how those events make most sense, including what aspects of them are most dramatic, most important, most likely to produce reactions from the audience, most easily digestible, and so on. The claim of 'that's the way it was tonight,' as Walter Cronkite put it in his nightly sign-off on *CBS Evening News*, is a claim by the media professional to have made as good sense as could be done in the time available of the preceding day.

Reality television, as the excerpt from *Big Brother* above shows, follows a very different logic in presenting us reality. This logic has two components. *Big Brother* deliberately minimizes the professional crafting of the real, showing us an unremarkable reality, with very little in the way of voice-over and little reworking of material, with even its evening highlights programmes (from which the excerpt above comes) showing little coherence. Other shows may be more selective in what they broadcast and may polish the material more with voice-overs and plot structures, imposing order on the televisual flow (*Vets in Practice*, for example), but still depend on a sense that the camera is following the ins and outs of real life. Yet at the same time, reality television programmes are clearly manufactured, because audiences are always aware of the camera. There is nothing natural about *Big Brother*, and no pretence that the house participants are leading a normal life. They are locked in a house and constantly monitored, so cut off from the outside world that during the first Dutch show the Dutch Institute of Psychologists worried they might suffer psychosis: 'They're away from their families, with no telephone, no TV, no radio. They're separated from real life. That makes the perspective of reality very blurred' (Martz 1999).

Likewise, in many reality shows there are complex rules which make the behaviour of their participants anything but naturalistic. Peter Bazalgette, creative director of Endemol, maker of *Big Brother, Ground Force, Ready Steady Cook, There's Something about Miriam*, and many other shows, argues that it is precisely the explicit constructedness which appeals to viewers:

> [W]e expose all [the documentary maker's] tricks. We're completely up-front about it. When we want [the contestants] . . . to talk about their first love, you hear Big Brother say 'hey – would you talk about your first love?', but documentary film makers have always manipulated their material both in the ways in which they edit it, and the ways they shoot it.
>
> (cited in Holmes and Jermyn 2004: 12)

The candidly manufactured reality is therefore presented as a more trustworthy representation of the real, because audiences are made aware of the process of capturing people and action on camera. As Bazalgette puts it, viewers get to see the rushes that are usually left in the edit suite and not just some final, polished product.

Baudrillard's term, the **'hyper-real'**, is used within cultural theory to attempt to describe this apparent paradox. He argues that people in contemporary western culture, surrounded by glossy images of the world, come to find greater value in the images themselves rather than in the referents of these images in the world. Plastic Christmas trees, modelled on idealizing Christmas cards, come to be preferred to straggly trees. The Las Vegas version of Venice comes to be preferred to the original because it fits the mass mediated construction of Venice better, and is therefore more pleasurable. Moreover, these representations are recognized as fakes or rather as not meant to be taken as real – their attractiveness does not arise from their representativeness of some external reality. Baudrillard points to the mass media which surround a consumer culture as responsible for producing such simulations and for shaping people's lives around them. Kellner (1989) writes: 'Baudrillard interprets the media as key simulation machines which reproduce images, signs and codes which constitute an autonomous realm of (hyper)reality and which come to play a key role in everyday life and the obliteration of the social.'

Reality television is, in this view, television of the hyper-real. It treats as real the virtual world created by the media, the 'pseudo-events' that only happen because a camera is there waiting to record them. That is, rather than treat filmed events as representations of the real world, the best approximation the director could do in terms of his or her professional judgements, it treats them as emphatically real because they were caught on camera. This kind of realness is about a quality of the image rather than a quality of the directing, a change perhaps motivated by an awareness of how much journalism constructs what it represents. This is a subtle distinction, but becomes clearer with examples. The court case is not a way of finding out O.J. Simpson's guilt, but is in itself the primary object of interest. The crowds at Princess Diana's funeral attend partly to mourn but partly to be part of history-in-the-making (Macdonald 2003: 21). The footage of a Concorde plane crash or the beating of the Los Angeles resident Rodney King are more real than the journalists' packages on the events. Thus, the report does not anchor the footage, for the footage has its own status as a hyper-real image. Like the themed venues in Las Vegas, there is a sense in which their status as hyper-real depends on them being spectacles, that is, seen within a heightened awareness that others are consuming the same images. This knowledge is central to the fame shows (*Popstars, Pop Idol, Fame Academy, America's Next Top Model*) where, as Dovey (2000: 11) points out, 'without the fame-conferring gaze, there would be no event worth filming, no reality'. As is discussed below, reality television gains much of its power from the way it positions audiences as participants in spectacles. Hyper-reality helps, then, account for the apparent paradox of *Big Brother*. The distance of the images and dialogue from polished documentary or realistic fiction reminds viewers constantly that they are watching a version of reality being produced in front of them.

This is about the status of televisual images of people. It seems that perhaps the visual representation of real events and people in general often makes sense not just as recording them, but validating them. Turner's *Understanding Celebrity* (2004) cites arguments that people's willingness to expose themselves on television has less to do with narcissism than with an awareness of how powerful these images are in society. 'Implicit here is the growing importance of the camera as a means of constituting and validating everyday reality' (Turner 2004: 62). The performance of self-disclosure can be read as a political act, one of the few ways for most people to get access to the centre of society which the media construct themselves as being (Couldry 2003). The power of television to make people feel valued extends into a fantasy of being famous, not for doing anything special, but for being on television. Turner observes that this desire for fame – a fantasy of being famous which underlies the whole fascination with celebrity – seems to motivate many of the contestants on reality television shows. He cites the huge number of contestants with little singing ability who queued up to be ridiculed on *Pop Idol* and similar shows. Later series of *Big Brother* show a similar motivation, with participants sometimes speaking directly to or winking at the camera. As Baudrillard (1983a) points out, some sense of the distinction between public and private must have collapsed for all this to make sense. Some divide must have broken down between our sense of self in interaction with others in roles such as citizens or employees and our intimate interaction with friends and family as private individuals. The private bourgeois space, where what people do is no one else's business and where they recharge the batteries of who they are, has become weak and less convincing as a site of locating the self. Today's citizens therefore don't want to read novels about people at home, they want to see them on television being private in public.

I see myself and I confess: The talk behind the surveillance

Scholarship such as Couldry (2003) and Baudrillard (1983a) suggests that reality television is less about reality than it is about television: the lens has the power to produce a particular sense of the real. Foucault is often turned to in order to conceptualize this power. To him, modern societies are characterized by what he calls disciplinary technologies – a term which invokes images of thumbscrews and manacles but which, in a rhetorical flourish, he describes as still more powerful than such merely physical punishment. These technologies include practices of surveillance, from the clocking on and off of staff to the arrangement of benches in rows in schools and factories so that everyone can be seen at once and the compiling of dossiers about individuals. The rational eye of the teacher, doctor, scientist and manager observes, not as an absolute ruler, who can be hated and resisted, but instead as someone who knows what is reasonable, what is normal, and what will allow us to lead fulfilled lives. This 'normalizing judgement' (Foucault 1991: 183) about such things as what normal sex is, what a normal body size is, what normal ideals are, regulates the behaviour of all of us.

Another key technology for Foucault is that of confession. Confession extends well beyond the acknowledgement of wrongdoing but produces a myriad of contexts where we speak about our own selves to others who can interpret and understand that self better than us, because of their access to such norms. Foucault (1990: 60) writes of 'all these voices that have spoken for so long in our civilization – repeating the formidable injunction to tell what one is and what one does, what one recollects and what one has forgotten, what one is thinking and what one thinks he is not thinking' (cited in Dovey 2000: 105).

Within Foucault's framework, analysis of reality television might look for the norms which are being enforced by people's performance before the surveillance of the camera and by their confession to the camera. MacDonald (2003) argues, from a Foucauldian position, that the gestures and ways of talking that people produce for television are far from being unique expressions but are in line with the conventions of behaviour they are aware of as appropriate on camera. They are aware that, if they get the performance right, particularly if they appear personable and sociable, there are the rewards of appearing successful and possibly even the chance of fame and wealth. She sees this normalization within conventions of style, behaviour and ultimately identity as deeply ideological (MacDonald 2003: 71, 82). *What Not to Wear* (BBC 2002–, BBC America/TLC 2003–) is a prime example of this power. Fashion victims nominated by their friends are videoed in secret before being confronted with this surveillance. They are then sent out to shop for a new wardrobe and equipped with fashion advice (long t-shirts accentuate the tummy, women should never wear black and white as it 'cheapens' both), this time aware that a camera is following them. The shift from the hidden footage of the failing individual to footage of him or her trying to become tasteful accentuates the consumer media norms which judge us by viewing us.

What is important here from a discourse analytic perspective is that, in order to understand the way power is deployed in reality television, we should place less emphasis on the fact that private lives are being seen by millions of viewers than on the ideas and statements which shape that viewing. In other words, the spectacle is not only talked about but comes into view because of how it can be talked about by society's rulemakers. If there are no doctors or psychologists here applying judgements of what is normal, there are Trinny and Susannah, the middle-class 'fashionistas' (Palmer 2004) of *What Not to Wear*, who know what looks good. The power at work here does not lie simply in the exposure of these people on television, but in the knowledge that lies behind it. Similarly, when the camera is pointed at individuals, they fill the silence not simply with an account of their thoughts and feelings, but with a confessional discourse that acknowledges the norms of the wider society who are their confessors. As Dovey (2000: 129) writes of video diary keepers in the BBC *Video Nation* project of the late 1990s, 'They are positioned in such a way that their mode of address has to speak from the individual to the general – this is a starting point for their participation.' What is important, then, to understand the way power is deployed in reality television is the statement surrounding the viewing of the fashion victims undressing, 'Look at her tits. They're like torpedoes!' or the voice-over explaining why *Big Brother* participants have been called to confess in the 'diary room'. Viewers must constantly be told what they are seeing and participants must be told what to confess to.

Palmer (2004) analyses the position of being filmed by reality television cameras as a moment of being objectified by their surveillance, and therefore sharing the look of the audience. He draws on French sociologist Pierre Bourdieu's (1989) notion of people struggling for distinction from each other to account for the power of that look. However, he argues that these looks, although shaped by general rules surrounding how social actors should look and act and ideas of correctness that are widely shared in society, are given particular force by the status of the experts on many reality shows. The reliance of *What Not to Wear* on two quintessentially upper-middle class young women – whose accents, dress sense, lack of worries about money and assuredness about giving orders places them firmly within a born-to-rule class – reinforces the role of the rich in establishing taste and correct behaviour. Palmer uses the programme to remind us that class structures (and therefore the need for class-based theory) are alive and well. Members of a society seek economic capital, they seek educational capital, but they also seek cultural capital – the possession of a kind of knowledge about what it means to have taste. For Bourdieu and for Palmer, taste maps tightly onto existing social hierarchies – Trinny and Susannah belong to a fraction of the upper-middle classes who are able to claim universal status for their sense of taste. Audiences' viewing – and the participants' self-observation – are organized by powerful principles of distinction and hence status in society. Surveillance carries power when people know how they should look and act, and that knowledge is signalled by the statements by the Trinnies and Susannahs of reality television. At the same time, Baudrillard's hyper-real reminds us that viewers are watching something that is more real than real. This is a spectacle for consumption, and therefore not directly about the viewer. In my viewing at least, there is always a distance between the fashionistas' responses to their victims' clothes and mine, so that I make judgements about the victim based on my own knowledge of people like them. Research is beginning to emerge on how audiences respond to reality television, which suggests their readings are often distanced and active in such a way (Hill 2000; Jones 2003).

To sum up, many discourse scholars would follow Barthes (1977a: 39) in arguing that the diffuse meaning of images must be fixed, usually by language, in order for its meaning-making potential to be unlocked: the 'tyranny of uncertain signs' must be anchored. Macdonald (2003: 71) uses the example of photos of the English nanny, Louise Woodward, convicted in Boston in 1997 for fatally maltreating the baby in her care. A *Boston Herald* photo of Woodward 'raising her head in anguish' at the verdict was sold round the world, and 'appropriated differently by those who thought her guilty and by British papers convinced of her innocence'. The spectacle therefore becomes 'a receptacle also of a range of viewer responses and interpretations' (Macdonald 2003: 71). Language gives definition to the image.

The grammar of images

Theorists of language tend to think of words and combinations of words as being a meaningful system which has some independence from the accumulated ways of using it, although those uses add to and inflect meaning. The word 'house' has a stable meaning within the set of rules of how language works, on top of which sit people's stereotypes and associations with houses. Do images have the same system or grammar underlying them? That is, can we use discourse analytic techniques developed to describe and explain language to understand still and moving images? Most theories of visual culture tend to describe its meaning in the semiotic or intertextual terms discussed in Chapter 2. So for Dovey (2000) the camcorder has strong associations with the closed circuit television recording of crime and surveillance and with the private context of home videos. He accounts for some of the appeal of reality television in the tension between these contrasting associations, one a machine-like, disembodied surveillance and the other embodied and emotionally loaded. A particular kind of image – grainy, unsteady, poorly lit and sometimes unclear video footage – suggests to us either or both of those antecedent contexts. However, the visuals of reality television clearly do a lot more than call up elements of context-specific cultural knowledge. Is what's left over to be described as simply **iconic**, that is, as looking like what we are used to seeing with our eyes? Or is there a grammatical system to visual images as well?

Kress and van Leeuwen (1996, 2001) argue that images and words work by different systems of making sense, and that images can say things which words cannot (and vice versa). A biologist's diagram of a cell, for example, has to put the nucleus somewhere, either in the middle or closer to the cell wall, although the nucleus is understood as moving around within that space. A written description need only say the nucleus is within the cell, and so can be both less precise but more accurate (Kress and Van Leeuwen 2001: 126). They describe this difference in terms of different grammars at work, and have also extended the principle to other modes, such as smell or sound. They argue that discourse analytic categories (and they draw particularly on Hallidayan linguistics) such as transitivity and **modality** also apply to images. This approach differs from the semiotic, pragmatic and intertextual approaches to images that were discussed in Chapter 2 in that Kress and van Leeuwen are trying to uncover principles of composition that have become established as conventions for both producers and consumers. They are looking for general rules rather than net-works of associations or banks of learned meanings. 'Grammar goes beyond formal rules of correctness. It is a means of representing patterns of experience . . . It enables human beings to build a mental picture of reality, to make sense of their experience of what goes on around them and inside them' (Halliday 1994: 101, cited in Kress and Van Leeuwen 1996: 2). In these terms, the principle that an image in the centre of a screen or page will have dependent or subsidiary elements scattered around it is a grammatical structure. This structure, in other words, is one of the basic ways of making sense that visual media have developed in western culture, and other elements such as typography, colour, the richness of images have their own compositional rules. There is a tension here. Kress and van Leeuwen (1996) argue that they are giving status back to the visual, disagreeing with Barthes that images depend on words for their meaning potential to be anchored. But they also draw upon linguistic categories to do this, and use of their analytical schemas must be aware that the visual is still being read through the lens of language-based theories.

Visual propositions

This section examines two aspects of their visual grammar: the ways that participants and processes are represented in images and the modality of images. The first aspect draws directly on Hallidayan grammar. Kress and van Leeuwen (1996) analyse images as if they were clauses, with clauses' two main elements: (1) participants (the nouns in a simple clause); and (2) the processes (usually the verbs). The *participants* within the image are the people or objects there which stand out as distinct – either by their position in the foreground, or by the distinctive use of colour, size or shape. These partici-pants are also identifiable because they are implicated in the second element, *processes*. (The image also implies interacting participants, that is, the viewer and the one who has constructed the view, and these may be left implicit or may be involved in the image's processes too.) Processes, as discussed in Chapter 3, may be about doing, saying, feeling or being, but most important in visual modes are doing processes, which Kress and van Leeuwen identify using the art theory term, 'vectors'. A vector usually cuts obliquely across the viewing. They write:

> The vectors may be formed by bodies or limbs or tools 'in action', but there are many other ways to turn represented elements into diagonal lines of action. A road running diagonally across the picture space, for instance, is also a vector, and the car driving on it an 'Actor' in the process of 'driving'.
> (Kress and Van Leeuwen 1996: 57)

A scene where one person talks to the other involves a vector between their faces. A scene where a person addresses the camera, by contrast, will contain no action but instead be a saying process addressed to the viewer.

This gives us a way of gathering evidence to analyse key aspects of how reality television makes sense. A major concern of critics has been that such television is voyeuristic: audiences are captivated by the sense of being able to see into other people's private lives. The notion of a 'hyper-real' suggests the situation is more complex, as categories such as real–not real and private–public become blurred, but Kress and van Leeuwen's (1996) terms allow us to be more specific. The voyeuristic act, in the literal sense of seeing people without them knowing they are being watched, is rare on television. It is indeed closely associated with the power relationships to be found in pornography. The (usually male) voyeur violates the (usually female) other by viewing her without her permission, and still more so at a private moment such as going to the toilet or undressing (Hughes 1999). The televisual images of women and children in a programme such as the BBC's *Child of Our Time* (2000–) allow viewers to see them in private moments – including in bed, when the parents are angry, and when the children do not think they are being observed – but is not voyeuristic in Hughes' terms because the parents have agreed to the filming and are aware when it is happening. The image itself, then, is placed within a quite different discursive frame.

But there are commonalities in the processes and the participants of these images. In both pornographically voyeuristic images and images from reality television, the participants rarely look at the camera. In both, the lens much more often observes the participants without that gaze being returned. The vectors of the participants' gazes, which to Kress and van Leeuwen (1996) are read by viewers as actions or reactions by participants, are directed towards each other or at objects. In reality television images, participants may at times gaze into space, suggesting private moments of internal mental processes. These vectors do not include the viewer as one of the participants and therefore establish distance. Both these and pornographic voyeurism project an 'outside', entirely independent of the viewer and therefore one that he or she can safely observe, opening up the possibility of what MacDonald (2003: 70) describes as 'the *frisson* of emotional excitement that comes in part from knowing that we are safe from a returning look'. MacDonald (2003: 99) calls this relationship a 'permitted voyeurism'. The viewer here is therefore constructed by the discursive context, and not by the image – it is a viewing not of the individual voyeur looking on a private scene but of the audience looking upon the hyperreal, on a stage set that is also the real world.

Once the camera zooms in, however, a different vector comes into being, one in which the viewer is implicated, as it stretches from our gaze down the narrowing view onto its object. An act of recognizing is performed by the camera. This is clearest in shows which use closed circuit surveillance television, where the panning and zooming are sudden and mechanistic, and therefore call attention to themselves. Jermyn (2004) quotes Tim Miller, series producer on *Britain's Most Wanted*, explaining why such footage is introduced by a dramatic zoom into the image: 'It's quite exciting. There's something about zooming in on something that is exciting in a way that just seeing it happen wouldn't be. It gives it added emphasis. And also when you zoom into something the image becomes bigger' (cited in Jermyn 2004: 79). The speed and suddenness of the zoom are important. The movement of the film camera is often described as pulling the viewer into identification with the gaze of that camera, and it can perhaps achieve that because it allows us to take part in the imagining of the narrative world. By contrast, the abrupt, shaky movement of the camcorder and the too-sudden zoom of the closed circuit television image remind us of the camera's presence in the world it is viewing. It becomes part of the action, accentuating the reality claim. The shaky camera intrudes on the world: it is not part of a narrative, not 'maximumly meaningful' in Wright's terms (Chapter 4). Instead, like the verbal reminders of what we are seeing discussed above, it disrupts any narrative or flow with the act of seeing, as if to make the statement, 'this is what you are looking at'.

By contrast, the hand gestures and gaze of the presenter of *Child of Our Time*, Robert Winston, are often directed at the viewer. The 'narrative visual propositions' (Kress and Van Leeuwen 1996: 62) associated with him bridge between the televisual and the watching contexts. The diary camcorder discussed below works within a similar visual semiotic, where the viewer is explicitly addressed as a participant.

The modality of the camcorder

The shaky or poorly-lit or out-of-focus camera communicates meaning in another way, affecting what Kress and Van Leeuwen (1996) call the modality of the image. This term too is drawn from Hallidayan linguistics. Modality describes the ways in which language communicates to us the speaker's attitude to what is being said or written. It may be indicated by a modal verb attached to a verb, as in 'It *could have been* me' or 'They *may* come back'. It may be indicated by an adverb, as in 'It was *possibly* me' or 'They're *definitely* coming.' Or it could also be expressed through tone of voice. Modality is usually talked about as on a continuum, from strong ('I believe this') to weak ('I'm tentative about this'). Visual discourse analysis finds modality also at work in images, through a visual grammar. Machin and Thornborrow (2003) argue that images in *Cosmopolitan* often display women with blurred backgrounds or in unidentifiable or very simple settings, and in pure, unmodulated colours. These features move the image from a sense of real people in real settings to a more abstract '*Cosmo*-land'. As in a fairy tale, these 'schematic and idealized' images allow glossy lipstick and fashion coordination to take centre stage without being subjected to the reality checks we might apply in more realistic settings (imagine a character in the naturalistic world of *The Bill* living by a set of *Cosmo* hot tips) (Machin and Thornborrow 2003: 459). The poor quality of some reality television camerawork signifies the opposite – that is, high modality – reminding the viewer always of the presence of the camera in a setting not purpose-designed for filming. These reminders are conventions – we learn to recognize a jiggling image in a war zone as a sign that the cameraman is running for safety, because we have learnt to expect steady cameras – but they are conventions that very strongly suggest a lack of staging. Dovey (2000: 55) observes that 'the low grade video image has become *the* privileged form of TV "truth telling" '. He goes on to argue that such images are 'indexical', that is, they lead viewers to presume 'a direct and transparent correspondence between what is in front of the camera lens and its taped representation' (Dovey 2000: 55). But the camera often communicates a sense of the real by failing to show it very well – you see Mark's back rather than his face in the *Celebrity Big Brother* excerpt – so is not straightforwardly indexical. Visual grammar suggests that instead it strongly modalizes the claim about what the camera saw, saying, if it were to be verbalized, this is what *actually* happened.

The diary shots of fashion victims coming to terms with Trinny and Susannah's advice about their wardrobe on *What Not to Wear* are a good example of the high modality of reality television. These images are shot by the victim her or himself, by holding the camera at arm's length or propping it up on a table. They are at steep upward angles, usually set in poor light and show the person unkempt and ready to go to bed, speaking in a low voice. The images are thus highly modalized, vouching for the actuality which has been recorded. A claim is constructed that we are seeing the person backstage, between the acts of the show, as it were, and with their guard down.

In describing the relationship of the camera to the reality it records, visual grammar again helps pin down the construction of a hyper-real image. Low-grade camcorder images record not just what happened, but a strong claim to authenticity in recording the events. But, as the banality of the 'I spy' game in the *Celebrity Big Brother* excerpt suggests, the emphasis in reality television is somewhat less on what was seen – on meaning – than on the process of seeing. The truth that is communicated is not anything about the four celebrities on their couch, but about truly seeing them. Friedman (2002: 7) notes that what distinguishes reality television is not necessarily that it shows anything that was not seen before on screen but in the marketing claim it now makes to show us real life, its 'open and explicit sale of television programming as a representation of the real'. In Baudrillard's terms, the hyper-reality of the visual spectacle lies at the heart of how it makes sense and of its enjoyableness. We must be pulled back constantly, reminded that we are watching authentic footage of reality in the making, so that the spectacle does not drift into a narrative with its own narratological world and characters.

Using visual grammatical analysis: *Double Take*

Double Take (BBC 2001, 2003) is a show about the fantasy that goes with images of reality. Using celebrity look-alikes and impersonators, along with fuzzy, unsteady camerawork reminiscent of hidden cameras, artist Alison Jackson purports to take us inside the private lives of celebrities from David Beckham to members of the British Royal Family and contemporary politicians. Like the reality television shows discussed above, *Double Take* seeks to attract viewers through the claim of the camcorder to show life as it 'really is', by showing it happening in its banal and most private moments before the camera. Unlike those shows, it also makes us conscious of the constructedness of that view, building on Jackson's art (including a video installation of a Princess Diana look-alike flirting with the camera) and her advertising images of celebrity doubles for Schweppes. We know these are not real, but they look real and they reflect what we know or would like to know about these celebrities. It is a satire not so much of the celebrities, but of the lenses within which they are produced as images. In one parody, Michael Jackson takes his children shopping for new noses at a plastic surgeons; in another, Tony Blair dances in a US military uniform, accompanied by Cherie Blair as a cheer leader; in another, David Beckham and goalkeeper David Seaman swap hairspray in the changing room. In another, Prince William is observed standing in front of a full-length mirror, naked except for the royal robes and crown he is trying on (Figure 5.1). These are 'real' images of tabloid fantasies. Jackson states that her art and television work aim to 'explore the blurred boundaries between reality and the

Figure 5.1 Alison Jackson's images confront viewers with tabloid fantasies presented within the conventions of reality television. Here a look-alike Prince William is posed as if the real prince was caught trying on the crown jewels
Source: Image courtesy of Alison Jackson, www.alisonjackson.com

imaginary' (Jackson n.d.). She cites Baudrillard (1994) to describe this blurring as a simulation. Unlike someone feigning illness, someone simulating illness takes the place of being ill for the moment of the simulating image or action. Baudrillard (1994) writes: 'simulation threatens the difference between "true" and "false", between "real" and "imaginary". Since the simulator produces "true" symptoms, is he ill or not? He cannot be treated objectively either as ill or not ill' (cited in Jackson n.d.). In contemporary media culture, where celebrity identity is a spectacle performed for the camera, the balance between real and fantasy is just waiting for Jackson to tip it right over.

At the textual level, Jackson's simulation of Beckham and Seaman in the dressing room uses the televisual grammar of realness. The camera is at a slight angle and the men do not look at us or even face us, positioning the viewer as looking through a voyeuristic camera's lens and positioning the scene as distanced from us, in the real world. Within the 'grammar' of television, this is not an imaginary world that we are asked to share but a real one that we are asked to watch unfold in front of us. The two participants are also identifiable real people, whose images are likely to be familiar to viewers, but whose context in a private space is not. Like an informal rather than formal label in language (see Chapter 1), this intimate image positions us as knowing their personal lives, talking about them on a first-name basis, as it were. The narrative visual proposition constructed by the vectors of the two men's gazes is clearly of them looking at themselves, engrossed in the private act of grooming. This is emphasized verbally by Beckham's humming to himself and by the men's talk in low and friendly voices, in relation to which the viewer is an overhearer. The poor sound, grainy and overexposed image and skewed angle produce a high modality to the image by ensuring the viewer is aware of the presence of the camera. This is *really* happening in front of us.

Jackson's point is not, of course, to pretend that the scene is real, but to destabilize the status of those visual conventions – to expose them as conventions – and to expose the illusion that we can get to know celebrities through such images. The point is not that the images are a lie or a fiction, it is rather that the line between real and fictional images is much less stable than reality television and the processes of celebrification pretend. In the parody, Beckham undoes Seaman's curlers, commenting on the lovely thickness of his hair (in a parody of the male sports locker room), lends him some hairspray and then, alone in the room, admires himself in the mirror before giving his reflection a kiss. This is, as one unimpressed reviewer put it, a hackneyed parody, a caricature already done many times over (Tyers 2003). That is indeed what Jackson is presenting the viewer with. We are confronted with Beckham-as-fantasy presented as Beckham-as-real, and challenged to unpick the real from the fictional. Unlike a normal parody, which would caricature the real Beckham, this

Baudrillardian parody of the celebrity image has no stable referent point: it is playing with all the paparazzi photographs, stories, football footage, Posh and Becks jokes and interviews which construct the celebrity, and the culture which is fascinated by them.

Discourse analysts are faced, therefore, with a double job in relation to such hyper-real images. The visual itself makes sense according to a set of conventions – a visual grammar – which cannot simply be reduced to a verbal account of the image or to the talk which surrounds it. The simulation happens at the level of the image, and in the double take of the viewer who looks, is not sure whether he or she believes, and looks again. We can give names to the participants in the scenes, placing them in language, but the visual image doesn't quite fit either of the labels 'real Beckham' or 'fake Beckham', remaining in a limbo of being seen but not fully identified. The interest and pleasure of this show – and, perhaps, of much reality programming – lie in what being on camera does to the people that it explores.

Yet the programme gains its meaning from the discursive context of a culture fascinated by celebrities and by claims of realness. If we were to regard its images as indexing the real world, the programme would be both voyeuristic and a lie. Instead it makes sense within a complex cultural moment which encompasses Foucault's confessional culture, the conscious performance of selfhood within consumer culture and a weakening of private–public distinctions. This is not explicitly said in *Double Take*, as it is in shows where there is a presenter or voice-over, or shows where the action, such as a garden make-over, is brought into sudden contact with the real world in a moment of the owner's surprised reaction. *Double Take* requires the viewer to bring the context to bear, or rather to attempt to read the images which work neither as real life nor as fictions. For, finally, the messiness or resistance of real images to making too much sense is important to the way they work. The claim of the camera is to show us what it saw, a claim which, as was discussed above, contrasts with that of documentary to interpret on our behalf, to fill in the gaps and give context.

What we see in *Celebrity Big Brother* as much as in *Double Take* feels real to the extent that it resists interpretation. As a result, hyper-real television must constantly move on to find new show formats and new performances of the real. Each new show quickly loses its appeal because it no longer stands outside television's sense-making genres and representations. As a parody, *Double Take* depends on the accumulated words about Beckham and other celebrities. But what it is parodying is something not quite verbalizable, and once it can be verbalized, the parody runs dry (the show won a BAFTA award in 2002 but was cut after two short runs in 2003). In the end, the visual and the verbal offer distinct but inter-related modes of knowing the world.

Discourse analysis is not just applicable to verbal language. As this chapter has shown, other modes, such as the visual, can be explored as ways of making sense of the world. Kress and van Leeuwen (1996) propose a grammar of the visual to do this. That grammar, applied to reality television, helps describe how the camera makes its claim to be showing us unmediated reality. However, the visual is never independent of the verbal and, as the analysis of *Double Take* suggests, the image is always very soon interpreted, overlaid again with language.

Further reading

Kress and Van Leeuwen (1996) explains their grammatical approach to the visual in detail. Their later book, *Multimodal Discourse* (2001), softens the claim to be finding a grammar when it discusses the way the conventions of verbal, visual and other modes work together. They have also analysed the grammar of colour (Kress and Van Leeuwen 2002), the grammar of sound (Van Leeuwen 1999) and Kress has argued that literacy should be seen as being about other modes as well as language (Kress 2003). One of the best accounts of the meaning of the visual, however, remains Berger (1972).

6 | THE POWER TO TALK: CONVERSATION ANALYSIS OF BROADCAST INTERVIEWS

The trouble is that most of what we see and hear is filtered through someone who is an expert in communication – maybe a producer, or a journalist, or an editor ... You just don't hear people who are actually working in industry talking in their own language about their lives and problems.

(Tony Benn, British MP)

Introduction

At first sight, the participation of a wide range of individuals in talk radio and television discussion programmes is empowering. Instead of being left as mere spectators on public debate, spoken for and about by politicians, business leaders, academics and other authorized voices, growing numbers of people are able to talk for themselves and talk about themselves live on air. This is a general and long-term shift in broadcasting (see, for example, Scannell and Cardiff 1991), indicative of a potential shift in power in society.[1] As one British MP reflects on the experience of appearing on the BBC's current affairs programme, *Question Time*: 'My impression now is they throw it out to the audience much more than they used to. It's become even more democratic, the public get even more of a say than they did before, and that that's no bad thing' (Boris Johnson, interviewed on BBC 2004).

Television shows such as *Question Time*, but also popular daytime shows such as *Kilroy, Dr Phil, The Oprah Winfrey Show*, and radio programmes from current affairs to phone-in radio shows, appear to have the potential to end both the politics of deference and the media's narrow range of sources, giving airtime and authority to many more people in society:

> The move from elite to participatory social and political arrangements [in current affairs broadcasting] is resulting in changes within the mass media from the paternalistic 'auntie' of elite programming to a potentially more responsive and open medium . . . These [shows] can be seen to challenge traditional oppositions between producer and audience, text and reader, expert and laity.
>
> (Livingstone and Lunt 1994: 14)

That potential to change media and politics is circumscribed, as Livingstone and Lunt and others quickly point out. The previous chapter suggested that 'ordinary people' appear on television more as spectacles of real life and less as authorities on their own lives. Talk on television and radio also follows tight rules. The presenter or host often 'directs, cajoles, re-interprets what partici-pants have said in order to heighten controversy, and provides a moralizing touchstone for the opinions being articulated' (MacDonald 2003: 84). Even with the most accommodating presenter, the broadcast studio 'defines the terms of social interaction in its own domain by pre-allocating social roles and statuses' (Scannell 1991b: 2). On the other hand again, the category of 'ordinary people' is also changing as broadcasting formats change. As another politician, Roy Hattersley, commented on *Question Time*, people now expect to be able to voice their opinions and are aware of the rules of broadcast studios: 'Originally I think the audiences were just people who came along as they might to any other programme, but now they are much more self-confident, much more articulate, know the rules of the game' (Hattersley, interviewed on BBC 2004). Knowledge about and ability to work within those rules are widespread.

The question about whether participatory broadcasting contributes to a democratizing of society is difficult to answer. Analyses of these programmes are also often caught up in wider theoretical debates about the relationship between citizenship and popular culture. Some critics argue the case for a 'DIY citizenship' in which the choices we face as media consumers are exercises in democracy, or rather a 'democratainment' that no longer sticks to the old categories of consumer and citizen (Hartley 1999). Others argue back that such 'empowerment' gives narrow neo-liberal rights to speak and consume but little in the way of social justice rights such as education, employment and housing (Dovey 2000: 86–8). Talking on live television or radio is, in the latter view, a right to be an individual consumer, leaving the big political issues to those already in power.

A number of discourse analysts argue that these claimed shifts in power can be studied best at the micro-level of individual interviews and talk. In order to do so, many have turned to conversation analysis, a method which analyses the smallest details of verbal interaction. This approach takes to its furthest defendable extent the claim of discourse theory which this book explores, that culture and social action happen through the details of language use rather than in larger abstract structures which are then instantiated in language. The talk on radio and television is not conversation, because the participants are filling quite rigid social roles of journalist and expert, of host and 'ordinary person', and because the talk is designed for the overhearing broadcast audience. But it can be contrasted with conversation, as will be discussed below, in order to see how it institutionalizes talk. Talk on air also gains its wider social power from the way it pulls in talk from other contexts (such as the home, government departments, business) and feeds back into people's talk in those contexts, and from the way it passes itself off as the talk of citizens. Cook (2000: 79) talks of the mythic power of broadcast talk, the power to shape the 'national conversation'. Conversation analysis of talk on air can, then, describe aspects of the distribution of power in society.

'Did you threaten to overrule him?' Identifying some social rules of news interviews

One of the clearest recent examples of the struggle for power in broadcast talk is the 1997 interview of then Home Secretary Michael Howard by Jeremy Paxman on the BBC *Newsnight* programme. Already with a reputation as a pugnacious political interviewer, Paxman challenged the account Howard had given in Parliament of a dispute between him and the head of the prison's service, which developed into a dispute also with Howard's junior minister, Ann Widdecombe. Paxman asked Howard whether he had threatened to overrule the civil servant (thus overstepping his powers), and when he received obfuscating replies, repeated the question a further 13 times. The interview led to complaints by politicians and won a media industry award. Here is an excerpt:

JP: Mr Lewis says <u>I</u> (.) that is Mr Lewis (.) told him what we had <u>decided</u> about Marriott and <u>he</u> (.) that is (.) <u>you</u> exp<u>lo</u>ded. Simply <u>mo</u>ving the governor was simply unpalatable it <u>sounded</u> indecisive it would be <u>seen</u> as a fudge. If I did <u>not</u> change my <u>mind</u> and suspend Mr Marriott he would <u>have</u> to consider overruling me.

MH: Mr <u>Marriot</u>[

JP: [You can't <u>both</u> be right

MH: Mr <u>Marriott</u> was <u>not</u> sus<u>pen</u>ded. I was <u>entitled</u> to express my <u>views</u> I was entitled to be consulted=

JP: =Did you <u>threaten</u> to overrule him?
MH: I I was <u>not</u> entitled to <u>instruct</u> Derek Lewis (.) and <u>I</u> did <u>not</u> <u>instruct</u> him
      (0.5) And
MH: [the <u>truth</u> of it
JP: [Did you threaten to over<u>rule</u> him?
MH: The <u>truth</u> of the matter is that Mr Marriott <u>was</u> <u>not</u>
            <u>suspended</u>[I <u>did</u> <u>not</u>
JP: [Did you threaten to overrule him?
MH: I <u>did</u> <u>not</u> overrule [Derek Lewis
JP: [Did you <u>threaten</u> to overrule him?
MH: I took <u>advice</u> on what I <u>could</u> or <u>could not</u> do[and I acted
JP: [<u>Did</u> <u>you</u> threaten to over-
                                      rule him Mr Howard?
MH: <u>scrupulously</u> in accordance with that

                                                              (BBC 1997)

Something in the norms of broadcast interviews breaks down in this excerpt. It
is not simply that the interview failed to draw out any meaningful information
about its topic, although that is in itself a problem. Nor is it just that Paxman
comes close to accusing Howard of lying ('You can't both be right'), for challenges are, as is discussed below, not uncommon in broadcast interactions, and
not read as personal accusations. Instead, for the interview to break down, as it
clearly did, there must be a set of usually invisible, taken-for-granted conventions about what each person does and says which were disrupted. And indeed
their disruption makes them easier to spot. The interviewer clearly should not
ask the same question repeatedly, but should move the interchange forward.
Part of the reason for that is to elicit information on behalf of the audience, and
part of it is to keep on the right side of a line between probing and being
aggressive. Talk in broadcasting is strongly shaped by conventional roles for the
interviewer, which relate to her or his status as a representative of the listener and
as a neutral figure. The interviewee, for his or her part, clearly should not
appear to be ignoring the question or seek to decide when it has been answered,
although public figures frequently do re-shape the question to their own ends.
The interchange breaks down, then, because the two people involved do not
stick to a set of conventional roles.

Conversation analysis suggests that interaction through talk – whether conversation or interview or some other speech event – requires a complex set of
such agreements between the participants, about who can speak, what can be
said and how the talk should be taken. Ultimately, in this view, any sense of
what the talk means arises out of the two (or more) participants reacting to
each other in such a way that each knows that the other understands and agrees

what kind of talk is happening here. Conversation analysts call this the local management of talk. Such analysis provides us with a technique to see what went wrong in the Paxman–Howard interview – on which more shortly – and to explore how power is sought and challenged by each. More generally, conversation analysis can contribute to understanding what kinds of social interactions are happening in broadcast talk.

Conversation analysis

In order to do this, the basic approaches of conversation analysis need to be explained. Conversation analysis began with the question of why everyday communication does not break down into chaos, why people know not to talk at the same time, how people know a conversation has started or ended, and how a conversation keeps going. Ethnomethodologists such as Sacks surmised that the answers to these questions would help explain wider questions of how social life goes on. The starting point of such analysis is therefore two-fold. The first is that people are competent social actors, not simply the results of structures but people who make choices, decisions and interpretations and shape the world around them. The job of analysis is not to know what people are 'really' doing, to probe to a deeper level, but to understand how they understand. Slembrouk (2003) writes that:

> For [conversation analysts], the crucial question is not how people respond to a social order and its normative constraints, but rather how that order is brought about in a specific situation, through activities in quite specific time and place. To understand the orderliness of social life, one does not need abstraction and aggregation, but instead one must turn to the fine-grained details of moment-to-moment existence and their sequential organization.

As a result, this approach to discourse focuses on micro-level details that might be regarded by other analysts as banal or as the kind of 'noise' to be read through, seeing those details as at the heart of how language works. Social order happens through pauses and ums and goodbyes as much if not more than through the substantive content of talk. The second starting point follows on from the first. Conversation analysts claim not to begin with theoretical assumptions or frameworks, but to begin with the attempt to understand interaction as it makes sense to those involved. The social context of talk – whether that is the gender of the participants or the job of a journalist or a cultural taboo – is only relevant to understanding the talk if the participants make it relevant, that is, if they talk as if they are gendered in particular ways or talk as journalists. Debate rages between conversation analysts and other discourse scholars about whether this is a tenable position to take (see Billig 1999 and Schegloff 1999). That said, it is an approach which has led to a number of insights, because of its concern for the details of what is said rather than what the analyst assumes is happening and because of its emphasis on how the interactants make sense of what they are doing. As Boden (1994) puts it, these scholars turn the problem of social order upside down (cited in Slembrouk 2003).

With a suspicion of the idea of predetermined social frameworks, conversation analysts have instead looked for some kind of social order in the sequences of talk. Unlike narratologists, for example, they are not interested in coherence in terms of an overall structure but in the **cohesion** that happens from one utterance to the next. The following (the closing words of a telephone call) is an example of the kind of talk they seek to understand:

J: . . . and uh, uh we're gonna see if we can't uh tie in our plans a little better.
B: Okay / / fine.
J: ALRIGHT?
B: RIGHT.
J: Okay boy,
B: Okay
J: Bye / / Bye
B: G'night

(Schegloff and Sacks 1973: 290)

For Schegloff and Sacks, the analytical problem here is two-fold. First, how do the two people here know when the phone call is over? If one simply stopped talking, the other would reasonably take it as a pause and fill that space with talk. If the phone call is not to become a nightmare of never-ending talk, there must be a way of the two agreeing when the conversation has ended. The second problem, of why the two spend so long saying goodbye, is the start of the answer to the first. What the participants appear to be doing is negotiating the end of the call. The way they do it introduces us to a key concept of the sequential ordering of talk: talk happens in pairs. At the start of the excerpt, J makes a fairly final statement. He then pauses, allowing B to come in. Conversation analysts observe that, as a general principle, statements are accompanied by responses, just as questions have answers and accusations have defences or confessions. An utterance by one party to an interaction requires another. B's response performs a key role in the local management of the interaction, for by doing so he shows that he acknowledges that J has just made a statement. Conversation analysts argue that this **adjacency pair** structure is the way that interactants manage to talk only one at a time rather than constantly interrupting each other, and the way that they know that the other interactants are on the same wavelength about what kind of talk is happening. The participants display to each other their understanding of what they and the other person are doing. Taking turns to talk in adjacency pairs is a basic kind of social glue.

B's brief response in this case performs a second role. Instead of using his response to lead into a statement of his own, he hands the floor back to J, signalling that he has nothing further to add. J opens another adjacency pair, this time a question making absolutely sure that B is in agreement that they have reached a good end to the topic, and B responds in kind, again handing the floor back to J. At this point, and only at this point, after B has had two turns without initiating any new topic, is J able to signal the end of the talk, 'Okay boy'. B can then do likewise and they can finally exchange goodbyes. Schegloff and Sacks (1973) note that this double ending to the topic is necessary because people often don't want to mark things as important by saying them immediately, because that intrudes too far on the other person, not leaving her or him open to negotiate the discussion. Instead they tend to leave off saying something until later, until it arises naturally in conversation. The repeated handing back of the speaking turn to the other we see above is not dithering, then, but mutual consideration and shared management of talk.

When talk is not conversational: Talking institutions

These kinds of exchanges are useful foils against which to define talk which happens in institutions. Conversation analysts have studied a wide range of institutional settings, from doctors' surgeries to courtrooms and media talk. The interaction above appears long-winded when written down but can be read as testimony to the equal positions of the two interactants. While one of them (J) has to lead, the interaction seems to operate by an acknowledgement by both that both of them have to agree to end the call. By contrast, broadcast interviews end abruptly. Paxman ends *Newsnight* interviews with no such 'pre-closings':

JP: There we must <u>leave</u> it (.) Michael Howard, <u>thank</u> you.

In the institutional setting of the news studio, the power to end the talk lies with only one of the parties. Were Howard to have said, 'Thank you, Jeremy, and goodbye', a fairly extraordinary breakdown of the studio's rules would have taken place. Paxman can also end the talk abruptly, without leaving Howard the opportunity to take the floor and initiate a topic, as J does for B, because the roles of questioner and answerer are rigidly defined by the institutional context. Neither of the parties in the studio expects to have to negotiate the ending, and so it can end quickly, without that brevity having particular meaning.[2]

Greatbatch (1998: 167) describes a number of differences of media interview talk from conversation and argues that many are due to the expectation that interviewers will not take sides or given opinions, but adopt a 'neutralistic stance'. The interviewer gains his or her power to ask questions as a representative of the news organization, not as an individual, and thus fills a well-defined social role. Paxman's role requires that he produce mostly questions rather than statements and if he does produce statements, he must distance himself from them by attributing them to others. He does this above, reading from a statement by the civil servant: 'Mr Lewis says I that is Mr Lewis told him what we had decided about Marriott.' Statements which are not attributed therefore tend to be readable as questions or at most challenges designed to elicit responses. The challenge, 'You can't both be right', which in everyday conversation could well be read as rude and as a sign that the challenger was no longer taking the other party seriously, can be read here within broadcasting conventions as robust questioning. Greatbatch (Heritage and Greatbatch 1991) also observes that interviewers characteristically do not affiliate or disaffiliate with interviewees. They avoid 'acknowledgement tokens' which listeners commonly make while speakers are still holding the floor, such as 'mm', 'uh huh', 'yes'. They also avoid 'news receipt objects' such as 'Oh, really' and 'Did you?', which fill pauses in speaker talk. Interviewers tend to listen silently or fill pauses with new questions, again behaviour that would be strange in a conversation, suggesting the person was not listening closely. Within the studio, however, they mark the questions and statements as produced on behalf of others. What is important within conversation analysis is that both participants read the distance from conversation in these ways, that they both orient towards and therefore locally manage a shared set of conventions.

As a result, conversation analysis is able to analyse when the expectations of broadcast studio talk are traduced. In the Paxman–Howard interview, then, we can see that the turn-taking of adjacency pairs is not always followed. Paxman does not wait until Howard has finished giving his responses before pushing in with a renewal of the question. The reason for this is clear: he is showing that he does not regard Howard's response as a valid answer to the question and is taking back the floor to restore the relationship of questioner and answerer. Howard, for his part, shows he does not recognize Paxman's authority to require him to answer the question. The interaction reaches stalemate – in ethnomethodological terms, the local management of the turn-taking collapses – as each refuses to give ground to the other's interpretation of how the talk should unfold. What makes the interview riveting viewing is that, extraordinarily, neither steps out of his role but continues to try to regard Paxman's repeated questioning and Howard's dissimulation as acceptable. At one point, just after the excerpt above, Paxman nearly acknowledges the breakdown: 'I'm going to be frightfully rude but did you threaten to overrule him?' However, Howard does not take this either as rude or as an apology for rudeness, but as a reformulation of the question (and I think most viewers would read it that way too, for if Paxman were apologizing or acknowledging he was stepping outside neutralism and being rude, he would surely not have asked the same question yet again). Cases can be found where politicians explicitly try to renegotiate the rules or refuse to accept the neutralism of the interviewer (Greatbatch 1998: 174). The risk for them in doing so is that they then appear to be avoiding answering the questions posed to them – in other words, that it is they and not the interviewers who are breaking the implicit contract.

Overheard conversations

Many of the differences of broadcast talk from other contexts are due to the presence of a studio audience and a wider broadcast audience. If this talk is like conversation, it is conversation overheard by and in the end designed for thousands or millions of other people. The interviewer asks questions on behalf of the audience, and will sometimes invoke the listening audience explicitly to gain power over the interviewee. As Clayman (2002) finds from a large sample of US news interviews, speaking for 'the people' allows journalists to ask the most sensitive and intrusive questions and to defend themselves against interviewees' accusations of unfair or biased questioning. When the British journalist David Frost interviewed Richard Nixon in 1977, in the US President's only television interview after the Watergate scandal, he quickly changed a question from a personal one, which could have been read as offensive, to one that gained legitimacy by being on behalf of the public:

I:: would like to hear you sa:y > I think the American people would like to hear you say..hh (.) O:ne is::, (0.7) the:re was probably mo::re (0.2) tha::n, (0.4) mista:kes there was:: (0.7) wro:ngdoing (0.2) whether it was a cri::me >or not=yes it may have been a crime< too.

(Clayman 2002: 202)[3]

The overhearing audience therefore legitimates a more intrusive, aggressive kind of talk, that is not intended to be taken as interpersonal aggression, but is intended as a public voice which the journalist is merely animating. Goffman's term **footing** is useful here: people, particularly when they fill institutional roles, often talk as the animator rather than the author (who composed the words) or the principal (whose ideas are being expressed) (Bell 1991: 37). In these terms, Frost was presenting himself as animator for ideas whose author was the 'American people'. Although he was clearly on one level also the author of the question, he sought to construct a social reality in which he had less responsibility for accusing the former US President of being a criminal. To the extent that Nixon accepted this, and Clayman's (2002) analysis of the interview tapes suggests he acted as if he did, then that social reality came into being. Sometimes the power of the studio to make its own social rules is made explicit. Livingstone and Lunt quote one audience member in a daytime discussion programme recalling that:

> Mike Scott said 'we like a lively debate, please don't be too polite, it makes good television if people are actually a bit rude and forget their British reserve and actually just push in, talk on top of each other, so please don't be typically Brits, don't be reserved, if you feel strongly then please speak up.' (Alice, studio audience)
>
> (1994: 164)

Here the programme producer presents his show as good television to the extent that it manages to act as the animator for individuals' stronger emotional responses. In order for that to happen, he tells the studio audience to suspend the social rules they are accustomed to.

For conversation analysts, the social world is about interaction, and comes into existence through talk such as that discussed above. That argument is strongest when we can see participants such as Nixon and the audience member quoted above, Alice, responding in terms of the footings and rules the broadcasters are trying to set up, and it attests to the power of those actions. Many analysts would, however, qualify the point, arguing that the context in which people take talk is sometimes established or managed within the talk but is sometimes not. For example, a fictional interview might sounds exactly the same as the *Newsnight* one above, but would have a fundamentally different context – everyone from the two men involved to the audience to the givers of industry awards would know it was not real. Conversation analysis is somewhat blind to that kind of externally managed context – or rather it says such contexts are merely analysts' readings into the material. This difference of approach to context relates to a wider difference between discourse analysts who regard objective description of society as possible and those who argue that analysts will always bring something of themselves to that description. The complaint of the critics is that conversation analysts will assume that conversational interaction is between social equals unless they find evidence in the transcript to suggest otherwise. As feminist discourse scholars in particular have noted, there is strong evidence that everyday relations are in fact far from free of power imbalances.

Powerful talk

Media discourse analysts interested in issues around power and public debate will often, then, make use of conversation analysis without following its principles to the letter. The method shows that interviewers build on the general social right that when we ask a question we tend to have the right to talk again after the answerer has spoken (Thornborrow 2001b). Within the institutional context of the studio, they build this into a considerable power to tell people who they are and to decide what they will talk about. Interviewees, in turn, get most of their power from their wider social status as public figures, using that status to leverage the power not to answer questions as they are posed, and using questions as opportunities to say what they have to say. This is arguably why interviewers often interrupt speakers – in order to regain control they must reassert their power to decide who talks and when. Both participants must recognize each other's roles in the talk for those moves to become part of the interaction.

This balance of power does not apply to people who come on air without high social status, whose messages would be unlikely to be missed by audiences if they were cut off and who would have little impact if they complained. Consequently, it is hard to argue that there is anything straightforwardly democratizing going on in participatory broadcasting. In the Paxman–Howard interview the participants had different but fairly well-balanced sources of power – Howard as a Cabinet Minister and the one in possession of the information, and Paxman as a key figure in the making and breaking of political reputations and the one in control of the unfolding talk. It is more common to find that the host or interviewer has much of the power. Hutchby (1996) points out that in radio phone-ins the host tends to take the second turn, using his or her first turn simply to prompt the caller to talk (they may be cut off if they don't get to the point quickly). This handing on of the speaking turn doesn't empower callers, but forces them to put forward arguments and to fill in the air time, while the host merely responds. As Cameron (2001: 163) says, 'Second speakers can win the argument by undermining their opponent's case; they are not obliged to produce a convincing alternative.' The way this power works becomes clear when one caller in Hutchby's sample breaks the rules, asking a question back, and the host accepts the question by coming up with a response: 'By choosing to make a substantive point of his own . . . the host "gives away" his advantage, enabling the caller to do to him what he has previously done to her – that is, challenge his point and return the floor to him using a question' (Cameron 2001: 164). Even when the caller fights for this discursive power, though, the host can still simply cut her off.

Livingstone and Lunt find that participants often experience broadcast discussions in terms of a very limited and not very satisfying empowerment of having their voices heard. One participant in a daytime discussion show told them:

> I felt that we were placed there a few minutes before, we hadn't had time to settle in to the surroundings, to even discuss or talk to people beforehand. I felt as though I knew no-one there. And so it wasn't like a real discussion, because no ice was broken, so to speak. Even the way it's set out, you have the seats facing the cameras, every one is facing forward. To talk to someone you have to look over the other side of the audience, it's not like any other situation we're usually in really. (Ruth, studio audience)
>
> (1994: 167)

For this person, the breach of conversational conventions, such as hello–hello adjacency pairs and sitting face-to-face, made the studio talk unsatisfying and ultimately of poor quality. Thus the studio's rewriting of social conventions was hard for this person to accept. It must be said, though, that this is not a universal response. Another participant interviewed for the same study felt a discussion show had 'more of a sense of real conversation' because of the way the host (Robert Kilroy-Silk, host of *Kilroy* (BBC 1986–2004)) managed the discussion in terms of interpersonal norms, so that the participants were not 'barracking' or talking past one another, as the participant expected from watching politicians interviewed on television (Livingstone and Lunt 1994: 168).

Being the right kind of talker

The local management of talk in broadcasting has some similarities to conversation and some rules of its own. The challenge for interviewees, particularly for lay participants such as people Livingstone and Lunt spoke to, appears to be in learning those rules and making use of them to their rhetorical advantage. Thornborrow (2001a) finds from studying the first words of callers on radio and audience participants in television talk shows that they tend to make the same kinds of first moves. On a talk show, speakers tend to start not with a hello but with personal information about themselves:

Host: Sir yes
Man: Yeah Esther I'm nineteen and (.) I'm quite lucky my parents have been married for twenty-five years [–]

(Thornborrow 2001a: 464)

By contrast, callers to the BBC Radio 4 *Any Answers* programme will start by launching into contributions to one of the topics under discussion. Thornborrow interprets this as participants building identities for themselves that are relevant to the discussion going on. Another interpretation is that lay people are usually well aware of the rules of each subgenre of broadcast talk and are adept at talking in ways that will gain them maximum effect within that. But knowing how to fit into a programme format does not necessarily mean that people are empowered. We could, on the contrary, read the talk show quoted by Thornborrow (2001a) as forcing people to disclose personal issues if they wish to talk successfully there. Lay people, as many media critics have pointed out, have a small range of allowable identities in the media, usually as people who experience life but not as experts on their lives. That expert role is often still in the hands of the doctors, psychologists, agony aunts, lawyers and others who sit on the panels of such programmes. By contrast, *Any Answers* allows callers to take on a public role, in which their opinions are more important than their personal details or life stories, but gives little space for the voices of those without a stake in public political culture. This is about the power – and responsibility – of broadcast talk hosts to allow different kinds of public identity to be expressed, as will be explored below in a case study of the British Virgin Radio *Nick Abbot Show*.

Conversationalization

To summarize, we can use conversation analysis to explore how the institutional talk of broadcasting contrasts with conversation. But we can at the same time explore how conversation is changing broadcasting, taking us further in exploring the myth that on-air talk propagates that it is 'real talk' (Cook 2000). Fairclough (1995) has identified what he calls the 'conversationalization' of public discussion through the media. He finds interviewers seeking to place themselves alongside listeners or viewers by becoming chatty and interviewees likewise trying to place themselves alongside 'ordinary people' or other popular cultural identities. Part of the struggle for power discussed above, therefore, is enacted through trying to draw on what these elite voices think of as the voice of the people. In this view, conversation has gained a powerful status in culture as 'the nation's conversation'. This is partly to do with the sense of closeness between governing and governed that broadcasting constructs as it beams straight into living rooms. Politicians and other public figures who speak in less formal modes come across best – Prime Minister Tony Blair is a good contemporary example in his performances of emotional sincerity (Montgomery 1999b). Lang and Lang (1983: 283) argue that television has forced greater changes on political actors than on other groups in society, because 'it forces them to be responsive to norms binding on other members of society' (cited in Livingstone and Lunt 1994: 33). The British Royal Family, for example, are represented in the media as having 'ordinary' qualities, partly because of their personal scandals which place them at just one remove from any other set of celebrities, but partly because the coverage of those scandals required them to justify their behaviour, to talk on camera, and therefore to cross the boundary from mythic monarchy to normal people (Abell and Stokoe 1999: 301).

Fairclough (1995) focuses on vocabulary rather than on the sequential structures that conversation analysts discuss. As a result, his claim is more about the broadcaster's style than the social action happening there. In an analysis of an interview on the BBC Radio 4 *Today* programme in 1992, he finds colloquial lexis (such as 'mate', 'fancy', 'bloke', 'fed up to back teeth'), colloquial use of pronouns ('an awful lot of people when *you* ask them') and the colloquial use of the present tense in telling a narrative ('he *comes* back to you and *says*'). He also finds facts compressed and left more implicit than might be expected in a formal news interview, again something he sees as conversational in style ('a lot of people have been saying oh well an October election') (Fairclough 1995: 142ff.). This is a 'simulated voice' of the ordinary citizen, a rhetorical effect which allows expectations and contexts that belong in conversation to become relevant to political interviewing. Fairclough argues for an ideological dimension to broadcast talk in much the same way as Cook does – the talk of elites passes itself off as the language of everyday people. It muddies the special voice of public debate on behalf of citizens with the kind of language used to address consumers. But he also recognizes a potentially democratic effect tangled up with the legitimation of elites and the 'marketization' of culture (Fairclough 1995: 149). Livingstone and Lunt (1994), in their study of television discussion programmes, reach a similar ambivalent conclusion: broadcast talk contains more ordinary voices, but puts these voices in an unequal relationship with institutional sites of power. It democratizes, but within the rules established by elite media figures.

Case study: The responsibility of the shock jock

Radio phone-in shows, or talk radio, have developed rapidly since the 1980s, particularly since the shift of music radio to the FM band in many markets, leaving vacant the MW/AM spectrum. These shows claim considerable democratic potential, often marketing themselves with slogans such as 'the place to have your say'. But they have quickly become identified also as the site of highly conservative political and cultural perspectives. Douglas notes that radio talk is dominated by men and argues that it has become a space where men who felt themselves marginalized by changes in public discourse in the wake of the women's and gay liberation movements could celebrate different values, including hedonism, disrespect, bad taste, sensationalism and disobedience (Douglas 2002). One such show was the *Nick Abbot Show* (Virgin 1215, 1993–4). A late night phone-in show, it was characterized by Abbot's rudeness to callers and their sometimes rude or eccentric behaviour back. In conversation analytic terms, the host and his regular callers between them developed a set of conventions in which offensiveness was humorous and in which callers could expect to be mocked and cut off. One fan-site (where clips from the show can be heard), called it 'a rude man taking the piss out of some poor caller'.[4] In one incident, Abbot told a teenager to dump his girlfriend because she wouldn't have sex with him. He was then criticized in a magazine review, whereupon he rounded on his attacker in terms that she regarded as sexual harassment, leading to a campaign by the reviewer that resulted in a £20,000 fine for the station and Abbot's transfer to a music requests show (Rayner 1995). This was a space where Douglas' characteristics of disrespect, bad taste and anti-authoritarianism were given full voice. In the following excerpt, Abbot deals with a caller keen to play by the programme's conventions of performing prejudice:

NA: Uhhh <u>W</u>orcester
Caller: (He)llo there <u>Nick</u>
NA: Hiya=
Caller: =Hello that <u>guy</u> who was going on there politically correct he was really <u>boring</u> wasn't he
NA: (.) Well he <u>had</u> a good <u>point</u> but uh
Caller: He <u>wasn't</u> he was I was <u>sat</u> here picking the <u>scabs</u> off my <u>cat</u> (0.5) the my <u>cat's</u> got all this <u>scabs</u> on it and I was sitting here picking them <u>off</u> because the guy was so bloody <u>boring</u>
NA: <u>I</u> uh preferred <u>him</u> uh t- than uh you talking about the scabs on your cat
NA: [hate to break the news to you
Caller: [(as) I say my cat has got some severe scabs [I really want to talk about
NA: [ehh
Caller: my <u>neigh</u>bour
NA: Well <u>any</u>thing but more cat
Caller: Nah I <u>came</u> in I <u>came</u> I <u>came</u> in this eve(ning) after watching this <u>really</u> brilliant band in <u>Worcester</u> called uh <u>Blog</u>nuff
NA: Right= [*slow*]
Caller: =Dead good
NA: Mm hm
Caller: And I <u>came</u> in and turned you on and=

NA: =Like that bloke in Romford would say <u>it's</u> the <u>nuts</u> mate

Caller: Yeah it's the <u>nuts</u>. I came in and turned you <u>on</u> (.) so to speak (.) and my next door <u>neigh</u>bour started knocking on the <u>wall</u>

NA: Well that's the first time somebody's turned me <u>on</u> and I haven't been aware of it my<u>self</u>=

Caller: =You <u>lucky</u> bugger (.) I came in but I've got to tell you about this <u>woman</u> I used to live with her sister who's a bit of a tub of <u>lard</u>

NA: What kind of thing is <u>that</u> to say about your <u>sis</u>ter?

Caller: <u>No</u> it's her my next door <u>neigh</u>bour's sister

NA: Right

Caller: My <u>next</u> my next door <u>neigh</u>bour's sister didn't like my next door neighbour (.) so she moved in with <u>me</u> and uh then she didn't like me so she moved out again

NA: Well I can under<u>stand</u> that

Caller: Mm well yes and (.) um what happened <u>then</u> it's a very interesting story um

NA: Yea-uh I'm sure it gets interesting any [moment now

Caller: [No uh she was telling me about her <u>sister</u>

NA: Uh huh

                                        (Virgin 1215 (UK) 1994)

The caller has the power here to initiate topics and attitudes, whether his cat's scabs, his interest in his neighbours or his attitude to women. But as Hutchby found, there is considerable power for the host here in forcing the caller to take the first turn position, which the host can then argue against. This power is evident in the way the caller changes topic as Abbot knocks him down, first on political correctness, then on his cat topic, the band he heard, his derogatory comment on 'lardy' women and lastly his claim to be saying something interesting, which leads to him being cut off shortly after this excerpt. When Abbot is not rejecting the topics, he is trumping the caller's jokes or providing the punchlines. The caller fills a sidekick role, saying something potentially funny ('I turned you on'), and calling attention to the double entendre of the phrase ('so to speak'), but needing Abbot's recognition of his intention and his expansion of it into a joke of his own for it to become one. Moreover, the caller is clearly orienting towards Abbot's control of the interaction, initiating topics and therefore inhabiting identities that might be thought to fit within the show: criticism of political correctness, derogatory comments about women, discussing inappropriate activities such as picking a cat's scabs. He is also quick to affiliate towards Abbot's mention of the 'bloke in Romford', one of the show's regular callers.

This places Abbot in a double position. He makes comments at the caller's expense ('I'm sure it gets interesting any moment now'), taking on not only the host's legitimate power as representative of callers, but claiming a non-accountable power to transgress rules of politeness, neutrality and reasonableness in his treatment of the caller. It is this transgression which gives this 'shock jock' show its claim to humour. But he also provides licence for callers to engage in similar unsocial behaviour to his. They therefore locally manage a suspension of rules about appropriate topics and comments, in a late night context when those policing society's moral strictures might be thought to be asleep. As one journalist commented sarcastically, 'Basically, the whole idea was that it went out without a seven-second delay and, as soon as kids found out they could swear on air, they did. He used to have his hand hovering over the kill switch. It was almost a test of speed' (Tedder 1999). This double position leads to inconsistency – he will encourage scatological and prejudiced statements but criticize callers who follow him – which adds to the appeal of the show for listeners. They can listen as Abbot wields his unreasonable power over callers and as callers verbally spar with him on air. Like similar shows in the USA, it is 'a verbal adjunct to street fighting' where what is said is less important than the fight for dominance (Douglas 2002).

Part of the local management of the talk here is also a complicity between caller and host in seeing how far poor taste and prejudice can be pushed. But, as his use of the cut-off switch suggests, Abbot is subject to institutional requirements from his employers and the radio regulator. His wielding of interactional power also inevitably places him in the position of enforcing social and cultural standards. By telling off the caller for calling a woman 'a bit of a tub of lard', he is making a set of social codes relevant. By giving minimal affiliations ('mm hm') in response to the caller's enthusiasm for the band he heard, he implicitly enforces standards of taste. That these standards are inconsistent is important, for Abbot therefore places himself in a position beyond the rules he enforces for others. There is a politics to this, similar perhaps to the politics that Palmer finds in *What Not to Wear* (Chapter 5). Abbot speaks in a geographically indistinct accent, allowing him the very middle-class claim to classlessness, while most of his callers have distinctive accents (the caller above has a Yorkshire accent). Tellingly, the only affiliative comment he makes in the excerpt is to speak in the words, and accent, of the bloke from Romford: 'It's the nuts'. The host here is mocking the class-based positions of callers (in another call the victim is mocked for her private school intonation), claiming a high degree of cultural capital. He positions himself as knowing how people should behave in the young, urban world of Virgin radio. Part of the pleasurableness of talk radio is the tension that neither listeners nor the host know what will be said next, that anything could happen next. There is a sense of risk and the potential for ordinary voices to momentarily evade the censors. But the 'shock jock' host, perhaps more than most, is about control of that talk. Like the crime news discussed in Chapter 1, these caller intrusions are raised only to be subject immediately to the rule of law.

Conversation analysis builds on one of the strengths of discourse analysis in general, its focus on the empirical detail of language use. It looks in the smallest details of people's talk for evidence of how normal, everyday language use works, drawing on the key ideas that people are highly skilled at communicating so that there must be good reasons for the way they talk and that speakers must recognize what other speakers are doing in order for talk to work. The analysis of turn-taking which emerges from that approach reveals the distance of broadcast talk from conversation and therefore casts light on the struggles for power that take place in live broadcasting.

Further reading

Cameron (2001) gives a good overview in her chapter on conversation analysis. She recommends Hutchby and Wooffitt (1998) for further detail. Clayman, Heritage, Greatbatch and Hutchby have done important conversation analysis analyses of media discourse. Further references and some of their work are found in Drew and Heritage (1992). The collection of papers in *Broadcast Talk* (Scannell 1991a) is the first major collection by other media discourse analysts to draw on that work. A good recent collection that draws on this research tradition is Tolson (2001). For more on the impact of a conversational ethos in broadcasting on politics, see Scannell (1992), Fairclough's analysis of politics in Britain (Fairclough 2000) and McLuhan's classic comments on the television medium's impact on US politics (McLuhan 1964). Crisell (1994) includes a chapter on radio phone-in shows.

RACISM AS SOCIAL COGNITION IN SPORTS COMMENTARY

Tonight 25 million viewers will watch a clash that is more than just a football match.

(*Daily Mail*, 17 June 2000)

The analysis of the 'unsaid' is sometimes more revealing than the study of what is actually expressed in the text.

(van Dijk 1991: 144)

Introduction

The BBC sports commentator John Motson once observed in a BBC Radio Five Live interview that from the commentary box football players are often hard to tell apart. He had a particular problem with black players: 'There are teams where you have got players who, from a distance, look almost identical. And, of course, with more black players coming into the game, they would not mind me saying that that can be very confusing' (cited in Boggan 1998). Many people did indeed mind him saying that. For Motson, it was apparent to them, black players tended to look the same when there are lots of them. This is clearly a statement of prejudice, a statement which implies black players are first and foremost blacks, and only second individual sportspeople. This chapter is about such prejudice and the communication of it through the media. However, it will not focus on individuals' comments, but rather the communicative context within which racism and other forms of prejudice 'make sense' in a pernicious manner. For Motson was not communicating any personal attitude towards black people, nor was he communicating any conscious sense of their difference to white players. Instead, like many media figures, he was drawing upon a common way of seeing people in terms of their difference from white skin within a predominantly white society. The prejudice – literally, in Latin, the pre-judgement – belongs in this view to a whole society. The way of thinking and the way of talking about black players which popped readily into this commentator's head did so precisely because it was socially shared knowledge and therefore readily available as a way of talking about the difficulties of his job. Racism, as it is discussed in this chapter, is social communication.

In particular, the chapter explores the work of a discourse analyst who has spent much of his career studying racism by theorizing prejudice as **social cognition**, Teun van Dijk. Drawing upon artificial intelligence research, he looks for linguistic evidence of ways of storing and recalling information in the mind that take part in socially shared stereotypes and other pre-judgements. Following van Dijk, we can interpret Motson's comment in terms of shared cognitive structures. The structure is within his mind: the statement suggests the speaker mentally lumps black players together, while he sees white players in terms of more individual characteristics. But in calling upon that cognitive categorization in a comment, the speaker asks listeners to recognize their own use of that categorization and to bring that into use in order to understand the comment. Comments such as Motson's, then, reinforce an already existing set of social categorizations, reminding us as listeners that it is unremarkable in British society to see black people's skin colour first and their other character-istics a distant second. A quick thought experiment makes the social nature of the thinking clear. If the commentator had said that teams with too many ginger-haired players were a problem, listeners to the Radio 5 Live interview might have regarded this as a quirky limitation of his, for that is not a widely shared recognition problem. But race-based identification – seeing people's skin colour first and thereby lumping them together – is common and was therefore easily understandable. Such racism is likely to have been further reinforced because it was an authoritative sports figure who voiced it and because it was reproduced to hundreds of thousands of listeners. Van Dijk (1988b: 169) gives particular emphasis to such media racism, citing a number of studies that have found people rely heavily on media accounts for their knowledge, beliefs and opinions about ethnic minorities.

Much of van Dijk's work has been on the reproduction of racism in the news. I will instead use sports coverage, and in particular live sports commentary, to explore the discursive production of racism. This is for a number of reasons. First, sport is deeply related to group identity, whether gender or national or regional identity, and with wider matters of power in society. It can be studied as a 'cultural theatre where the values of the larger society are resonated, dominant social practices are legitimized, and structural inequalities reproduced' (Sabo and Jansen 1992: 173). Sport, particularly in its interdependent relationship with the media, is an important theatre where who we are, and therefore who we are ethnically, is played out. Second, sports commentary produced live and in the heat of a sports event is likely to contain more unguarded statements, less self-monitoring, and may therefore give a particularly rich description of the shared cognitive structures which van Dijk theorizes. Third, sport claims a populist and apolitical status which many other public genres, full of elite figures and talk, have difficulty doing. It opens up for us aspects of shared social life which official public life can miss. In the terms of Billig et al. (1988), it allows us to study lived ideology as well as the intellectual ideology of coherent systems of discourse and their institutions. But, fourth, sport is also a site of struggle, often pulled into politics, whether it is campaigns to eradicate sectarianism from Scottish football or boycotts of South African sport during the Apartheid era. Precisely because of sport's populist status and its links to national identity, sports commentary is often criticized both by fans and by political figures, and is therefore a kind of talk where much has to be negotiated. Motson, for example, was forced to justify himself on BBC radio the morning after his interview and was roundly criticized for undermining anti-racist education in British football (Latham 1998). To analyse sports coverage is therefore to analyse an important site of society's struggle over issues of what is often termed 'race'.

The discursive production of 'race'

Discourse analysis is particularly well adapted to understanding the idea of 'race' because it is centrally concerned with meaning as a social activity and with social life as constructed through language. 'Race' fits squarely within these research assumptions, indeed, you could argue that it makes little sense outside them. Genetics can find no empirical evidence for claims that there are well-defined races, and specifically that some different genetic potential among people in different parts of the world leads to differences in terms of cultural categories such as rationality, capacity for hard work and cleanliness. The American Association of Physical Anthropologists released a statement in 1996 rejecting the nineteenth-century scientific study of different races and stating that: 'The peoples of the world today appear to possess equal biological potential for assimilating any human culture. Racist political doctrines find no foundation in scientific knowledge concerning modern or past human populations' (AAPA 1996).

In fact, there seems to be some consensus that about 85 per cent of the total genetic variation in the human species can be found in any population, and only about 7 per cent can be accounted for by the differences between geographic regions of the world. Thus, 'any given European (or African, Asian, etc.) is genetically far more similar to many Africans, Asians, Native Americans than to some other Europeans' (P.D. Welch 2003). 'Race', as a notion that people with different skin colour are fundamentally different, is clearly an almost entirely cultural category. It is one group's act of making sense of another through gross generalizations about what all the members of that group are like. For this reason it is not separable from the category of ethnicity: the act of saying that all blacks are excessively sexual is more pernicious, but not essentially different, from the act of saying that all Italians are passionate.

Why racism arises, if it has no basis in biology, is a fraught question. It is clear, however, that categorizing others by their skin colour is closely tied to a sense of group identity. Structuralism has proposed that a group's sense of who they are is often more clearly articulated as a sense of who they are not. Thus, Englishness is poorly defined, whereas foreignness or otherness is constantly talked about and reinforced. By constructing an opposition, a cluster of binaries under which 'they' are represented as strange, bad, uncultured, dangerous, childlike, and so on, 'we' can, without it ever being said, see ourselves as the opposite of those terms. Said's (1978) account of Orientalism, a term which implied some unity to a huge swathe of the world's cultures from the Ottoman Turks to the Japanese, is a classic example in western European culture. That construction of otherness, through cultural products from Fry's Turkish Delight to Jane Austen's *Mansfield Park*, is then available for Europeans to make sense of everything from what despots look like to a sense of the exotic. Such categorizations have a history within a colonial past, but are by no means merely historic. J.K. Rowling's Harry Potter series, with its Central Asian-sounding horror of Azkaban and its Islamic-sounding names for villains such as Salazar, shows that it is alive and well. The Germans are another favourite category for British culture to gather together characteristics against which it defines itself. English football, in particular, is often defined in popular media representations against a German football that merges into German militarism. Germans, as constructed through a century of propaganda, boys' comics and war films, represent a tidy, well-delineated enemy for England. England, in the shadow of that Germany, can find its finest hour. Ferguson (1998) quotes the following call to arms from the tabloid *Daily Mirror*:

'Ve haf vays', 'Filthy Hun', 'You haf been warned'
England's old enemy, defeated in two World Wars and one World Cup.
We have decided to teach the Hun a lesson.
Herr we go again.

> The Germans hate being reminded of their failures. Like eating well-matured cheese for breakfast. Or nicking all the sunloungers in the Mediterranean. But what they hate most is being reminded of that glorious day in 1966 when England made them the sourest of sour-krauts.
>
> (*Daily Mirror*, 26 June 1996: 2, cited in Ferguson 1998: 136)

The fact that the German coach, Jürgen Klinsmann, was previously a popular Tottenham Hotspurs player did not change the paper mocking him as 'Mr Hitman' (in a reference to the song, 'Who Do You Think You Are Kidding, Mr Hitler?'). An ethnic discourse sweeps aside other modes of representation in setting up an absolute and simple opposition between 'them' and 'us'.

Racism can be described in terms of a binary between an in-group and an out-group, a structure that is central to the interests of the dominant groups in a society. Scholars have, however, pointed out that people draw upon different categorizations of others in different contexts. Stereotypes are flexible, sometimes there and sometimes not. This is what the *Daily Mirror* was doing with Klinsmann. Ferguson notes that one article contains a reference to him as a 'former Spurs star', yet elsewhere he is synonymous with Hitler. Moreover, racism is often much more about the latter half of the 'us' and 'them' binary, and indeed the 'us' category often disappears entirely from sight in discourse (Ballard 2002). While binaries or opposites or contrasts are sometimes deployed, they are one rhetorical tool among a range of ways of talking about ethnic minorities. It might be better, then, to think of racist discourse as a way of deploying ideas of race or nation or ethnicity in certain ways at some times rather than others. It is not so much a fixed them/us binary as a way of talking, a social action that establishes relationships between the speaker and an in-group audience and between that audience and others. Potter and Wetherell (1992) suggest that there are shared 'interpretative repertoires' available within a society for talking about particular issues in particular contexts. Racism in this view is all about resources that come easily to hand to explain away a whole host of problems from unemployment to crime to cultural change ostensibly in terms of other people's characteristics. Potter and Wetherell therefore focus on the ways of talking, particularly the ways of describing and explaining, that people have available to them, rather than on hypothesizing some underlying racist attitude towards outsiders. Racism makes sense of the world for us:

> If a researcher really wishes to get to grips with racism then a vital part of their activity must be the investigation of how description and explanation are meshed together and how different kinds of explanations assume different kinds of objects or supply the social world with varying objects.
>
> (Potter and Wetherell 2001: 209)

The category of whiteness is not well defined because it is not used as such an explanatory category. In New Zealand, for example, Maori, Pacific Islands and Asian people often identify themselves and others identify them according to ethnicity, while white New Zealanders often simply call themselves New Zealanders, because the white European culture holds the status as the national culture and there is no social need to assert it. Whiteness elides into New Zealandness, and while it logically exists in a binary relation to 'other' ethnicity, it rarely exists socially.

This way of thinking of racism as an action performed through talk has the additional benefit of reminding the critic that at the heart of racism lies the power to define someone else, to make 'their' identity in the shadow of 'ours'. One strategy of anti-racism has been to tackle such definitions overtly – to bring to the surface and to challenge the role that language plays in racism. The label 'nigger' used by a young black person to address his or her friends is a strategy to take the words away from a racist white culture, load it with positive in-group identification, and thus reduce a little the racist culture's power to put down the speaker as black. How far a subculture's slang can change the meanings of a word for the rest of the language and culture and how long an ironic reappropriation of a word remains radical are debatable (see Cameron 1995).

This way of thinking also reminds the critic not to take racism out of the context of all the other ways of representing with which it is tied up in actual language use. Very rarely are people talked about in derogatory ways simply and only because of their skin colour. The New Zealand television host Paul Holmes called United Nations Secretary-General Kofi Annan a 'cheeky darkie' in a racist dismissal that was part of a wider comment on the UN criticism of the US doctrine of pre-emptive military action (*New Zealand Herald*, 24 September 1993). 'Race' was invoked, or to spell it out, the implication that black Africans are cheeky to speak up against the white people who run world affairs, was invoked alongside a whole range of other arguments. Thus, 'the expression of racism is an integral component of a wider, historical process of racialization which is interlinked with exclusionary practices and with the expression of other forms of exclusionary ideology' (Miles 1989: 98, see also MacDonald 2003: 53).

'Race' and the media

The media are one among many cultural institutions which may reproduce racism. But the forms of representation they reflect are held by many critics to be particularly powerful in perpetuating wider social structures, because they operate within a claim to speak to and for large groups – the whole country, in the case of many broadcasters – and to reflect an objective reality. Hall writes:

> What [the media] 'produce' is, precisely, representations of the social world, images, descriptions, explanations and frames for understanding how the world is and why it works as it is said and shown to work. And, amongst other kinds of ideological labour, the media construct for us definitions of what *race* is, what meaning the imagery of race carries, and what the 'problem of race' is understood to be.
>
> (cited in MacDonald 2003: 14)

In helping to produce a society's concept of 'race', the media inevitably produce a quite limited set of meanings – in Potter and Wetherell's terms, a limited interpretative repertoire. Cottle (1999: 193) summarizes 40 years of British criticism on representations of 'race' in the media as follows: 'Across the years and seemingly as a matter of routine, Britain's black and ethnic minorities have tended to be depicted in terms of a restricted repertoire of representations and within contexts characterized by conflict, controversy and deviance.' This repertoire has included:

- public health scares;
- muggings and inner-city disorder;
- problems of 'numbers';
- attacks on anti-racism campaigns;
- ignoring social inequalities.

Van Dijk has found strikingly similar repertoires in the Dutch media. In one study of the coverage of the arrival of a small number of Tamil asylum-seekers in the 1980s (van Dijk 1988b), he found they were talked about consistently as either having problems (such as being targeted by criminal gangs) or causing problems (such as abusing the Dutch social welfare system). In both ways, they tended to be criminalized by a constant association with deviance, crime, making false asylum claims, drugs and homelessness. In a string of studies, he has consistently found that the media present an 'ethnic consensus in which the very latitude of opinions and attitudes is quite strictly contained' (van Dijk 1991: 246).

Sport has been a context where gross generalizations about outsiders using ideas of 'race' have been prevalent and tacitly sanctioned as a way of celebrating in-group identity. This is related to its status as an area where 'overt emotional engagement remains publicly acceptable in ways in which this would be unthinkable in other contexts' (O'Donnell 1994: 354). Talk about sport is full of passionate statements about who 'we' are as a social group which merge into explanations and justifications of why we do or not do well in competitions. It easily accommodates and perhaps even requires an interpretative repertoire that establishes fundamental differences between categories of people. Major sporting moments, such as Australia's winning of the Americas Cup, often become imbued with in-group significance. Indeed, it is only when people can feel they are coming together as a nation through moments such as the shared watching of a media event that the nation becomes tangible. At these moments authority figures and spokespeople are able to project backwards from them to traditions and well-defined national characteristics that suddenly were 'always there'. 'These stereotypes signify as ethical norms, mobilized to advocate, shape and generate new habits amongst the citizenry' (Rowe et al. 1998: 121). What it means to be part of the nation and what the nation itself means are reinforced through such moments. National characteristics can also be challenged at such moments, particularly in international competitions. When the Chinese athlete Liu Xiang won the men's 110 metre hurdles at the 2004 Olympics, he talked of his victory partly as a challenge to interpretative repertoires in other countries about East Asians: 'My victory has proved that athletes with yellow skin can run as fast as those with black and white skin' (Wang 2004).

At times, the game being played becomes obscured as its symbolic function in performing ethnicity comes to the fore – quite literally, the football game is described without reference to the ball. Studies over a large number of years have shown consistently that television commentators talk differently about black and white players (and more recent studies have looked at similar patterns in coverage of Hispanic and Asian American players). Rainville and McCormick argued in a classic 1970s study of NFL commentary that:

> In his description of play, the announcer is building a positive reputation for the white player by more frequently praising him during play, more often depicting him as the aggressor and more often granting him more positive special focus. The announcer is, at the same time, building a negative reputation for the black player by negatively comparing him to other players, making negative references to his past achievements, and depicting him as the recipient of aggression.
>
> (Rainville and McCormick 1977: 24–5)

Other studies (see Davis and Harris 1998, for a review) have found black players talked about by commentators more in terms of the 'brawn' of natural athletes and white players in terms of 'brains' and hard work, of blacks as selfish players and whites as team players. Off the pitch, black sportsmen attract descriptions that draw on a fear of black men as over-sexed and violent (although black sportswomen do not) or descriptions of them as hip or as role models for blacks.

In recent years, such studies have suggested that sport is becoming a place where 'race' is seen as a less legitimate categorization, as sports clubs and broadcasters accept a responsibility to produce talk which draws upon different interpretative repertoires. Davis and Harris (1998) cite studies which found that the patterns which Rainville and McCormick (1977) found are no longer so clear-cut. There is also anecdotal evidence. O'Donnell (2003) notes that Scotland's most popular sports radio programme, *Saturday Super Scoreboard*, cold-shoulders callers who invoke the century-old sectarian rivalry between (Catholic) Celtic and (Protestant) Rangers football clubs. Those who draw on sectarian interpretative resources to discuss the competition between Celtic and Rangers are demoted from being addressed by their first names to 'caller', with one informed he was part of 'the narrow-minded minority in Scotland' (O'Donnell 2003: 216). The programme positions their contributions outside the shared, acceptable way of talking. However, McCarthy et al. (2003), also studying the UK sports media, found a mixed picture. In their sample of football commentary on the BBC and the Sky Sport channel, black players were, in general, no more likely to be evaluated negatively than white players, or to be commented about in terms of psychological attributes such as determination or skill. They were, however, much more likely to be praised for their physical attributes. Thus, 94 per cent of the commentator remarks about black players' physical characteristics were positive, and only 6 per cent negative, while 75 per cent of comments on white players' physical attributes were positive (McCarthy et al. 2003: 226). To the authors, the praise of black physicality suggested a racist ideology at work, but one which could not be expressed openly. They cite Birrell's (1989: 222) conclusion that such references play a major role in constructing 'dominant images of racially-defined groups, and thus a major mechanism for the reproduction of racial relations' (cited in McCarthy et al. 2003: 226).

Prejudice and social cognition

The content analysis studies cited by Davis and Harris look for racism in the content of talk, and find a number of forms of racism disappearing. But many scholars who study racism are sceptical that this means that those same racist cognitive resources are no longer relevant to social life. Van Dijk (1999) argues that a characteristic of racism today is that is has become less explicit as racism has lost its scientific status and acceptability in public debate, but that 'inferential' racism is still a powerful shaping factor in discourse. Bonilla-Silva and Forman (2000) point out that some interview-based studies in the USA show higher levels of racism in the population than survey-based studies. People may avow themselves to be not racist, aware of the social opprobrium that those perceived as racists attract, but then immediately afterwards express comments which arguably are racist, such as opposition to 'mixed-race' marriages. To reconcile this semantic conflict, they draw on what van Dijk (1999) calls mitigation strategies – statements of the 'I'm not racist but' variety. These include constructing discriminatory practices as being for a minority's 'own good', arguing that the practices are fair and not discriminatory, justifying practices in terms of facts (e.g. claims that mixed-race marriages are more likely to lead to divorce) and blaming minorities for their situation.

This racism is therefore harder to identify. However, van Dijk's semantic theory provides a number of tools to probe inferential racism, that analyse the way statements draw upon shared or background knowledge. Van Dijk argues that all language use is just the visible tip of a large iceberg of implicit world knowledge. Thus the statement denying racism can be unpacked to show racist presuppositions.

Van Dijk provides a full theory and set of analytical terms to discuss how such world knowledge is produced and called up in language use and to point to its use in discriminatory practices. He writes:

> Words, clauses and other textual expressions may imply concepts or propositions which may be inferred on the basis of background knowledge. This feature of discourse and communication has important ideological dimensions. The analysis of the 'unsaid' is sometimes more revealing than the study of what is actually expressed in the text.
>
> (1991: 144)

There are parallels between this concept of background world knowledge and Potter and Wetherell's term, 'interpretative resources'. Both terms describe socially shared ways of thinking and talking, which no one individual needs to claim as expressing his or her personal attitude but which can be easily deployed because 'everyone' knows this. However, Potter and Wetherell are closer to conversation analysts (Chapter 6) in focusing much more on the social relations established in talk than on what is happening within individuals' minds – 'not on individuals in [social] interchange, but on what is distributed between them' (Condor and Antaki 1997: 335). They in fact are suspicious of attempts to study memory, perception or emotion by looking for 'hidden inner processes' behind people's words, arguing that 'psychology is constructed in language' (Billig 2001: 211–12). Van Dijk, by contrast, aims to understand the socially shared by theorizing the link between knowledge inside our heads and the language we use to share that knowledge. He aims thereby to link cognitive psychology to social and cultural analysis. To do this he draws on a range of forms of analysis, including labelling (Chapter 1) and transitivity analysis (Chapter 3) but also on an explicitly cognitive theory of the way information is stored and retrieved in the mind, which I discuss briefly below.

Van Dijk focuses upon the ways that the meanings of sentences or utterances are organized into larger structures of sense, which he terms 'macrostructures'. A single unit of meaning, he suggests, is not remembered by readers, but is reduced down into 'macropropositions' or 'topics' which the reader is able to store and later remember. 'Experimental research has repeatedly shown that topics are usually the best recalled information of a text' (van Dijk 1991: 73). He argues we remember long stretches of information, such as stories, by remembering the gist of the story:

> [L]anguage users can summarize fairly complex units of information with one or two sentences, and these sentences are assumed to express the gist, or theme, or the topic of the information. In intuitive terms, such themes or topics organize what is most important in a text. They, indeed, define the 'upshot' of what is said or written.
>
> (van Dijk 1985: 74)

He argues that it is often in these larger structures – in the way that verbal material is boiled down into briefer topics – that we find socially shared and prejudicial ways of construing other people.

He developed his analysis of macrostructures in the critique of newspaper discourse (e.g. van Dijk 1988a), arguing that headlines work to sum up stories and attract readers to them because they represent the story reduced down its gist – to a macroproposition or topic. Sub-editors are pre-digesting the story for readers, in other words, doing the reduction of meaning down to a single proposition that readers would do in their heads. Sports commentary does not have headlines. Instead, like the narratives which Labov (1997) describes (see Chapter 4), commentary combines description of action with moments of evaluation, pauses in the action when explanations are made about what is going on and why. It is at these moments of evaluation that we might expect to find the topical statements of the commentary: the sense of what is really going on in the sports event, why the action has happened and what world knowledge is relevant to understanding the game or sports display. Thus, van Dijk provides theoretical justification for the studies of commentators' evaluations of black and white players discussed above. In van Dijk's terms, we could interpret the positive physical descriptions of black football players found by McCarthy et al. (2003), first, as a denial of racism. The racism lies in the perception of the black players as defined in terms of their physicality, but that is expressed in positive terms, with the negative corollary, the racist attitude that black players are not characterized by high mental sporting ability, omitted. Second, we could seek to trace the macrostructure at work by working back from the evaluations (these included 'very athletic player', 'strong in the tackle', 'great leaping ability') to the verbal and visual propositions – the play-by-play commentary and the action on the pitch – that these evaluative comments are seeking to give the gist of.

To trace topical statements back to the propositions they summarize, you would need to watch the games from which the comments came (a fuller analysis of commentary on a game is given in the case study below), so the following analysis is somewhat tentative. Van Dijk (1988a) suggests that material is reduced down to topics by three 'macro-rules': deleting, abstracting and generalizing. Thus, a phrase, 'great leaping ability', has *deleted* large amounts of information about the player's action, information such as his leaping to challenge another player for possession of a high ball or other moments of play. The phrase has *abstracted* from the player's many moments of play this one detail, marking it out as one that represents his playing, and it has *generalized* from actual leaps and their successful outcomes in terms of playing the game to an ability, a general characteristic of the player.

In formulating an evaluative phrase such as this one, the commentator would need to omit many other possible ways of summarizing the player's actions. In a critical analysis, this moment in analysis is the crucial one, for it is here that we can identify the larger macrostructure or pyramid of meaning, and therefore the ideological dimension to the shaping of understanding. A player praised for his physical prowess is one who is not being praised for his endurance or intellect, although arguably these are just as important elements in the decision to jump and the act of jumping for the ball. The 'natural ability' macrostructure appears, from the evidence of analyses such as McCarthy et al. (2003), to be one that is used more frequently for black players than for white ones.

But why should broadcasters reach for processes of summarizing that end up in phrases such as 'great leaping ability', and how can they be confident that listeners to their commentary will be able to follow those cognitive processes? Van Dijk argues that summarizing works because people share a large amount of knowledge about the world and about the available ways of making sense of it. He calls this shared knowledge 'scripts' and 'models'. Summarizing information into topics tends to take place along well-worn paths of meaning-making that are signalled to the audience in a few key words. He writes:

> Models are mental structures of information that, besides the new information offered in a news report, feature information about such a situation as inferred from general knowledge scripts. Thus, when reading about the 'riot' in Handsworth, readers make a model of this particular disturbance on the basis of the information in the news reports, but 'know' much more about it than the newspaper now tells them, because they have

more general knowledge about such disturbances or the place where they occur.

(van Dijk 1991: 74)

In van Dijk's news examples, when the journalist uses language such as 'riot' and 'black youths' a small number of cognitive scripts immediately become relevant to the reader to link them together into a model of the current situation. The journalist need not state (and would not need to be conscious of the assumption) that blacks are 'known' to be naturally violent to explain the event, but provides information which makes sense in terms of that script, and omits or downplays information which suggests other factors. In another study, this time of Dutch reporting on Tamil refugees from the Sri Lanka civil war (van Dijk 1988b), he found that the crisis the refugees were escaping from was mentioned in news articles, but was buried, while news headlines, such as 'Thousands of Tamils Smuggled into Country', communicated a sense of large numbers of people arriving in the Netherlands illegally. Van Dijk writes:

A coherent semantic system was construed by the press that happened to be remarkably similar to the prevailing ethnic prejudice [scripts] against all existing minority groups. In other words, the press made it 'easy' for prejudiced readers simply to apply such existing prejudices in their own evaluation of the new immigrants.

(1988b: 185)

Underlying media discourse, then, van Dijk finds ethnic prejudice in the scripts by which they make sense. Further, he argues that such scripts must be present in speakers' and hearers' minds for the language to make coherent sense.

Similarly, in sports commentary, it is no surprise to come across a black sportsman described as physically adept, because we have all seen many such images interpreted in such ways before. Images from Jesse Owens in the 1936 Berlin Olympics to Haile Gebri Selassi, Carl Lewis, Ben Johnson and other black sportsmen in more recent Olympics, to boxer Muhammed Ali and basketballer Michael Jordan, contribute to a script of a 'natural' black male sporting prowess. Scripts of black sporting intellect, endurance or hard work, on the other hand, are much less common. This situation can be accounted for in ideological terms. Van Sterkenburg and Knoppers write that: 'Since (white male) dominance in western societies is usually based on a hierarchy in which mental qualities are valued above physical qualities, this discourse primarily supports the privileged position of many white men' (2004: 303).

The sports commentator, faced with rapidly unfolding events on the pitch, and provided with a ready-made and coherent semantic system by which to make sense of it, is unlikely to reach for other interpretative frameworks. Just as poststructuralists argue that discourse speaks the subject, van Dijk's cognitive semantics proposes that prejudices can circulate within a society through such headlines and evaluative comments and become reinforced as shared knowledge without anyone claiming ownership of them. We cannot read off the racism of the individual journalist or commentator from the text (Cottle 1999), but we can read off the scripts or system of shared knowledge which underpin the communicative activity of news and commentary.

One criticism of van Dijk is that his analysis of socially shared cognition is limited as a critique of ideology because it reduces it down to structures of ideas. Van Dijk has countered with a book called *Ideology* (1998), but the criticism remains. Montgomery (1999a) argues that van Dijk sees ideology too much in terms of the rational and not enough in terms of people's emotional investment in social practices and the forms of power which bind them together. His view of ideology is a little too voluntaristic, too much about efficient communication, and not enough about power, the formation of identity and other social phenomena. It also suffers from the assumption that people are 'cognitive misers', that is, that they will always reduce information down to its most easily stored form. Billig shows that cognitive psychology's focus on generalizing and categorizing is only half the story (Abell and Stokoe 1999). People also describe things as unique or atypical, remembering a piece of music in relation to one strong experience or years later being able to remember a detail of a childhood scene but nothing of the context. The human mind is, in other words, not a machine.

Sports talk as the tip of the iceberg

Social cognition is, perhaps, not sufficient as a theory of how power works in society. But a strength of the approach is that it allows analysis to be precise in describing the unstated dimension of communication, to describe the iceberg on the basis of its visible tip. As O'Donnell (1994) notes, stereotypical categorizations of sports figures and teams are characteristically brief references, leaving much to be inferred. He quotes a headline (originally in Castilian) from the Spanish sports daily *As*:

PANZERS VERSUS ARGENTINA

(*As*, 8 July 1992)

He states: 'Little effort is required to reconstruct the narrative set in motion in the reader's mind by such a headline' (O'Donnell 1994: 369). Using van Dijk's cognitive semantic analysis, it is possible to describe in more detail what is going on here. 'Argentina' is a straightforwardly abstracted reference to the Argentinean football team which contemporary sports readers would have known was playing in the football World Cup at the time. 'Panzers' refers of course to German tanks from World War II, which are clearly not at issue here, and so generalizes from the military efficiency and skill of the Wehrmacht to Germany as a whole. There is an obvious clash between the image of a tank battalion and a football team, suggesting a mismatch at the level of how the two teams regarded and played the game. This might be a witty rhetorical play with our expectations, to be recognized as merely metaphorical, were it not for the consistency with which O'Donnell and other scholars have found German sportspeople represented in this way in other countries' media. Germans are repeatedly characterized by a military efficiency, controlled aggression and rational calculation, which is implicitly at odds with common scripts of how the game 'should' be played. While sports commentary often draws upon military metaphor, German sportspeople frequently attract such language. Bishop and Jaworski (2003) suggest that this kind of sporting reference helps build the nation as a shared experience of history, a sense of looking back collectively on the Germany of World War II (particularly important for countries which fought against Germany). According to O'Donnell (1994: 354), most countries' teams and sportspeople are represented in such severely limited ways in 'an astonishing uniformity both within and across national boundaries', each with its own repertoire of stereotypical attributes.

Part of the power of the *As* headline above is that it stereotypes the German team for the duration of the whole text. However, in van Dijk's (1991: 76) analysis, the macroproposition is never a single concept, but is a whole clause, the most important and over-arching action of the larger text it is summarizing. So stereotypes do not stand alone, but arise as meaningful resources within this proposition, as topic actors who engage in macropropositions. Similarly, for Bishop and Jaworski (2003), the typification or stereotype does not make sense alone but works the way it does because it also expresses a sense of separation – a rhetoric of 'us' and 'them' – and a sense of conflict. The *As* headline invokes a stereotyped Germany as it thematizes the whole text in terms of a clash between militarism and the gamesmanship of the Argentineans. We are thus to understand from *As* that what is most important about the game previewed in the article is that it is a battle of Argentina against the German national character.

Case study: Latin temperaments v. Third World coaches

In a brief case study below I analyse some of the evaluative comments in the Eurosport television commentary by Gary Bloom on the 1998 football

World Cup match between Spain and Nigeria (13 June 1998; Nigeria won 3:2) to explore what topics arise in these moments and how they might be analysed within van Dijk's theorization of racist talk. In turn, the pre-match commentary, commentary on players' abilities and comment on the fans are discussed.

The commentary begins with pre-kick-off discussion of the teams, their players and the coaches. Pre-match commentary often sets up expectations for the game, and is therefore important in developing a set of themes about how the game will progress and, implicitly, why. The pre-match commentary below is dominated by two themes: the tactical advantage to Spain of rain and Spain's underachievement. Nigeria is talked about only little, and then in quite limited ways.

> Spanish coach Javier Clemente wanted rain for today's match. And how his prayers have been answered. Clemente feels that the Nigerians will be better suited (.) to more humid conditions. and that is hardly what we've got today it's been raining hard when I arrived this morning in this beautiful city (.) and at one stage there were real fears that this game (.) would have to be called off but the good news is that in the last hour the rain has ceased but it's rather overcast and humid now. But the playing surface I think you'll find is very very wet indeed . . .
>
> *[details of the teams omitted]*
>
> Well this man said we want rain. This is what he said yesterday. And as you can see from the Perspex (0.5) which surrounds the dugout there's plenty of it about. Javier Clemente trying to lead Spain to some sort of success at a major championships for the first time (1) Spain have so often underachieved (.) on the international scene (0.5) and yet they have such outstanding players. Now you've probably seen him before [the camera shows the Nigerian coach, with the caption, 'Coach B. Milutinovic']. He's the coach of Nigeria but he's the former national coach of Mexico Costa Rica (0.5) and the USA (2) Luis Enrique kisses his ring for good luck (4) And very shortly we'll be off and running.

Not only the majority of the statements (e.g. 'Clemente wanted rain', 'Enrique kisses his ring for good luck') but also the evaluative, summarizing clauses are about Spain ('Clemente trying to lead Spain to some sort of success'), although the images show both teams. The game, in this commentary, is about the Spanish team, and in particular about the team making good on the natural talent of their players. O'Donnell (1994) notes that southern European teams are often stereotyped as possessing natural talent but lacking discipline. That is not stated, but against the background, which Bloom gives, of Spain's lack of international success and the talent of its players, it adds coherence to the commentary. Thus, the partly stated topic of the pre-match commentary is a tension between Clemente's coaching and the Latin footballing character.

The Nigerians are described (aside from in reference to the team line-ups, omitted here) in just two ways in the pre-match commentary: in terms of benefiting from humidity and in a jokey aside on their second-hand coach, 'You've probably seen him before.' Although the viewer sees many images of Nigerian players and cheering fans that do not suggest a one-sided game, what she or he hears, and therefore the evaluative discourse by which to make sense of those images, is fairly dismissive of them. The second reference, particularly as it follows a detailed discussion of the Spanish coach's task, remains at the level of a stereotype of Third World countries which can only afford second-hand coaches. Both these references do nothing to build on or amend the script of 'Third World team' which is called up.

As the match begins, two kinds of evaluative comments about players begin to build up. First, the talk about Spanish achievements is continued, in a number of references to the successes and histories of individual Spanish players and their club sides and in references to previous World Cup games involving Spain. Indeed, most of the talk is about the Spanish team, both evaluative and action talk. When Spain has the ball, it is often commented on, and when Nigeria has the ball, there is often silence. In the following, for example, the focus is on the Spanish attack rather than the Nigerian defence:

Good header by Nadal, Raul, Nadal for Spain. Luis Enrique calling for the ball, Raul, Hierro. Oh but it was just behind (.) Hierro who did well to rescue the situation and pick out Ferrer FERRER'S CROSS (1) and Kiko's (.) or rather Raul's header hits (.) the frame of the goal (2) Lovely cross and Raul (.) put (.) the full weight of his body into the header and smacked it into the crossbar (.) and twice now Raul has come close (3) Bit of a let off there for Nigeria.

By contrast, when Nigerian players are on the attack, the focus of attention tends to be shared. Thus commentary explores the topic established in the pre-match commentary of Spain making good on its potential. This is not an over-riding concern. So there are few statements along the lines of 'A patient build-up here by Spain', which directly thematize Spanish play in terms of discipline over individual talent. But the commentary makes sense of the play in terms of the Spanish task.

Second, the commentary focuses a little more on the Spanish when they play well yet focuses more on the Nigerians when they do not. When Spanish players shoot unsuccessfully at goal, they are often putting the Nigerian goalkeeper under pressure or are coming close to success (as in the example above). When Nigerian players shoot, their shots are often coded as failures. During a replay, the commentator says:

> There's that shot again by Ikpeba. I thought that was a poor effort on goal because if Ikpeba could have just held that ball up there for a couple of colleagues to run into the box who knows what might have happened.

A topic of Spanish success clearly shapes the commentary.

The commentator talks differently about Nigerian and Spanish fans. The Spanish are particularized, such as in the image of 'Manolo', a famous, loyal supporter who has banged a large red drum at every Spanish World Cup appearance since 1982. By contrast, the commentator describes Nigerian fans as follows:

> A marvellous occasion for the Nigerians. Nigeria, Africa's most populated nation (2) They are really daft about their football. And on the way to the stadium (.) this morning all I could see were Nigerians off the train (.) heading to the stadium in their numbers (.) and obviously awash with green flags.

While the Spanish fan is individualized, the Nigerians are described as a mass. We are – like a Spanish player at one point – 'surrounded by green-shirted' people who are rarely individualized.

Is this racist? On one level, the emphasis on Spanish play and success at the start of the game is simply the commentator doing his job of building tension and watching it play out. And it is true that once the Nigerians began getting more possession and passing better further into the game, the patterns changed slightly, with more talk about Nigerian skill and fewer negative comments. Some of the talk is about expectations of the match, which evolve with the action. At one point the commentator states, after some nifty dribbling of the ball, 'They're so skilful, the Nigerians.' This may indeed simply be praise for skilful play. However, the skill of the Spanish is represented more as something listeners to the commentary already know, embedded inside other statements or left unstated, or is a matter of the skill of individual players. The overt statement of a collective Nigerian skilfulness suggests that this is news, that it goes against what 'everyone' knows. In the context of a World Cup game, and where the Nigerians are the current Olympic football champions, a phrase such as 'Beautiful play' would have sufficed.

The negative comments about the Nigerians are classic cases of the prejudicial commentary noted by Rainville and McCormick on NFL matches. Black and white players – in this case, black and white teams – are spoken about within expectations of greater white skill and determination to win, expect-ations which are rarely allowed to be challenged.

There are textual clues, then, that the text is built upon scripts and back-ground knowledge, mobilized in the overall topics and in the evaluations which explore those topics, that Europeans are skilful and that an African team is unlikely to do well. There is, as with Motson, no deliberate or overt prejudice at work. But the semantic structures that are present make most sense within inferential structures and scripts which emphasize white actors as the ones to be interested in and emphasize their positive attributes.

There is, moreover, not much done to add to or revise prior knowledge about Africans. Much more knowledge is given about the Spanish players and team, giving them greater specificity. When a Spanish footballer plays well, he is praised. When, as in the example above, a Nigerian footballer does well, the whole team is praised as skilful. Moreover, references to Nigerian players are often in terms of a European knowledge. The Nigerian team 'includes several players with European experience'. When Nigeria scores, the commentator says, 'Spain's lead is wiped out within four minutes and there is terrific celebra-tions going on there inside this stadium because Mutio Adepoju who plays his club football in Spain has headed Nigeria level.' The game is known in European terms.

Such sports commentary is not just telling us about an attitude to Nigerian football. The inferential structures we can detect here are much more general. Sport is, as discussed above, often a **metonym** for the nation, a site at which national characteristics and expectations are established and renewed. In a sporting context, national and ethnic identity and pride are very much at stake. Moreover, much of what we know about other countries is formed in asides and inferences in contexts such as sport, fiction and celebrity gossip. As Philo (2001) notes, some countries only ever get into British news if a hot air balloon with the celebrity businessman Richard Branson in it floats over their territory. Therefore the social cognition in World Cup commentary intersects with much wider ideological forces.

This chapter has analysed racism within the argument that while explicit racism is rare, it is present as a set of inferential structures to make sense of cultural practices. Van Dijk's analysis of the themes or macropropositions of a text allow us to make a text accountable for the semantic resources which it draws on. It also provides a way of theorizing how a text draws on socially shared background knowledge. That analysis was applied to broadcast sports commentary to argue that, although 'race' is rarely explicitly mentioned there, it forms a key part of the shared cognition of broadcaster and audiences about what is going on in sports events.

Further reading

A concise account by van Dijk of his analysis of semantic macrostructures is his chapter in *Discourse and Communication* (1985). He has applied his analysis in fuller detail to news discourse in *News as Discourse* (1988a) and has written many books and articles on racism (e.g. van Dijk 1993), including an account of people's discursive strategies to deny racism (van Dijk 1999). A similar social cognitive approach is taken by Wodak in studying nationalism and prejudice in Austria (e.g. Wodak 1996). Wetherell and Potter (1992) represent an alternative major approach to racist discourse.

CONNECTING WITH NEW MEDIA: WEBLOGS AND OTHER INTERACTIVE MEDIA

One of the things I'm sure about in journalism right now is that my readers know more than I do . . . To the extent that I can take advantage of that in a way that does something for everyone involved – that strikes me as pretty cool.

(technology journalist and weblogger, Dan Gillmor)

Introduction

In January 2002, the then Director-General of the BBC, Greg Dyke, used an *Observer* journalist to float the idea of adding a fourth pillar to the corporation's 80-year-old founding ethos: from now on it would 'inform, educate, entertain and connect' (Arlidge 2002). BBC websites such as 'Where I Live' began to spring up, featuring stories, opinions and even sports results written by people in their local areas. Television and radio programmes began featuring web-chats after the programme, they invited viewers or listeners to send in ideas and their comments were read on air. New jobs for 'iPresenters' were created. These developments were not unique to the BBC, but represent a particularly clear example of a more general and significant change in the mediascape. The news and entertainment media we have become used to critiquing since the first mass circulation newspapers emerged in the mid-nineteenth century are no longer straightforwardly mass media, as media users choose the way they receive content, answer back to producers and are addressed in new ways. This raises questions about the notion of publicness, the distinction between media producers and audiences, the role of the media in nation-building and much else: digital media provide different answers to such old questions. But they also require distinctive forms of analysis, and Dyke's word 'connect' signals a key component of what is different.

As critical scholars have pointed out, much about 'new' media is in fact little different from the 'old', which is as we might expect, given that they arise in the same societies. Cornford and Robins write: 'In reality the new media are far from being the anarchic, decentralized infrastructure of a new social and political order. There are clearly new players in the media sector, but the game that they are playing is much the same as it always was' (1999: 112).

However, one area where there is good evidence for a significant departure from existing media practices is the relationship set up between the producer and consumer of the text. New critical terms have in fact been required to describe those we call 'audiences' or 'viewers' or 'readers' in other contexts, with a consensus emerging that people in the new media context are media 'users' (Livingstone and Lievrouw 2002). Among others, theories of interactivity and online community have been developed to account for the textual practices engaged in by users and theories of networked individualism and cosmopolitan societies invoked to account for the impact of these textual practices on the social (see Further reading). While digital media by and large reproduce the corporate structures of offline media, they do so according to different textual dynamics.

Online media form an immense field, with a correspondingly immense range of kinds of discourse. This chapter focuses primarily on online journalism, allowing contrasts and parallels to emerge with the other chapters which also focused on journalism (Chapters 1, 3 and 7). It begins by contrasting an online news product with its televisual counterpart, before accounting for some of the discursive differences by critically exploring the often loosely used idea of interactivity. Interactivity is used in much the same sense in media sales, journalism and new media scholarship. Jensen (1999: 201) defines it as the degree to which media forms 'let the user exert an influence on the content and/or form of the mediated communication'. Implicitly, for many who use the phrase, 'interactive media' stand in contrast to 'old media', where broadcast or printing technology allowed only one-way communication. However, if we are to make use of the term as an analytical tool, it is important to observe that interactivity is neither this simple nor this new. As the chapter explores, there are two major dimensions to the interaction that takes place, control over navigation and over content. Moreover, all media texts set up relations between people. If some digital media reveal new textual dynamics, it is not because they are newly interactive, but because they enable interactivity or connectivity in distinctive and particularly rich ways. A number of examples are discussed to specify just how news journalism as a form of knowledge about the world is becoming rearticulated in some highly interactive media. The chapter ends by exploring the interactivity of a **weblog** produced by a journalist in Iraq.

Relationships: Mass media and new media

A number of researchers in the 1980s thought of the new Internet media of email, Usenet and file transfers (the world wide web was yet to develop) as existing outside both the social and the commercial worlds. This 'new world' attitude, perhaps fed by science fiction fantasies such as William Gibson's *Neuromancer* (1984) which first began to interpret the phenomenon, has slowly dissipated as the Internet has become more and more important in the lives of people in western countries. By the end of 2003, the 'media time' that Europeans spent online exceeded that spent reading magazines, at 10 per cent (EIAA 2003). Online activities are as much part of many people's lives as reading newspapers or going downtown to shop, and are subject to much the same social rules. However, social practices are changed as they go online – partly because of the cybercultural expectations which people have about some parts of the Internet, leading to distinctive discursive practices, and partly because the medium itself provides different opportunities.

Media aimed at young people, which position themselves as cutting edge, often provide the clearest examples of this distinctiveness. The chapter begins with one such site in order to specify how computer-mediated discourse differs from discourse in other media, and in particular to pin down the key concept interactivity or connectivity. In New Zealand, the national public service broadcaster, TVNZ, ran a substantial website alongside its young people's current affairs show, *Flipside* (TV2 (NZ) 2002–04).[1] The daily current affairs programme, which presented the news in an informal manner and ran stories aimed at the 18–39 age group who tend not to watch news programmes, was pulled in December 2004 during a ratings war with commercial channels. While it ran, the show sought to involve its television viewers by inviting them to phone or text in competition entries and views. However, it overwhelming positioned viewers as an audience for content which the producers ordained, in the order they ordained it, and at a set time in the television schedule. The website, by contrast, invited users to become reporters for the show, to compete against each other in 'photoshopping' competitions, to share their views in discussion boards and to choose what content they consumed, and in what order (Figure 8.1). From the first interaction between producer and consumer, the physical click on a link or bookmark to the website or the typing in of its web address to call up the site, the relationship required a much more active

Figure 8.1 A screenshot of the New Zealand youth current affairs show *Flipside*, showing features that encourage greater interaction from users
Source: Image courtesy of Television New Zealand

consumer. The relations set up by the two media texts can be contrasted as shown in Table 8.1.

This relationship can be characterized in terms of the degree of interactivity. The television version is minimally interactive. As Thompson notes of mass media in general, it provides a 'quasi-interaction' between producers and receivers who do not share the same space (they can be literally a world apart) and who often do not share the same time either (as with televised tributes after the death of the British Queen Mother in 2002, when some of those interviewed were dead by the time the pre-recorded tributes were aired). Thompson writes:

> For the vast majority of recipients the only way in which they intervene in
> the quasi-interaction is by deciding whether to initiate it by turning on the

Table 8.1 Contrast between the two media texts

'Flipside' (TV2 (NZ))	flipside.nzoom.com
one-way interaction	two-way
decisions on content centralized in producers	decisions distributed among producers and users
all watch the same	individual browsing
daily ritual	watch when you want
time constraints on content	no time constraints

> TV, to continue it by leaving it on and paying some degree of attention, or to close it down by ignoring it, changing channels or turning it off.
>
> (1995: 96)

As a result, he describes a significant 'structural asymmetry' in mass media, in which recipients are less constrained to pay attention but can have little impact on what's said and producers regard recipients as anonymous spectators whose attention needs to be grabbed. If we begin from a model of conversation, television and other mass media are a strange and unsocial kind of interaction. The website does not provide co-presence either – the immediacy of the to-and-fro of talk in which conversational interaction is built (as discussed in Chapter 6) – and it can, like mass media, be consumed at a distance and in a different time from its production. But it meets Jensen's (1999) criteria of interactivity because it allows the user a wide choice in how to consume *Flipside* online and allows the user some opportunities to produce her or his own content. In Thompson's terms, the interaction is more symmetrical, or closer to the interaction found in conversation.

A number of new media analysts have sought a more precise description of the way websites perform interactivity. One typology of the different kinds of interaction possible in a text builds on Bordewijk and van Kaam's (1986) model of power in mass communication: we can talk of 'allocution', where one person at the centre speaks to many at the periphery (Thompson's quasi-interaction), 'consultation', where an individual looks for information from a central store (as when a user looks up a book or a database), 'registration', where an individual sends information to the centre, and 'conversation'. Only in the last do information and power over the talk flow both ways (Bordewijk and van Kaam 1986). Apart from conversation, however, these categories look to a discourse analyst like parts of interaction, not whole interactions. When a reader looks up a dictionary, he or she 'consults' but also does something more complex, entering a social relationship with the implied author of the dictionary. The distribution of power is not determined just by the direction that information moves – it can be one of deference to the dictionary's authority or one of flicking through looking for strange words, or any other of a range of activities. Interactivity therefore needs to be a measure of the social activity that the producers and users of something like *Flipside* are entering into, about how the chain of communicative actions unfolds. It is also a term that is perhaps best used to describe the responsiveness of the participants to each other. McMillan (2002) sees two parts to that responsiveness. A text, such as a website, may be interactive in the sense of giving people considerable power to choose what they do – what information is communicated, when it happens, and so on. In this sense, the dictionary is quite an interactive form of social action, because users get to decide how they use its material. A text, may, second, be interactive in the sense of allowing material to move both ways. The dictionary gives the reader no voice at all, and in fact takes on huge 'oracular' power, as Bourdieu (1991: 212) terms it, in speaking on behalf of the society and the language in ordaining 'correct' English. Websites which feature discussion boards, email contacts and forms to fill in distribute that power. These two kinds of interaction, which go under a number of names but I will call 'navigational' and 'functional' interactivity, are examined below.[2]

However, the interaction in a text, while enabled by the way the text is produced, is also about social conventions emerging around those texts and is about the social and cultural context in which those texts are consumed. A text isn't interactive, but the discursive practices of which the text is part may be. McMillan (2002) has found, for example, that different readers assess the same features differently in terms of interactivity. In other words, interactivity as a measure of the text's *features* differs markedly from interactivity as a measure of people's *use* of those features. It is therefore a complex phenomenon, and we need a definition which describes it in terms of that complexity in order to bring features and use together. Rafaeli defines interactivity as: 'an expression of the extent that, in a given series of communicative exchanges, any third (or later) transmission (or message) is related to the degree to which previous exchanges referred to even earlier transmissions' (1988: 111). That is, the more a text refers back to previous things said, acknowledging the ongoing interchange between the participants and responding to that, the more interactive it is. On this criterion, the conversational practices discussed in Chapter 6 are highly inter-active. A user's path through the *Flipside* website, responding to links by click-ing on them and getting in turn different web pages or pieces of video, is less so but still fairly interactive, with the site's material unfolding in tandem with the user's interests. More interactive still is a website which changes as a result of users' interactions with it, so that a chain of communicative acts takes place involving different people. What is of greatest interest to many new media discourse analysts is how the different degrees of complex and reciprocal language events lead to different kinds of knowledge and different distributions of power in society.

Knowledge and the surfer

The web surfer who clicks on a link is telling the computer to download a copy of a file to display on the screen. The web is a 'pull' medium, a long way from 'push' media where the newspaper copy or broadcast signal is sent out with little initiative from those who will receive it. But what kinds of discourse emerge from this technological affordance? The answer is far from simple. Sometimes, as with hypertext novels, where users click on different links to take a story in different directions, the technology clashes with the conventions of the genre. As Miller notes, print novels are read within the assumption that they will make sense, that the author is taking the reader somewhere, that the text will be coherent:

> Because print promises – however deceptively – to make coherent sense, it becomes the reader's responsibility to try to hold it to that promise and catch it when it reneges. Moulthrop claims that '[b]reakdowns always teach us something' ... But hyperfictions don't break down: they are broken to begin with.
>
> (Miller n.d.)

The communicative act, in the case of a novel, is the whole novel, and we attempt to understand it as a whole. As the philosopher Gadamer (1979: 238) puts it, understanding requires that the person doing the understanding assumes that the other person has said something that makes sense to him or herself. If the reader is given a list of possible outcomes and asked to choose from them, taking the plot one way or another, that act of trying to understand breaks down.

News stories are, however, already much less coherent. As White (1995) has found, while the headline and introduction are required for the text to make sense as texts, most of the other paragraphs of a text could be reordered with little effect on the meaning. He describes these paragraphs as satellites orbiting around the introduction, expanding on the story summarized there and providing evidence in paragraphs of background or quotation (White 1995). The story is constructed this way so that it can be cut down easily in order to fit the 'news hole' available after the ads have been placed (Bell 1991). The coherence of the news text is established much more, as was discussed in the Introduction and Chapter 7, in terms of the social categories and shared knowledge of the readers which are made relevant in the labelling or key words provided. It is for this reason that news websites are able to produce complex hypertexts, comprised of many smaller texts on a particular issue linked together into a 'special topic' or 'in depth' section. The BBC Online special sections on elections (such as 'Vote USA 2004'[3]) allow users to choose which of dozens of stories to read on the election, to read and post in a discussion section, to listen to audio or video clips from correspondents or to read background material, including profiles of the presidential candidates, profiles of each state, opinion polls, information on the voting system and a guide to the candidates' views on key election issues. Even when there is little attempt to make such hypertexts coherent, as in a number of news sites' use of automated software to produce a page that links to all their stories on a subject, the text is still meaningful.

What is affected, however, in news hypertexts, is the *way* it is meaningful, that is, the way knowledge is produced out of the text. It has, to start with, a slightly different relationship to time. A user who clicks on her or his favourite website to get the latest headlines is doing something similar to the listener who turns on the radio on the hour to catch the news. Both are consuming information within a context where the timeliness of the news is important. But a user who seeks out information on a topic, such as the US presidential elections, is likely to be as concerned with factors such as relevance to the questions or interests that she or he has as whether the text comes from today or last week. 'Vote USA 2004', for example, provides an interactive graphic with poll data from three different polling agencies over the nine months before the election (http://news.bbc.co.uk/1/hi/world/americas/3658490.stm). The information is up to date, but its nine-month timeframe indicates a wider notion of temporal relevance. The polls graphic also illustrates a different relationship of such texts to the real. The three polls show close but different results: a week before the election date, the ABC/*Washington Post* poll put Kerry ahead on 48 per cent, the CNN/*USA Today*/Gallup poll put Bush ahead on 49 per cent and the CBS/*New York Times* poll put the two leading candidates level on 45 per cent. The interactivity of the graphic, allowing the user to choose which poll to look at for which time period, reduces the claim of each poll to represent the real situation, highlighting that each of them is both approximate and a hypothetical version of voters' intentions.

The job of the journalist becomes reoriented slightly when the news organization seeks to provide such multiple ways of finding out about the real. Bardoel (1996: 296) suggests we add to the current 'orientating' role of journalism – giving background, commentary and explanation – another role of 'instrumental' journalism, providing interested users with the specialized material they are looking for. Many news websites actually offer few links, particularly outside their domains, but those which do thereby help contribute to a model of knowledge in which the truth of what is happening in the world cannot be channelled exclusively through one news text. One clear example is the British *Guardian* newspaper's news weblog, which each day provides fresh links to news articles from around the world which its editors think noteworthy. The webpage is not an authoritative news source on what happened yesterday, for it provides often conflicting perspectives on the same event. It produces instead a different kind of claim to authority in its use of multiple links. The news weblog's linking to an article vouches for that text's value, while the status of the *Washington Post* or the Human Rights Watch article linked to reinforces the weblog's authority (Matheson 2004a). The rich linking of such sites inserts the user into a network of knowing, placing these sites as key 'nodes' in that network, and placing their users as part of the global 'informational elite' who are 'in the know' (Castells 1996).

Intertextuality entails, as a result, a 'disaggregating' of the news audience. The website with many links assumes that not all users are looking for the same thing, and they do not all have the same expertise or background knowledge – assumptions that are forced on the newspaper editor, who must decide on one front page article and has room for one poll graphic. Ward (2002: 121) writes that the online user's 'pattern of consuming information is a haphazard zig-zag rather than a line. And every pathway created by every user can be different.' Bardoel's (1996) instrumental journalist is writing for a much smaller audience, whose members are acting much more individually than media practitioners and researchers have tended to think of media audiences. In his view, this is a transformation of a quasi-objective representation of the latest world news into a service for users, where knowledge is gained in the interaction between website and user.

To other critics, however, it is a further extension of the consumer society into the news media. The relationship between the editor and the reader is transformed into one between the content provider and the consumer, and the editor's decisions about what is in the public interest and important that the public should know are elided into a wide array of attractive informational choices. Williams (1998: 39) warns that such a news service 'becomes just one step in an informational quest by the consumer, one that may be harder and harder to distinguish from other sorts of information seeking'. The special roles of the journalist to hold the powerful to account or to represent the views of the people are perhaps weakened, as news journalists write less for a public than a market niche. The logical extension of navigational interactivity within a consumerist logic is that the website, through **cookies** that tell it of the users' identity and preferences, pre-selects the kind of news which the user has read in the past or which the user has told the site to gather for him or her. Sunstein writes of these 'Daily Me' services:

> The market for news, entertainment, and information has finally been perfected. Consumers are able to see precisely what they want. When the power to filter is unlimited, people can decide, in advance and with perfect accuracy, what they will and will not encounter. They can design something very much like a communications universe of their own choosing.
>
> (2002: 5)

To him, the diversity of information resources on the Internet is contributing to the fragmenting of public spaces and a weakening of public life.

I will, however, give the last word here to a discourse analyst. Lemke (2003) argues that the use made of such consumerist spaces is not necessarily consumerist. He proposes that the hypertext provides a similar opportunity to the television remote's control of the flow of the televisual. Users are able to 'traverse' the space of the web, making new meanings precisely because, as Miller noted, there is no expectation of final meaning to the text. Instead there is a chain of cohesive links between elements, which he sees as fundamentally the same as the intertextual links that readers or viewers make in all texts. This he sees as politically liberating. If we live under a consumer capitalist hegemony which has colonized many aspects of culture, providing us with relationships through our consumption of things and producing spaces of identity through conformity, the space for personal creativity is reduced:

> As those spaces become less and less available to us, and afford us less and less opportunity, we have begun to turn to another possibility: to make our meanings across rather than between institutional spaces. Instead of seeking out the cracks, the not-yet-colonized spaces of everyday life, we can seek to make traversal meanings by appropriating elements from multiple institutional spaces and catenating them together along a unique traversal that affords us a very large space of potential new meanings to be made.
>
> (Lemke 2003)

Lemke is suggesting that, when we come across a news story during surfing, we are not entering deeply into the news genre, accepting the role of the news institution, but in surfing across its surface, glancing, clicking, moving on, we are producing new, distinctive texts.

Media that connect: Functional interactivity

This book has suggested in a number of places that knowledge is not constructed by individuals themselves, but is a social accomplishment through discourse. To know something involves talking about it with others by building on frameworks that are shared with them. It is perhaps for that reason that 'Daily Me' services have not proved as successful as both their makers and their critics thought. For the Internet has not developed as a solipsistic device, taking people out of society into a world of their own making. Instead, research suggests that it contributes to communicative processes in the wider society. Indeed, interactivity can be understood as an increase in interconnections between forms and sites of knowledge.

As noted above, early theorists of the Internet saw it as a space apart, as a cyberspace with its own rules. Herring writes:

> Many early researchers believed that computer-networked communication was a 'cool' medium well suited to the transfer of data and information, but poorly suited to social uses ... Others saw in CMC [computer-mediated communication] a utopian, egalitarian potential – with social status cues 'filtered out', anyone could participate freely in open, democratic exchanges ... The social life that teems on the Internet in the late 1990s bears out neither of these idealized visions.
>
> (2001: 620)

This is particularly the case in online forms where users can post their own words, images and sounds. Turkle's (1995) ethnographic work on online gaming groups such as multi-user dungeons (MUDs) provides one example of this 'teeming' life. She argues that online relationships are as 'real' as offline ones and positive relationships developed online can then provide people with the resources to develop similar relationships offline. Wellman et al. (2003) reach similar conclusions, on the basis of the 'Netville' study in a new Toronto suburb, where some residents received free fast Internet access. They argue that the people who were connected tended to know more people, tended to be more social and tended to be more involved in the community because the interactions they had online enhanced rather than replaced offline interactions. Some research on peer-to-peer file-sharing networks such as Napster and eDonkey suggests that users find as much satisfaction in the act of sharing files with others as in getting free music, in 'the impulse to add oneself to the community as a quest for social integration' (Giesler and Pohlmann 2002: 3). The ability not only to locate but also to contribute to media content online, what is called functional interactivity above, provides opportunities for as rich and as complex social interactions and connections between people as any other social context.

We must look hard to find journalistic discourse where functional interactivity has had an impact, for it poses a significant challenge to news practices. Riley et al. (1998) quote journalists horrified at the thought of having to interact with readers instead of getting on with the next story. Dan Gillmor, a Californian technology journalist and weblogger or 'blogger', however, talks of new forms of journalism emerging in the daily online diary on technology news he keeps: 'I frequently hear from readers after a column, saying, "That was interesting, but have you thought about this or that angle?," and often the answer is no, I hadn't, so the next time I return to the subject the missing piece makes its way into the article' (cited in Lasica 2001). For Gillmor, his journalism is changed by such interaction not only because the news items he produces are enriched, but because the line between the journalist and the audience is blurred. The journalistic fiction that reporters know what is going on in the world better than audiences is severely dented as it becomes clear that, individually, many readers know a lot more than the journalist. M. Welch (2003) quotes the similar experience of an Australian freelance journalist and blogger, Tim Blair, who asked his military-knowledgeable readers to comment on a claim by the *Independent* correspondent Robert Fisk during the 2003 invasion of Iraq that the serial numbers on a metal fragment from an explosion in a Baghdad market linked them to the US military. Welch writes:

> Within twenty-four hours, more than a dozen readers with specialized knowledge (retired Air Force, former Naval Air Systems Command employees, others) had written in describing the weapon (U.S. high-speed antiradiation missile), manufacturer (Raytheon), launch point (F-16), and dozens of other minute details not seen in press accounts days and weeks later. Their conclusion, much as it pained them to say so: Fisk was probably right.
>
> (Welch 2003, cited in Allan and Matheson 2003)

Once new media forms provide opportunities for interactions between members of the public, such critics are suggesting, a better quality public communication emerges.

But just what kinds of interactions are taking place? Is journalistic discourse being produced when a reader interacts with a journalist, or is this a new kind of public communication? Gillmor suggests that an improved kind of journalism emerges, but from a discourse analytic perspective his weblog looks like something quite different to journalism. It is personal and sometimes opinionated, much of the time it comprises notes and comments rather than fully formed news stories and it sometimes alludes to a number of stories in one posting. Moreover, as a number of critics and participants in online discussion point out, people who post online are producing something that is neither a mass media form, for the readerships of even popular discussion sites or weblogs rarely number more than ten thousand, yet nor is it an interpersonal form, for the content is placed in a public domain. One weblogger on public affairs I have interviewed talked of rings of readerships, from the seven or eight people he regularly interacted with through reading each other's weblogs and emailing, a wider online 'conversation' on public life in which his weblog was taking part, a still wider 'audience' for weblogs on public affairs and beyond that a 'public debate' to which he was contributing (Matheson 2004b). In writing his blog he has to negotiate all these levels. Bregman and Haythornthwaite (2003) argue that people taking part in online discussions find themselves unsure how to behave in communication contexts that are like conversational interactions but which have to be written down and, unlike conversation, remain publicly available on the web afterwards.

From a discourse analytic perspective, a key issue is the way a discursive context is negotiated between participants online and the way participants perform particular selves in their interactions through the forms of language deployed. Bregman and Haythornthwaite (2003) put particular emphasis on this matter of 'visibility', or self-presentation, through talk, arguing that the newness of many online contexts for their participants and the constantly shifting group memberships require users to consciously work on the self being projected. The following text comes from iVillage,[4] a British website which covers much the same topics as a women's consumer magazine but which contains large amounts of text contributed by iVillage participants as well as paid-for journalists' contributions. The text comes from a section of the site devoted to discussions of workplace problems:

Title: Please help! Don't know how to handle th

Argh I am so upset and stressed about my work, please if any one can hlep I'd like to kow how.
My counsellor has advised me not to talk to my boss, but I'm feeling a bit vicitmised. Bascially 7 months ago, I started and she was relaly jealous cos her bf said he liked me 'to wind her up' and I know it's bothered her since as everybody says how obsessed she is with him.
[post continues]

The writer opens with a statement that she is upset. Unlike a magazine writer, who already has the authority to tell people about the world, this writer must first position herself within the discussion group context before she can tell them something. She does so by projecting a primarily emotional personhood and an individual who needs someone to talk to, rather than as someone with an experience that might be of benefit to others or as someone with advice to give, or as someone who comes from a particular part of society (we never learn, for example, what her job is). By doing this, she opens up a role for readers of being trustworthy, caring individuals able to give that advice. She also, by the use of the abbreviation, 'bf', addresses readers as members of an in-group which uses such words (in the iVillage section on adultery, the abbreviation 'OW' (other woman) works still more so as a badge of group identity). Such group markers are common in online social groups (Herring 2001). The invocation of these personal and group identities in the opening lines of the post are actions within the discursive space of iVillage, placing the writer as similar to previous posters who took on the same kind of identities and who asked readers to fill caring listener roles. Much of the discursive work of the text can be interpreted, like the file-sharing on Napster, as an attempt to open up a particular connection with others, one where a public space is made into a space of the personal and the interpersonal.

These matters of identity and relationship must be actively negotiated because of the fluidity of computer-mediated communication, where personal and public meet in complex combinations, and where there is some leeway with respect to social rules and practices. This is nothing unique to the Internet: people from different parts of society and even nations who become friends briefly in a holiday resort are in a similar space outside normal social relationships. But this discourse does stand in stark contrast to the projections of self to be found in most print or broadcast genres. The broadcast interviewers and interviewees discussed in Chapter 6 did not need to establish their respective identities, but inhabited roles that were pre-defined by the media institution. In online contexts where functional interactivity is prevalent, therefore, it is not only the media content which is partly produced by non-professionals but the whole discursive context of the interaction.

Slevin (2000) proposes that the kind of interactivity to be found on the Internet is symptomatic of wider changes to society in late modernity. To him, the Internet does not primarily work to form new kinds of communities, as many Internet theorists argue (and as iVillage's title claims), but a kind of social interaction that is 'post-traditional', characteristic of a society in which slowly established and deeply embedded communities are replaced by relationships between 'intelligent agents' (Slevin 2000: 97). He cites the sociologist Giddens:

> Being in an *intelligent relationship*, Giddens writes, 'means living along with others in a way that respects their autonomy'. Consequently, individuals who are thus associated 'are not partners or colleagues in an enterprise with a common purpose to pursue or a common interest to promote or protect . . . They are related in terms of a practice.'
>
> (cited in Slevin 2000: 97)

The 'cosmopolitan' who relates to others in this way is not someone who rejects the social rules established by communities, but someone who accepts responsibility for the ideas or attitudes he or she holds, and who is therefore ready to negotiate these ideas in interaction. The discursive negotiation of the iVillage post or of the journalist weblogger can perhaps be understood in these terms.

Case study: The blogger and interactive media

In this final section, a weblog will be used to explore further how the interactive media of the Internet enable certain kinds of discourse. Blogs are web diaries based on simple – and often free – software. The 'blogger' simply logs into his or her website, types a new entry, and the software then posts it at the top of the site with a datestamp, pushing previous entries down the page. Because such pages are so easy to produce, blogs are to be found across the Internet and are well suited to producing daily comments and to topical discourse in informal styles. Blogs have also developed a convention of rich linking to other websites, with many bloggers using their pages to tell others about interesting sites they have found and to quote and comment on the content of those sites. In terms of the definitions of interactivity discussed above, blogs are, then, highly interactive.

However, as also discussed above, the discourse analyst is interested not just in the technology and the kinds of texts it makes possible but in the uses to which it is put, in the identities and forms of knowledge produced and in the social life that is led through them. In exploring these issues, I will use an excerpt from one blog, Back to Iraq 3.0, written by a freelance US journalist in Iraq, Christopher Allbritton (October 19 2004; see Figure 8.2).

The site is similar to a number of journalistic weblogs on the Iraq war in its immediacy, telling the user what the journalist knows at that moment, and in its focus on the journalist's daily experience of reporting rather than on a final, objective news text. The process of telling the news is foregrounded in such websites rather than some final, authoritative product. Like Gillmor's evolving stories, we can look to the interactivity of the communicative process around the blog to account for this emphasis. A blog requires readers to come back each day, deliberately selecting the website from the countless other online offerings available, in order to read it. Each day, then, the communicative interaction between Allbritton and his regular users is renewed through the navigational interactivity of them surfing back to his site. Over days and week, that communicative relation develops. The user becomes knowledgeable about the unfolding text, as it expresses various analyses and responses to different situations in Iraq. A relationship can develop between the text and the user. The

O c t o b e r   1 9 ,   2 0 0 4

Bugged Out

AMMAN -- Well, as you can see from the dateline, I'm out of Baghdad. I evacuated after we learned of further threats against journalists. And just this afternoon, upon landing at Queen Alia International Airport, I learned that Margaret Hassan, the top CARE official in Iraq, has been kidnapped. She was taken while driving to work.

Her abduction fits a pattern. She did not employ armed guards and, like my friend John, was a "soft target." It's tragic, because she has done more for the Iraqi people than these insurgents ever will. She's been in the country working for children's issues and other health-related causes for more than 25 years. My heart goes out to her family.

Even so, I'm not happy to be out. It's cutting and running, and it feels like crap. I want to cover the story, as best I can, and I really don't like leaving my friends and colleagues behind. My fixer and translator have no work now, although I'm trying to find them another journalist to work with while I'm gone. I plan to return after Ramadan or whenever we hear that it's safe(r) again.

To answer some questions: The journalists are clumped together because we only endanger ourselves that way. Kodia asked me why we didn't disperse and stay with families.

- It's more difficult to secure their houses (blast walls, guards, etc.);
- We can't trust the neighbors not to rat us out;
- I don't trust any Iraqi I don't know well;
- And most important, we endanger them by staying with them -- they would be branded as collaborators.

So our options are limited in terms of where we can stay. Anyway, I'm going to be exploring my options for the next few weeks -- and watching the American campaign closely. Talk about a nail biter. I won't be coming back and "stumping" for anyone; that's not what I do. I report what I see. What you guys do with that information is up to you.

Cheers for now,
Christopher

Posted by Christopher at 07:13 PM | Comments (40) | TrackBack (1)
Categories: Commentary | Iraq

Figure 8.2 Freelance journalist Christopher Allbritton claimed his weblog, where he posted daily observations and reporting of the 2003 invasion of Iraq on a blog, enabled a much richer interaction with his audience than news journalism usually achieves

Source: Courtesy Christopher Allbritton, www.back-to-iraq.com

persona performed in the text, moreover, is often quite personal. As Figure 8.2 shows, Allbritton writes predominantly in the first person, and writes of his response to events as much as about the events themselves: 'I'm not happy to be out. It's cutting and running, and it feels like crap.' Like many bloggers, he writes of 'sharing' material with people, a quite interpersonal motivation. Thus, one of Allbritton's readers comments that the blog interests her not because of any claim to objective knowledge, but because of its personal, embodied knowledge. There are: 'No agendas except your own, which is perfectly acceptable to me. No one is totally objective, but you gave more personal perspectives of "behind the scenes" of what it takes to do what you do, which was terribly fascinating to me' (cited in Allbritton 2003: 83). Through the chain of communicative interactions, the user is able to get to know Allbritton, or at least get to know his persona. Allbritton (2003: 83), for his part, speaks of the personal connection which he has been able to develop through these postings. The consistent relations established are very close to those discussed by theorists of trust. Shaw (1997: 10) argues that trust develops in organizational networks when participants follow certain conventions:

- what we reveal to others reflects what we know;
- what we say is aligned with how we behave;
- our behavior is consistent across situations;
- our behavior is consistent across time.

News organizations tend to rely on a trust in the masthead – in the institution's authority and consistency. Blogs such as 'Back to Iraq' appear to depend more on a case-by-case discursive negotiation, just as the iVillage posters do, to establish relationships. As Slevin (2000) argues, the social relations here are not those of traditional communities, but of intelligent agents, that is, people actively placing themselves in a particular network.

However, Allbritton's readers do much more than browse each day. His site gained fame for his successful call to his blog's readers to raise the money and equipment to send him to Iraq in 2003 – in total, 320 readers sent in money, while one lent him a laptop. Each post on 'Back to Iraq' is followed by a large number of comments by readers, who advise Allbritton on what to do next, propose questions to ask of his sources and comment on the analysis he makes. The reporting on the site is all Allbritton's, but happens in direction interaction with those who read it. Again, as with the relationship which develops, the content develops across the complex and multiple communicative interactions between him and users.

Interactivity – a sometimes vague term – can be specified in terms of navigational and functional dimensions in order to analyse in detail what is distinctive about some new media forms. This chapter has emphasized that it is not the text which is interactive, but the use made of the text – the relationships and ways of understanding the world which people come to participate in through such forms. Thus, the interaction or connection doesn't just happen as a result of the technical affordance of the Internet, it is something that is established by the weblogger and his or her readers over time, by the iVillage participant or by the surfer traversing the web.

Further reading

A major discourse analyst of new media language in general is Herring (2001). She has also written on the emerging genre of weblogs (e.g. Herring et al. 2004). Interactivity has been analysed in relation to online news, although rarely from a discourse analytic perspective (see Massey and Levy 1999; Schultz 1999). On the argument for understanding online interaction in terms of communities, see Watson (1997).

APPENDIX: TRANSCRIPTION CONVENTIONS

The following standard transcription conventions were used in this book.

you   underlining indicates emphasis
[indicates overlapping talk
=   indicates one speaker follows the other with no gap
(.)   indicates a slight pause
(0.5)   indicates a pause of 0.5 seconds (or whatever number of seconds is
           stated in the brackets)
?   upward intonation (usually marking the end of a question)
[. . .]   indicates unclear material
CAPITALS   capitalized text indicates increase in volume

GLOSSARY

Accountable: an important idea in the study of social interactions is that people act in certain ways because they know that other people will attach a particular meaning to the action. This is the accountable meaning of the action. So when I wave at a bus driver, the accountable meaning is that I would like the bus to stop so I can get on, because I know that the driver knows that I know what waving at bus drivers means. The driver holds me accountable for waving at her or him by stopping, and so its social meaning is reinforced.

Adjacency pair: hello–hello, question–answer, accusation–defence (or confession), giving–thanking are all adjacency pairs. Conversation analysts put great importance in these pairs as the way people show each other they recognize what kind of talk is going on: if the second speaker responds to the first speaker's first part (e.g. a question) with the second part (e.g. an answer), social interaction is taking place.

Clause: the main syntactical unit of language, bigger than a phrase because it includes a noun unit and a verb unit. There are main clauses, which could stand on their own as sentences, and dependent clauses, which expand on an aspect of a main clause (the two clauses beginning 'which' in this sentence are dependent clauses). Clauses are identified most easily because there is usually one verb per clause. They are important in critical linguistics and other Hallidayan approaches because they are seen as a basic building block of meaning.

Cognitive: the world of thought and of mental processes. Discourse analysts are divided on how far cognition can be posited as something separate from language. Some (e.g. Billig 2001) argue that psychology is something people produce through their talk.

Coherence: the difference between a list of items and a series of items that has some order. Narratives, adjacency pairs and arguments all hang together, or cohere, by different logics, which are often not explicit in the words, but must be read into the text. So the narrative coherence of 'The queen died and the king died of grief', is that the second event was because of the first, although this isn't actually said (see

Chapter 4). Coherence involves, then, both the text and the reader and both know-ledge of **genres** and knowledge of how the world works (see Chapter 7).

Cohesion: some linguists distinguish cohesion from **coherence**. Cohesion describes the links that are established between **clauses** by the words used, such as using a name in one clause, followed by the pronoun 'she' in the next, or linking clauses with text-organizing forms such as 'But' or 'Second'.

Collocation: 'the habitual juxtaposition of words with other particular words' (*Oxford Dictionary of English Grammar*). Linguists focus on collocations where words tend to occur directly beside each other in a particular context, such as 'everyday life' or 'running and jumping', but some discourse analysts also talk of collocations as words which are often found fairly close together within a body of text in order to show how similar words accumulate to establish particular emphases or frame-works of thought.

Conversation analysis: analysis of the social interaction that takes place through the details of talk, developed by **ethnomethodologists** as part of their agenda of uncovering how people 'do' social life and the identities they perform. Terms such as **adjacency pairs, accountable** actions and the local management of interaction belong to this approach. In media analysis, it is used most often to explore how talk on air differs from conversation and therefore to explore what the media institution does to social interaction. See Chapter 6.

Cookies: a feature on some websites which asks the user's computer to send information back to the computer hosting the website. This is used to tailor websites to the browser we are using or the choices we made last time we visited and to make website shopping baskets work, among other uses. It therefore has implications both for the **interactivity** between the user and the site and for the privacy of users, who may not even know their computer is divulging information about them (which is why some people tell their browser to turn cookies off).

Co-text: the text which sits alongside the text an analyst is studying. It may be joined to that text to make a larger meaning, but may not be.

Critical discourse analysis: discourse analysis which is used to critique social structures and the distribution of power in society. Major thinkers include van Dijk, Fairclough, Wodak, who all write with a political commitment, and who often focus on media texts because of their role in mediating social and cultural power. This is not, though, a coherent school, because they draw on different techniques (see Wodak 2001).

Critical linguistics: beginning with Fowler et al. (1979), critical linguists have argued that analysis of how linguistic categories (from labels to transitivity to modality) are deployed in language use reflects ideological forces. Its major problem was its inability to see other reasons for textual choices than ideology and for its difficulty in dealing with how audiences make sense of texts differently. For these reasons, it has been largely subsumed within **social semiotics** and critical discourse analysis.

Deixis: from the Greek for pointing, means words such as 'you', 'there', 'now', 'this long' that refer to the speech situation or context for their meaning. They are important in constructing coherence in a text, because they require readers to link the piece of text they are in with the world or with other surrounding bits of text.

Discourse: you will find the word used in many (sometimes vague) senses in academic writing. Most scholars using it agree that it means 'language in use', that is, language being used by real people in real social contexts: so media discourse is all the language we find used in the media. That differentiates it from **text**, which refers only to the words or symbols, and from linguistics' traditional conception of language as sets of rules such as grammar and phonology. But discourse is also often used by social researchers, following Foucault, to talk of the power of language to shape society and culture. Discourse in this sense is about the way statements link up with other statements to make up a **discursive formation**.

Discursive formation: the accumulated and interlinked statements about a topic, which between them comprise a particular way of talking and thinking that shapes how we understand the topic, and which sets the terms for more statements on the topic. The term, then, describes how repeated language use constructs social realities. Cameron uses the example of discourses on drug-taking. Since the criminalization of heroine in the 1960s in Britain, taking the drug has been surrounded by a dominant way of talking that links it to lack of will-power, failure to cope with reality, corruption of young people and self-destruction. That discursive formation competes with other discursive formations on taking heroine, such as with ideas of freedom and self-exploration and with medical discourses on the effects and uses of the drug (Cameron 2001: 15–16, her whole chapter, 'What is Discourse', is recommended).

Ethnomethodology: beginning with Garfinkel (Garfinkel 1967), the study of 'the link between what social actors "do" in interaction and what they "know" about interaction' (Coupland and Jaworski 2001a: 175). It looks at people's competence in everyday social encounters to show how social structure, meaning and power all happen through people's joint orientation to those things. The observation that rules are only rules if people act by them has been powerful in discourse analysis more widely, but in particular has led to an entire approach to spoken discourse, **conversation analysis**.

Footing: describes the relationship of the speaker to what is being said: the words express the ideas or values of the 'principal', they are devised by the 'author' and they are produced or disseminated by the 'animator'. Media professionals often claim the status of only animating (being the messenger), but the blurring of that footing into the other categories is one way to describe the discursive power of the media.

Genre: based on the classical literary division of texts into poetry, prose and drama, genre describes the different language use appropriate to different social activities. Part of people's communicative competence is to know what genres are appropriate to what situations, and thus describing genre helps analysts to describe how people are orienting to social rules about language use, and what social groups people belong to (see Swales 1990).

Hallidayan linguistics: see **systemic functional linguistics**.

Hermeneutic: an interpretative approach to meaning, drawing on **phenomenological** thinking that we become conscious as we attempt to understand things from our particular place in the world. Since Heidegger, hermeneutics has placed emphasis both on what authors intend, emphasizing that people read in order to understand others, and on the diversity of interpretations that people make, which are not simply right or wrong. In this view, the meaning of something does not lie in the thing or in one person's mind but in the sharing of meaning between people through language. This thinking underpins much poststructuralist critical theory and study of social life in interaction, which in turn shape much discourse analysis. See Gripsrud (2002), Chapter 5, for an excellent introduction.

Hyper-real: a slippery concept used by Baudrillard to suggest how the meaning of things is changed in societies saturated by consumer media. In hyper-reality, glossy images come to be preferred to the real object, a preference that includes an awareness that they are simulations. See Chapter 5 for application of the concept to reality television.

Iconic: signs such as images which are like the thing they are representing, as opposed to symbolic signs, where the link between the signifier and the idea is conventional. Barthes noted that iconic signs are also, however, symbolic, as even objective records such as photographs are posed according to social conventions, so it is better to talk of some signs as having an iconic aspect to them (see Chandler 1995a).

Ideational function: also called representational function. In Hallidayan grammar, part of the function of any piece of text is to represent some object or idea, at the same time as it performs **interpersonal** and **textual functions**. Tracy and Coupland (1990) talk similarly of the 'instrumental', or exchanging information, as one function of talk. Critical analysis of ideation in media texts is often about looking for **ideology**.

Ideology: this can mean simply a coherent and powerful set of ideas, but tends to mean systems of representations which work in the interests of certain groups, often the most powerful, and which present themselves as unmotivated and commonsensical. It is a more structural notion than discourse (on this, see MacDonald 2003). On ideology generally, see Eagleton (1991) and Thompson (1984).

Interactivity: the extent to which the two (or more) parties to a communication event interact with each other. In new media studies, it is often claimed that digital technologies are new interactive media, because people can choose material and answer back to media producers. However, in discourse analytic terms, all communication is interactive, if to differing degrees. **Conversation analysis**, for example, can be thought of as the study of how society exists through interactivity. See Chapter 8 for a fuller discussion.

Interpersonal function: in Hallidayan grammar, any piece of text is about establishing a relationship between the speaker and hearer (or writer and reader, etc.) at the same time as it is about communicating some content. Sometimes talk, as in the goodbye sequence quoted in Chapter 6, is almost wholly about this dimension. In media discourse, looking for interpersonal dimensions provides clues to which audiences are being addressed, and in broadcast talk, how studio interaction is balanced with performing that talk for an overhearing audience.

Intertextuality: a term used by a number of theories of meaning that seek to show that the meaning of a word or text depends on its calling up previous texts rather than drawing on some dictionaries in our minds. Fairclough's analysis of generic heterogeneity is an important extension of the idea to show that texts draw on previous genres as well as previous texts (Fairclough 1995: 86ff). Corpus linguistics (see Chapter 1), semiotics and the analysis of genres all draw on the idea.

Lexis/lexical items: content-carrying words and phrases, as opposed to grammatical words such as 'from' or linking phrases which gain their meaning from the way they link lexis. The distinction breaks down to an extent in the notion of lexico-syntax, that the content of a word depends on the way it is used and the words around it. But close attention to lexical items on their own is still valuable, particularly in texts such as the news where **ideational** meaning is to the fore.

Metaphor: a word or image which is able to stand for another, because it is analogous to it in some aspect, but is not usually connected with it. It therefore works rhetorically to emphasize that aspect.

Metonym: a word or image that is used to stand for something that is associated with it. The appeal of ads is often discussed as metonymic in this way, particularly in psychoanalytic terms: an ad may feed our desire for power by selling us a fast car as a metonym for that power.

Modality: describes aspects of language that tell listeners (or readers etc.) how much the speaker vouches for or attaches him or herself to what is being said. See Chapter 5 for detail and for discussion of how Kress and Van Leeuwen (1996) extend the concept to the visual.

Multimodal: Kress and van Leeuwen argue that all texts, whether words written down or images on a screen, are made up of multiple modes (image, sound, word, smell, texture, colour) and that contemporary texts (such as a glossy brochure) are increasingly multimodal. In their later work, they argue for discourse analysis that tracks how these modes interrelate (Kress and Van Leeuwen 2001).

Nominalizations: processes which have been turned into nouns, thereby making an action into a thing and often into an abstract thing. They allow the speaker or writer to leave out who did the action to whom, and when or how it happened, and critical linguists pointed out the ideological value of sometimes doing that. So the phrase 'the settlement of Australia' is a nominalized form which glosses over who arrived where and when, information which might lead readers to remember that the country was already settled by Aboriginal peoples.

Ontological: philosophical questions about what it means to be who we are in the world are ontological. 'Any way of understanding the world, or some part of it, must make assumptions (which may be implicit or explicit) about what kinds of things do or can exist in that domain, and what might be their conditions of existence, relations of dependency, and so on' (*Oxford Dictionary of Sociology*).

Phenomenology: a major twentieth-century philosophical school concerned with how people's awareness of what they are doing shapes social life ('Phenomenology', *Encyclopedia of Sociology*). Its major impact on sociology and related fields such as discourse analysis has been to emphasize that the social world exists through people's subjective experiences of it. This idea underpins theories of language use from Foucault (see Chapter 3) to conversation analysis (see Chapter 6).

Pragmatics: a branch of discourse analysis that is concerned with how people know what words mean in a particular context. It has led to the idea that we work by more-or-less principles of meaning rather than rules and that the context of words is all important. The classic example is that the statements, 'Shut the window' and 'It's cold in here' are both requests for the same thing, and both are easily understandable as the same, even though the words are very different. An excellent introduction is Thomas (1995).

Processes: in Hallidayan linguistics, processes are seen as the basic unit of meaning. These are usually carried by the verb and are divided into four or more categories. In Chapter 4 I follow Martin and Rose's (2003) distinction of doing, saying, thinking and being processes, each of which shape different kinds of clause and determine what kinds of meanings can emerge in the clause.

Realism: while 'reality' refers to what is actually out there, realism refers to the act, whether in a painting or television programme or political manifesto of trying to represent reality. It usually means, therefore, a rejection of subjective responses and of idealized or Utopian representations but still includes a dimension of imagining how the real world is (and so journalists would not appreciate being called realist, because they see themselves as writing about reality).

Received Pronunciation: 'the form of speech associated with educated speakers in the southern counties of England' (*Fowler's Modern English Usage*).

Register: a term used by some discourse analysts to describe the kind of language appropriate to a certain situation. So the register of the news includes the topics, arguments and ideas appropriate there, the kinds of relationships that can be signalled there between journalist and audience, and the ways it is appropriate for the text to be shaped. The category blends into **genre**.

Relevance theory: Sperber and Wilson argue that speakers and hearers are able to communicate because they both are thinking in terms of what is relevant to that interaction. Relevance is therefore at the heart of **pragmatics** (see Sperber and Wilson 1986).

Representation: see **ideational function**.

Semantic: to do with meaning, often opposed to the formal dimension of language. So the phrases 'after our discussion' and 'when we talked' are quite different in form but semantically close.

Semiotics: the study of signs, particularly as a system of signs governed by rules of how they relate to each other. Semiotics has been successful at accounting for how social structures shape the way words and other symbols make sense, but less so at accounting for how people make sense with that system.

Social cognition: cognition is something that happens within the mind, but most social science argues that anything that can be recognized as meaningful is meaningful because others can think it too. So common meanings for words, common 'scripts' of what happens in particular contexts, common ways of organizing concepts in hierarchies in our minds are all aspects of social cognition.

Social semiotics: a school of analysis that has grown out of critical linguistics and semiotics, which argues that signs gain their meaning not from a system of meaning but from the interrelation of sign systems with their social and cultural contexts. Hodge and Kress's *Social Semiotics* (1988) includes some analysis of media texts and Jensen has produced a textbook on *The Social Semiotics of Mass Communication* (1995).

Sociolinguistics: the study of how language works in use. It owes its birth to the invention of the tape-recorder, which showed that people did not speak in the grammatical sentences of traditional linguistics and were in fact competent in much more, talking differently in different contexts. Although not primarily interested in issues of social hierarchy and power, pioneering analyses such as Hymes (1972) and Labov (1972) forged much early ground for discourse analysis.

Symbolic systems: language is only one among many ways of symbolizing the world. So a word, e.g. 'smile', along with the linguistic rules that put that word together with others and the social rules about when it is appropriate to use the word, belongs to the complex of symbolic systems that we call language. The same meaning can also be expressed through graphic symbols, even non-verbal sounds such as music. Semiotics has sought to analyse symbolic systems as independent from the real (any symbol would do for 'smile' as long as we all agreed), but discourse theory is more interested in how symbols obtain their meaning in social contexts.

Syntax: the rules for combining grammatical items (nouns, verbs, and so on) into meaningful clauses are the rules of syntax.

Systemic functional linguistics: an influential theory of language for critical discourse analysis, whose founder is M.A.K. Halliday. Systemic grammar emphasizes the function of language rather than its form, and analyses language in terms of a large number of categories which perform different functions. Terms such as **coherence, cohesion, ideational function, interpersonal function, textual function, register** and **modality** all belong to systemic grammar. See Halliday (1994).

Teleological: to do with the ends or purpose of something. So a teleological account of a narrative looks at the action in terms of the ending and the coherent whole it contributes to.

Text: any object that is symbolic – it carries meaning – and can therefore be analysed by semiotic or discourse analytic methods. Texts range from news articles to pictures to Sony Walkmen. The text is not the meaning but the symbolic object that carries the meaning.

Textual function: in Hallidayan grammar, every bit of text contributes to the whole through the way it takes part in an overall organization of the message.

Transformative generative grammar: the grammar associated with Chomsky, which thinks of the potential for language as a genetic human attribute, and which therefore analyses languages in terms of general rules, including rules about transformations between different forms of the same word or clause. The major philosophical difference between Chomsky's grammar and discourse analysis is that Chomsky is interested in language as a system that people are competent in, and is not interested in studying how that language is used.

Transitivity: the analysis of **processes**.

Weblog (or **blogs**): an Internet **genre**, which depends on cheap or free software that makes it easy for people to create websites made up of diary entries. Some blogs are personal diaries; others are collections of links to websites, usually with commentaries attached.

NOTES

Introduction

1 There is some confusion about the authorship of some books written by Bakhtin's colleagues, particularly over Valentin Vološinov's authorship. See Tihanov (2000: 9).

1 News and the social life of words

1 The linking together of lexical items through grammatical words becomes important in analysis of transitivity (Chapter 3) and propositions (Chapter 7).
2 Along with 'saying' and 'thinking', functionalist grammar regards these as the basic **processes** of the English language (see Glossary).
3 She makes a similar finding from analysis of the articles' transitivity (see Chapter 3).

2 Advertising discourse: Selling between the lines

1 At the time of writing, the ad was available online at au.playstation.com/assets/downloads/videos/mountain.wmv
2 The film screened on television mostly as a cut-down 30-second ad, with the crushing scene removed, partly because of an awareness that it would make some viewers uncomfortable (personal communication, Irena Tolj, senior brand manager for Sony Computer Entertainment Australia). The existence of an uncut version, used mostly in film theatres and on the Internet, adds further to a sense of being a member of an exclusive club.
3 Sue Tait, personal communication.

4 The stories they tell us: Studying television as narrative

1 URL: news.bbc.co.uk/1/hi/world/americas/1634614.stm
2 Thomas (1995) gives a detailed discussion of why discourse analysts favour 'principles' of discourse over 'rules'. She points out that rules are all or nothing, while principles are more or less; rules are exclusive of other rules, while principles can co-occur; rules constitute meaning, while principles regulate it; and rules are conventional, while principles are motivated to get something achieved. She cites Leech (1983) arguing that, as a result, rules give the impression of intellectual rigour but in the end do not describe most language use very well.
3 URL: www.tvtome.com/tvtome/servlet/GuidePageServlet/showid-146/epid-1468/
4 'Gaff' is a London slang term for a house (see www.LondonSlang.com/db/g/).

5 Making sense of images: The visual meanings of reality television

1 The housemates were: Goldie, Anne Diamond, Melinda Messenger, Sue Perkins, Mark Owen, and Les Dennis.

6 The power to talk: Conversation analysis of broadcast interviews

1 Bonner (2003: 61–2) calculates that in the UK and Australia people are now more likely to have been on television – whether as participants or members of live audiences – than not. She estimates that British television shows feature a quarter of a million people a year, with over 20,000 of them having speaking roles (cited in Turner 2004: 53).
2 Clayman (1991) analyses the openings of broadcasting interviews in a similar way. In the cases he analysed, the interviewer would tell the audience who the guests were, then start by asking them questions, often without even saying hello, and would leave the guest no room to negotiate the topic of conversation. These studio openings are at a considerable distance from conversation, where talk must begin with a meeting of gazes or a shouted hello or the ringing of a phone to establish the communication channel between the interactants, where it would be strange to baldly tell others who they are and what their social positions are, and where topics are a matter for negotiation.
3 Clayman (2002) uses the following transcription conventions in addition to those listed in this book's Appendix:

hh strings of 'h' mark audible breathing
: colons indicate the prior sound was prolonged
> greater and less than signs indicate speeding up or slowing down of speech

4 URL: w2s.co.uk/nick-abbot

8 Connecting with new media: weblogs and other interactive media

1 URL: www.flipside.nzoom.com
2 Guay (1995), whose terms these are, actually differentiates between three levels of interactivity: navigational, functional and adaptive. In the latter, the user can adapt the website to his or her goals or personality, customizing its appearance or content. This does not seem to me a fundamentally different discursive activity from the other two, so I have omitted it.
3 URL: news.bbc.co.uk/2/hi/in_depth/americas/2004/vote_usa_2004/default.stm (accessed 27 Sept. 2004).
4 URL: www.ivillage.co.uk

REFERENCES

Abell, J. and Stokoe, E. H. (1999) 'I take full responsibility, I take some responsibility, I'll take half of it but no more than that': Princess Diana and the negotiation of blame in the 'Panorama' interview, *Discourse Studies*, 1(3): 297–319.

Allan, S. and Matheson, D. (2003) Weblogs and the war in Iraq: journalism for the network society? Paper presented at Digital Dynamics conference, Loughborough University, 6–9 November.

Allbritton, C. (2003) Blogging from Iraq, *Nieman Reports*, Fall: 82–4. www.nieman.harvard.edu/reports/03-3NRfall/V57N3.pdf.

Allen, R.C. (2004) Making sense of soaps, in R.C. Allen and A. Hill (eds) *The Television Studies Reader*. London: Routledge.

Althusser, L. (1971) Ideology and Ideological State Apparatuses, in L. Althusser, *Lenin and Philosophy and Other Essays*. New York: Monthly Review Press.

American Association of Physical Anthropologists (AAPA) (1996) AAPA statement on biological aspects of race, *American Journal of Physical Anthropology*, 101: 569–70. www.physanth.org/positions/race.html.

Arlidge, J. (2002) Dyke's new mantra for the future BBC: only connect, *Observer*, 6 January.

Bakhtin, M. (1981) Discourse in the novel, in M. Holquist (ed.) *The Dialogic Imagination*. Austin, TX: University of Texas Press.

Ballard, R. (2002) Race, ethnicity and culture, in M. Holbron (ed.) *New Directions in Sociology*. Ormskirk: Causeway Press.

Ballaster, R., Beetham, M., Frazer, E. and Hebron, S. (1996) A critical analysis of women's magazines, in H. Baehr and A. Gray (eds) *Turning It On: A Reader in Women and Media*. London: Arnold.

Bardoel, J. (1996) Beyond journalism: a profession between information society and civil society, *European Journal of Communication*, 11(3): 283–302.

Barker, C. and Galasiński, D. (2001) *Cultural Studies and Discourse Analysis: A Dialogue on Language and Identity*. London: Sage.

Barthes, R. (1974) *S/Z*. New York: Hill and Wang.

Barthes, R. (1977a) *Image-Music-Text*. London: Fontana.

Barthes, R. (1977b) Introduction to the structural analysis of narratives, in R. Barthes, *Image-Music-Text*. New York: Hill and Wang.

Bastick, J. (2004) The gay cannibal, *FHM*, 76 (August).

Baudrillard, J. (1983a) The ecstasy of communication, in H. Foster (ed.) *Postmodern Culture*. London: Pluto Press.

Baudrillard, J. (1983b) Hyperreal America, *Economy and Society*, 22(2): 243–52.

Baudrillard, J. (1994) The procession of simulacra, in B. Wallis and M. Tucker (eds) *After Modernism: Rethinking Representation*. Boston: David R. Godine.

Bauman, Z. (1992) *Intimations of Modernity*. London: Routledge.

BBC (1997) *Newsnight*, BBC2, 13 May.

BBC (2004) *The Best of 'Question Time'*, BBC1, 16 September.

Becker, A.L. (1983) Correspondences: an essay on iconicity and philology, mimeo, Department of Linguistics, University of Michigan.

Bell, A. (1991) *The Language of News Media*. Oxford: Blackwell.

Benwell, B. (2003) New sexism? Readers' responses to the use of irony in men's magazines, in T. Holmes and D. Matheson (eds) Proceedings of *Mapping the Magazine*, School of Journalism, Media and Cultural Studies, Cardiff University.

Berger, J. (1972) *Ways of Seeing*. Harmondsworth: Penguin.

Bignell, J. (2002) *Media Semiotics: An Introduction*. Manchester: Manchester University Press.

Bignell, J. (2004) *An Introduction to Television Studies*. London: Routledge.

Billig, M. (1999) Whose terms? Whose ordinariness? Rhetoric and ideology in Conversation Analysis, *Discourse and Society*, 10: 543–57.

Billig, M. (2001) Discursive, ideological and rhetorical messages, in M. Wetherell, S. Taylor and S.J. Yates (eds) *Discourse Theory and Practice: A Reader*. London: Sage.

Billig, M., Condor, S., Edwards, D., Gane, M., Middleton, D. and Radley, A.R. (1988) *Ideological Dilemmas: A Social Psychology of Everyday Thinking*. London: Sage.

Birrell, S. (1989) Racial relations theories and sport: suggestions for a more critical analysis, *Sociology of Sport Journal*, 6: 212–17.

Bishop, H. and Jaworski, A. (2003) We beat 'em: nationalism and the hegemony of homogeneity in the British press reportage of Germany versus England during Euro 2000, *Discourse and Society*, 14(3): 243–71.

Boden, D. (1994) *The Business of Talk: Organisations in Action*. Cambridge: Polity Press.

Boggan, S. (1998) Black players look alike, says Motson, *The Independent*, 5 January.

Bonilla-Silva, E. and Forman, T.A. (2000) 'I am not racist but . . .': mapping white college students' racial ideology in the USA, *Discourse and Society*, 11(1): 50–85.

Bonner, F. (2003) *Ordinary Television: Analyzing Popular TV*. London: Sage.

Bordewijk, J.L. and van Kaam, B. (1986) Towards a new classification of tele-information services, *Intermedia*, 14(1): 16–21.

Bourdieu, P. (1989) *Distinction*. London: Routledge.

Bourdieu, P. (1991) *Language and Symbolic Power*. Cambridge: Polity Press.

Boyd-Barrett, O. and Newbold, C. (eds) (1995) *Approaches to Media: A Reader*. London: Arnold.

Bradby, H., Gabe, J. and Bury, M. (1995) 'Sexy docs' and 'busty blondes': press coverage of professional misconduct cases brought before the General Medical Council, *Sociology of Health and Illness*, 17(4): 458–76.

Branston, G. and Stafford, R. (2003) *The Media Student's Book*. London: Routledge.

Bregman, A. and Haythornthwaite, C. (2003) Radicals of presentation: visibility, relation and co-presence in persistent conversation, *New Media and Society*, 5(1): 117–40.

Brunsdon, C. and Morley, D. (1978) *Everyday Television: Nationwide*. London: British Film Institute.

Butler, J. (1990) *Gender Trouble: Feminism and the Subversion of Identity*. New York: Routledge.

Cambridge International Corpus (2004) Cambridge: Cambridge University Press. uk.cambridge.org/elt/corpus/cic.htm (accessed 26 May 2004).

Cameron, D. (1995) *Verbal Hygiene*. London: Routledge.

Cameron, D. (1999) Performing gender identity: young men's talk and the construction of heterosexual masculinity, in A. Jaworski and N. Coupland (eds) *The Discourse Reader*. London: Routledge.

Cameron, D. (2001) *Working with Spoken Discourse*. London: Sage.

Casey, B., Casey, N., Calvert, B., French, L. and Lewis, J. (2002) *Television Studies: Key Concepts*. London: Routledge.

Castells, M. (1996) *The Rise of the Network Society*. Oxford: Blackwell.

Chandler, D. (1995a) Denotation, connotation and myth, in *Semiotics for Beginners*. www.aber.ac.uk/media/Documents/S4B/sem06.html (accessed 5 Nov. 2004).

Chandler, D. (1995b) Intertextuality, in *Semiotics for Beginners*. www.aber.ac.uk/media/Documents/S4B/sem09.html (accessed 16 June 2004).

Chibnall, S. (1977) *Law-and-Order News: An Analysis of Crime Reporting in the British Press*. London: Tavistock Publications.

Chilton, P. (ed.) (1985) *Language and the Nuclear Arms Debate: Nukespeak Today*. London: Pinter.

Chouliaraki, L. and Fairclough, N. (1999) *Discourse in Late Modernity: Rethinking Critical Discourse Analysis*. Edinburgh: Edinburgh University Press.

Clark, K. (1992) The linguistics of blame: representations of women in The Sun's reporting of crimes of sexual violence, in M. Toolan (ed.) *Language, Text and Context: Essays in Stylistics*. London: Routledge.

Clayman, S.E. (1991) News interview openings: aspects of sequential organization, in P. Scannell (ed.) *Broadcast Talk*. London: Sage.

Clayman, S.E. (2002) Tribune of the people: maintaining the legitimacy of aggressive journalism, *Media, Culture and Society*, 24: 197–216.

Collins Cobuild (1995) *Collins Cobuild English Dictionary*. London: HarperCollins.

Condor, S. and Antaki, C. (1997) Social cognition and discourse, in T. van Dijk (ed.)

Discourse as Social Process. Discourse Studies: A Multidisciplinary Introduction, Vol. 1. London: Sage.

Cook, G. (1992) *The Discourse of Advertising*. London: Routledge.

Cook, J. (2000) Dangerously radioactive: the plural vocalities of radio talk, in A. Lee and C. Poynton (eds) *Culture and Text: Discourse and Methodology in Social Research and Cultural Studies*. Sydney: Allen and Unwin.

Corner, J. (1986) Codes and cultural analysis, in R. Collins, J. Curran, N. Garnham, P. Scannell, P. Schlesinger, and C. Sparks (eds) *Media, Culture and Society: A Critical Reader*. London: Sage.

Cornford, J. and Robins, K. (1999) New media, in J. Stokes and A. Reading (eds) *The Media in Britain: Current Debates and Developments*. Houndsmills: Palgrave.

Cottle, S. (1999) Ethnic minorities and the British news media: explaining (mis)representation, in J. Stokes and A. Reading (eds) *The Media in Britain: Current Debates and Developments*. Houndsmills: Palgrave.

Couldry, N. (2003) *Media Rituals: A Critical Approach*. London: Routledge.

Coupland, N. and Jaworski, A. (2001a) Conversation analysis, in P. Cobley (ed.) *The Routledge Companion to Semiotics and Linguistics*. London: Routledge.

Coupland, N. and Jaworski, A. (2001b) Discourse, in P. Cobley (ed.) *The Routledge Companion to Semiotics and Linguistics*. London: Routledge.

Crisell, A. (1994) *Understanding Radio*. London: Routledge.

Cronick, K. (2002) The discourse of President George W. Bush and Osama bin Laden, *Forum: Qualitative Research (Forum Qualitative Sozialforschung)*, 3 (3). www.-qualitative-research.net/fqs-texte/3-02/3-02cronick-e.pdf.

Currie, D. (2001) Dear Abby: advice pages as a site for the operation of power, *Feminist Theory*, 2(3): 259–81.

Daily Express (2002) Germans go through in shame game, *Daily Express*, 12 June.

Davis, L.R. and Harris, O. (1998) Sport and ethnicity in US sports media, in L.A. Wenner (ed.) *Mediasport*. London: Routledge.

Douglas, S.J. (2002) Letting the boys be boys: talk radio, male hysteria and political discourse in the 1980s, in M. Hilmes and J. Loviglio (eds) *The Radio Reader: Essays in the Cultural History of Radio*. New York: Routledge.

Dovey, J. (2000) *Freakshow: First-Person Media and Factual Television*. London: Pluto Press.

Drew, P. and Heritage, J. (1992) *Talk at Work: Interaction in Institutional Settings*. Cambridge: Cambridge University Press.

Du Gay, P., Hall, S., Janes, L., Mackay, H. and Negus, K. (1997) *Doing Cultural Studies: The Story of the Sony Walkman*. London: Sage.

Eagleton, T. (1991) *Ideology*. London: Verso.

EIAA (2003) Pan-European research shows that Internet constitutes 10 percent of Europeans' media consumption, EIAA Press Information, 2 December. www.eiaa.net/press-information/shwPress-information-releases.asp?id=22 (accessed 27 Oct. 2004).

Ellis, J. (1992) *Visible Fictions: Cinema, Television, Video*. London: Routledge.

Ellis, J. (1999) Television as working through, in J. Gripsrud (ed.) *Television and Common Knowledge*. London: Routledge.

Endemol (2004) Record viewing figures for UK Big Brother, Endemol press release, 1 June. www.endemol.com/newsitem.xml?id=335

Ericson, R.V., Baranek, P.M. and Chan, J.B.L. (1987) *Visualizing Deviance: A Study of News Organizations*. Milton Keynes: Open University Press.

Fabb, N. (1997) *Linguistics and Literature: Language in the Verbal Arts of the World*. Oxford: Blackwell.

Fairclough, N. (1992) *Discourse and Social Change*. Cambridge: Polity Press.

Fairclough, N. (1995) *Media Discourse*. London: Edward Arnold.

Fairclough, N. (1997) *Critical Discourse Analysis: The Critical Study of Language*. London: Longman.

Fairclough, N. (2000) *New Labour, New Language?* London: Routledge.

Fairclough, N. (2003) *Analysing Discourse: Textual Analysis for Social Research*. London: Routledge.

Ferguson, M. (1983) *Forever Feminine: Women's Magazines and the Cult of Femininity*. London: Heinemann.

Ferguson, R. (1998) *Representing 'Race': Ideology, Identity and the Media*. London: Arnold.

Feuer, J. (1992) *Genre Study and Television*. Chapel Hill, NC: University of North Carolina Press.

Feuer, J. (1995) Narrative form in American network television, in O. Boyd-Barrett and C. Newbold (eds) *Approaches to Media: A Reader*. London: Arnold.

Fishman, M. (1980) *Manufacturing the News*. Austin, TX: University of Texas Press.

Fiske, J. (1991) Television: polysemy and popularity, in R.K. Avery and D. Eason (eds) *Critical Perspectives on Media and Society*. London: Guilford.

Fitch, K. (2001) The ethnography of speaking: Sapir/Whorf, Hymes and Moerman, in M. Wetherell, S. Taylor and S.J. Yates (eds) *Discourse Theory and Practice: A Reader*. London: Sage.

Foucault, M. (1980) *The History of Sexuality,* Vol. 1: An Introduction. New York: Vintage.

Foucault, M. (1989) *The Archaeology of Knowledge*. London: Routledge.

Foucault, M. (1990) *The Will to Knowledge: The History of Sexuality*. London: Vintage Books.

Foucault, M. (1991) *Discipline and Punish: The Birth of the Prison*. Harmondsworth: Penguin.

Fowler, R. (1991) *Language in the News: Discourse and Ideology in the Press*. London: Routledge.

Fowler, R., Hodge, B., Kress, G. and Trew, T. (1979) *Language and Control*. London: Routledge and Kegan Paul.

Frazer, E. (1987) Teenage girls reading *Jackie, Media, Culture and Society*, 9: 407–25.

Friedman, J. (ed.) (2002) *Reality Squared: Televisual Discourse on the Real*. New Brunswick, NJ: Rutgers University Press.

Fuller, J. (1996) *News Values: Ideas for an Information Age.* Chicago: University of Chicago Press.

Gadamer, H.-G. (1979) *Truth and Method.* London: Sheed and Ward.

Garfinkel, H. (1967) *Studies in Ethnomethodology.* Englewood Cliffs, NJ: Prentice Hall.

Gee, J.P. (1999) *An Introduction to Discourse Analysis: Theory and Method.* London: Routledge.

Gergen, K.J. (1991) *The Saturated Self: Dilemmas of Identity in Contemporary Life.* New York: Basic Books.

Gergen, K.J. and Gergen, M. (1983) Narratives of the self, in T.R. Sarbin and K.E. Scheibe (eds) *Studies in Social Identity.* New York: Praeger.

Gibson, W. (1984) *Neuromancer.* London: Gollancz.

Giddens, A. (1984) *The Constitution of Society: Outline of the Theory of Structuration.* Berkeley, CA: University of California Press.

Giesler, M. and Pohlmann, M. (2002) The anthropology of file sharing: consuming Napster as a gift, *Napsterresearch.com.* www.napsterresearch.com/gift.htm (accessed 27 Sept. 2004).

Goddard, A. (1998) *The Language of Advertising.* London: Routledge.

Goffman, E. (1981) *Forms of Talk.* Oxford: Oxford University Press.

Gough-Yates, A. (2003) *Understanding Women's Magazines: Publishing, Markets and Readerships.* London: Routledge.

Gramsci, A. (1971) *Selections from the Prison Notebooks.* London: Lawrence and Wishart.

Greatbatch, D. (1998) Conversation analysis: neutralism in British news interviews, in A. Bell and P. Garrett (eds) *Approaches to Media Discourse.* Oxford: Blackwell.

Grice, H. P. (1975) Logic and conversation, in P. Cole and J.L. Morgan (eds) *Speech Acts.* New York: Academic Press.

Gripsrud, J. (2002) *Understanding Media Culture.* London: Arnold.

Guay, T. (1995) Web publishing paradigm. Information Technology Group project, April. hoshi.cic.sfu.ca/~guay/Paradigm/Paradigm.html (accessed 27 Sept. 2004).

Gubrium, J.F. and Holstein, J.A. (1995) Individual agency, the ordinary and postmodern life, *Sociological Quarterly,* 36(3): 555–70.

Gülich, E. and Quasthoff, U.M. (1985) Narrative analysis, in T. van Dijk (ed.) *Handbook of Discourse Analysis.* vol. 2: *Dimensions of Discourse.* London: Academic Press.

Gumperz, J.J. (1982) *Discourse Strategies.* Cambridge: Cambridge University Press.

Gumperz, J.J. and Levinson, S.C. (1996) *Rethinking Linguistic Relativity.* Cambridge: Cambridge University Press.

Hagart, J. (2003) The creaming of Manchester. www.subliminalworld.org/cream.htm (accessed 6 June 2004).

Hall, S. (1980) Race, articulation and societies structured in dominance, in UNESCO, *Sociological Theories: Race and Colonialism.* Paris: UNESCO.

Hall, S., Critcher, C., Jefferson, T., Clarke, J. and Roberts, B. (1978) *Policing the Crisis: Mugging, the State, and Law and Order.* London: Macmillan.

Halliday, M.A.K. (1994) *An Introduction to Functional Grammar.* London: Edward Arnold.

Hallin, D. (1987) The American news media: a critical theory perspective, in *Mass Communication Review Yearbook*. London: Sage.

Hartley, J. (1990) *Understanding News*. London: Methuen.

Hartley, J. (1999) *Uses of Television*. London: Routledge.

Harvey, D. (1996) *Justice, Nature and the Geography of Difference*. Oxford: Blackwell.

Heidegger, M. (1971) Language, in *Poetry, Language, Thought*. New York: Harper and Row.

Heritage, J. and Greatbatch, D. (1991) On the institutional character of institutional talk: the case of news interviews, in D. Boden and D.H. Zimmerman (eds) *Talk and Social Structure*. Cambridge: Polity Press.

Herring, S.C. (2001) Computer-mediated discourse, in D. Schiffrin, D. Tannen and H.E. Hamilton (eds) *The Handbook of Discourse Analysis*. Oxford: Blackwell.

Herring, S.C., Kouper, I., Scheidt, L.A. and Wright, E.L. (2004) Women and children last: the discursive construction of weblogs, in L. Gurak, S. Antonijevic, L. Johnson, C. Ratliff, and J. Reyman (eds) *Into the Blogosphere: Rhetoric, Community, and Culture of Weblogs*. Electronic book, University of Minnesota. blog.lib.umn.edu/blogosphere.

Hill, A. (2000) Fearful and safe: audience response to British reality programming, *Television and New Media*, 1(2): 193–213.

Hodge, R. and Kress, G. (1988) *Social Semiotics*. Cambridge: Polity Press.

Hodge, R. and Kress, G. (1993) *Language as Ideology*. London: Routledge.

Hoey, M. (2001) *Textual Interaction*. London: Routledge.

Holmes, S. and Jermyn, D. (2004) Introduction: understanding reality TV, in S. Holmes and D. Jermyn (eds) *Understanding Reality Television*. London: Routledge.

Hughes, D.M. (1999) Pimps and predators on the Internet: globalizing sexual exploitation of women and children, *Coalition Against Trafficking in Women*. www.uri.edu/artsci/wms/hughes/pprep.htm.

Hutchby, I. (1996) Power in discourse: the case of arguments on a British talk radio show, *Discourse and Society*, 7(4): 481–97.

Hutchby, I. and Wooffitt, R. (1998) *Conversation Analysis: An Introduction*. Cambridge: Polity Press.

Hymes, D. (1972) Models of interaction in language and social life, in J.J. Gumperz and D. Hymes (eds) *Directions in Sociolinguistics: The Ethnography of Communication*. New York: Holt, Rinehart and Winston.

Iser, W. (1978) *The Act of Reading: A Theory of Aesthetic Response*. Baltimore, MD: Johns Hopkins University Press.

Itzkoff, D. (2002) Lad no more: my escape from *Maxim, New York Press*, vol.15(3) (June). www.nypress.com/print.cfm?content_id=6365.

Jackson, A. (n.d.) Art. www.alisonjackson.com/art2.htm (accessed 30 Sept. 2004).

Jackson, P., Stevenson, N. and Brooks, K. (2001) *Making Sense of Men's Magazines*. Cambridge: Polity Press.

Jaworski, A. and Coupland, N. (eds) (1999) *The Discourse Reader*. London: Routledge.

Jensen, J. (1999) Interactivity: tracking a new concept in media and communication studies, in P.A. Mayer (ed.) *Computer Media and Communication*. Oxford: Oxford University Press.

Jensen, K.B. (1995) *The Social Semiotics of Mass Communication*. London: Sage.

Jermyn, D. (2004) This is about real people: video technologies, actuality and affect in the television crime appeal, in S. Holmes and D. Jermyn (eds) *Understanding Reality Television*. London: Routledge.

Johnson, R. (1986) The story so far: and other transformations, in D. Punter (ed.) *Introduction to Contemporary Cultural Studies*. London: Longman.

Jones, J. (2003) Show your real face: a fan study of the UK 'Big Brother' transmissions (2001, 2002, 2003), *New Media and Society*, 5(3): 400–21.

Katz, J. (1987) What makes crime 'news'? *Media, Culture and Society*, 9: 47–75.

Kellner, D. (1989) Baudrillard: A new McLuhan? *Essays*. www.gseis.ucla.edu/faculty/kellner/flash/kellneraug8.swf (accessed 16 Sept. 2004).

Kellner, D. (1995) *Media Culture: Cultural Studies, Identity and Politics between the Modern and the Postmodern*. London: Routledge.

Kibble-White, J. (2002) And the beat goes on: Jack Kibble-White on 'The Bill' and Police ensemble dramas, *Off the Telly 2004* (August). www.offthetelly.co.uk/drama/cops.htm.

Klein, N. (2000) *No Logo: Taking Aim at the Brand Bullies*. New York: Picador.

Kress, G. (1983) Linguistic and ideological transformations in news reporting, in H. Davis and P. Walton (eds) *Language, Image, Media*. Oxford: Basil Blackwell.

Kress, G. (2003) *Literacy in the New Media Age*. London: Routledge.

Kress, G. and Van Leeuwen, T. (1996) *Reading Images: The Language of Visual Design*. London: Routledge.

Kress, G. and Van Leeuwen, T. (2001) *Multimodal Discourse: Modes and Media of Contemporary Communication*. London: Arnold.

Kress, G. and Van Leeuwen, T. (2002) Colour as a semiotic mode: notes for a grammar of colour, *Visual Communication*, 1(3): 343–68.

Kuiper, K. (1996) *Smooth Talkers: The Linguistic Performance of Auctioneers and Sportscasters*. Mahwah, NJ: Lawrence Erlbaum Associates.

Labov, W. (1972) The study of language in its social context, in P.P. Giglioli (ed.) *Language and Social Context*. Harmondsworth: Penguin.

Labov, W. (1997) Some further steps in narrative analysis, *Journal of Narrative and Life History*, 7(1–4): 395–415. www.ling.upenn.edu/~wlabov/sfs.html.

Labov, W. (1999) The transformation of experience in narrative, in A. Jaworski and N. Coupland (eds) *The Discourse Reader*. London: Routledge.

Labov, W. and Waletzky, J. (1967) Narrative analysis: oral versions of personal experience, in J. Helm (ed.) *Essays on the Verbal and Visual Arts*. Seattle: University of Washington Press.

Lang, G.E. and Lang, K. (1983) *The Battle for Public Opinion: The President, the Press and the Polls during Watergate*. New York: Columbia University Press.

Lasica, J.D. (2001) J.D.'s web watch: weblogs: a new source of news, *Online Journalism Review*, 1 May. ojr.usc.edu/content/story.cfm?request-588 (accessed 8 July 2001).

Latham, A. (1998) Motson in a hole. *Blind, Stupid and Desperate: Watford FC Site*. www.bsad.org/articles/motson.html (accessed 6 Oct. 2004).

Leech, G.N. (1983) *Principles of Pragmatics*. London: Longman.

Leiss, W., Kline, S. and Jholly, S. (1986) *Social Communication in Advertising: Persons, Products and Images of Wellbeing*. London: Methuen.

LeMahieu, D.L. (1988) *A Culture for Democracy: Mass Communication and the Cultivated Mind in Britain Between the Wars*. Oxford: Oxford University Press.

Lemke, J. (2003) Traversing discursive worlds: spaces, places, pacing and timing in discursive activity. Paper presented at DeXUS Summer Institute of Discourse Studies, Aalborg, 18–23 August. www-personal.umich.edu/~jaylemke/papers/DeXUS 2003.htm (accessed 3 Apr. 2004).

Lippmann, W. (1922) *Public Opinion*. New York: Macmillan.

Livingstone, S. and Lievrouw, L. (2002) Introduction: the social shaping and consequences of ICTs, in S. Livingstone and L. Lievrouw (eds) *Handbook of New Media: Social Shaping and Consequences of ICTs*. London: Sage.

Livingstone, S. and Lunt, P. (1994) *Talk on Television: Audience Participation and Public Debate*. London: Routledge.

Lord, A.B. (1960) *The Singer of Tales*. Cambridge, MA: Harvard University Press.

Lowe and Partners Worldwide (2003) New 'Diet Coke®' TV ad. *Press Releases*. www.loweworldwide.com/displayData.html/GPressReleases2003NewDietCokeAd 26.06.03.pdf?type=pdf&id=111 (accessed 17 June 2004).

Luke, A. (2001) Introduction: theory and practice in critical discourse analysis. www.gseis.ucla.edu/faculty/kellner/ed270/Luke/SAHA6.html (accessed 18 July 2004).

Lury, C. (1996) *Consumer Culture*. Cambridge: Polity Press.

MacDonald, M. (1995) *Representing Women: Myths of Femininity in the Popular Media*. London: Arnold.

MacDonald, M. (2003) *Exploring Media Discourse*. London: Arnold.

Machin, D. and Thornborrow, J. (2003) Branding and discourse: the case of *Cosmopolitan*, *Discourse and Society*, 14(4): 453–71.

Machin, D. and Van Leeuwen, T. (2004) Global media: generic homogeneity and discursive diversity, *Continuum*, 18(1): 99–120.

Mannheim, K. (1936) *Ideology and Utopia: An Introduction to the Sociology of Knowledge*. New York: Harcourt, Brace and Co.

Martin, J.R. and Rose, D. (2003) *Working with Discourse: Meaning Beyond the Clause*. London: Continuum.

Martz, L. (1999) Holland's 'unreal world', *wired*, 28 September. www.wired.com/news/culture/0,1284,31528,00.html.

Marx, K. and Engels, F. (1997–8) Ruling class and ruling ideas. *The German Ideology*. Marx/Engels Internet Archive. www.ex.ac.uk/Projects/meia/Archive/1845-GI/ruling.htm (accessed 16 May 2004).

Massey, B. and Levy, M.R. (1999) Interactivity, online journalism, and English-language web newspapers in Asia, *Journalism and Mass Communication Quarterly*, 76(1): 138–51.

Matheson, D. (2004a) Weblogs and the epistemology of the news: some trends in online journalism, *New Media and Society*, 6(4): 443–68.

Matheson, D. (2004b) Negotiating claims to journalism: webloggers' orientation to news genres, *Convergence*, 10(4): 33–54.

Maybin, J. (2001) Language, struggle and voice: The Bakhtin/Vološinov writings, in M. Wetherell, S. Taylor and S.J. Yates (eds) *Discourse Theory and Practice: A Reader*. London: Sage.

McCarthy, D, Jones, R.L. and Potrac, P. (2003) Constructing images and interpreting realities: the case of the black soccer player on television, *International Review for the Sociology of Sport*, 38(2): 217–38.

McKee, A. (2003) RE: (csaa-forum) re:ideology. csaa-forum@lists.myspinach.org. (accessed 26 June 2003).

McLuhan, M. (1964) *Understanding Media: The Extensions of Man*. London: Routledge and Kegan Paul.

McMillan, S.J. (2002) A four-part model of cyber-interactivity: some cyber-places are more interactive than others, *New Media and Society*, 4(2): 271–91.

Meinhof, U.H. and Smith, J. (2000) *Intertextuality and the Media*. Manchester: Manchester University Press.

Miles, R. (1989) *Racism*. London: Routledge.

Miller, J. (n.d.) Why hyperfiction didn't work. *M/C Reviews*. reviews.media-culture.org.au/sections.php?op=viewarticle&artid=126 (accessed 29 Oct. 2004).

Montgomery, M. (1995) *An Introduction to Language and Society*. London: Methuen.

Montgomery, M. (1999a) On ideology, *Discourse and Society*, 10 (3): 451–4.

Montgomery, M. (1999b) Speaking sincerely: public reactions to the death of Diana, *Language and Literature*, 8(1): 5–33.

National Union of Journalists (NUJ) (2003) NUJ guidelines on reporting the traveller community. www.nuj.org.uk/inner.php?docid=205 (accessed 23 May 2004).

New Zealand Herald (1993) Holmes' comments insulting, says Race Relations Commissioner, 24 September. www.nzherald.co.nz/storydisplay.cfm?storyID=3525205&thesection=news&thesubsection=general

Norton-Taylor, R. and Watt, N. (2003) The language of war, *Guardian* (UK), 14–28 March. www.guardian.co.uk/Iraq/Story/0,2763,914093,00.html.

Ochs, E. (1997) Narrative, in T. van Dijk (ed.) *Discourse as Structure and Process*. London: Sage.

O'Donnell, H. (1994) Mapping the mythical: a geopolitics of national sporting stereotypes, *Discourse and Society*, 5(3): 345–80.

O'Donnell, H. (2003) Fitba crazy? *Saturday Super Scoreboard* and the dialectics of political debate, in A. Bernstein and N. Blain (eds) *Sport, Media, Culture: Global and Local Dimensions*. London: Frank Cass.

Olson, S.R. (2004) Hollywood planet: global media and the competitive advantage of narrative transparency, in R.C. Allen and A. Hill (eds) *The Television Studies Reader*. London: Routledge.

Palmer, G. (2004) The new you: class and transformation in lifestyle television, in S. Holmes and D. Jermyn (eds) *Understanding Reality Television*. London: Routledge.

Pateman, T. (1990) How is understanding an advertisement possible? *Selected Works.* www.selectedworks.co.uk/advertisement.html (accessed 11 June 2004).

PBS (Public Broadcasting Service) (2003) Frontline: the persuaders: interview with Kevin Roberts, 15 December. www.pbs.org/wgbh/pages/frontline/shows/persuaders/interviews/roberts.html (accessed 5 Jan. 2005).

Petrovic, D. (2004) SONY PlayStation® 2 commercial – fun anyone? *analogik.com.* analogik.com/article_ps2.asp (accessed 1 June 1994).

Philo, G. (2001) An unseen world: how the media portrays the poor, *The Courier (UNESCO)*, November. www.unesco.org/courier/2001_11/uk/medias.htm.

Pinker, S. (1994) *The Language Instinct: How the Mind Creates Language.* New York: Harper Collins.

Postman, N. (1993) *Technopoly: The Surrender of Culture to Technology.* New York: Vintage Books.

Potter, J. (2001) Wittgenstein and Austin, in M. Wetherell, S. Taylor and S.J. Yates (eds) *Discourse Theory and Practice: A Reader.* London: Sage.

Potter, J. and Wetherell, M. (1992) *Mapping the Language of Racism: Discourse and the Legitimation of Exploitation.* New York: Columbia University Press.

Potter, J. and Wetherell, M. (2001) Unfolding discourse analysis, in M. Wetherell, S. Taylor and S.J. Yates (eds) *Discourse Theory and Practice: A Reader.* London: Sage.

Propp, V. (1968) *Morphology of the Folk Tale.* Austin, TX: University of Texas Press.

Rafaeli, S. (1988) Interactivity: from new media to communication, in R.P. Hawkins, J.M. Wiemann and S. Pingree (eds) *Advancing Communication Science: Merging Mass and Interpersonal Process.* Newbury Park, CA: Sage.

Rainville, R.E. and McCormick, E. (1977) Extent of covert racial prejudice in pro football announcers speech, *Journalism Quarterly*, 54: 20–6.

Rayner, J. (1995) Revenge on the air Virgin 1215, *Guardian*, 30 January.

Reah, D. (2002) *The Language of Newspapers.* London: Routledge.

Riley, P., Keough, C., Christiansen, T., Meilich, O. and Pierson, J. (1998) Community or colony: the case of online newspapers and the web, *Journal of Computer-Mediated Communication*, 4(1). www.ascusc.org/jcmc/vol4/issue1/keough.html.

Rimmon-Kenan, S. (1983) *Narrative Fiction: Contemporary Poetics.* London: Routledge.

Robinson, D. (1997) Linguistics and language, in M. Groden and M. Kreiswirth (eds) *The Johns Hopkins Guide to Literary Theory and Criticism.* Baltimore, MD: Johns Hopkins University Press.

Rose, B. (2003) TV genres re-viewed: introduction, *Journal of Popular Film and Television*, 1(31): 2–4.

Rowe, D., McKay, J. and Miller, T. (1998) Come together: sport, nationalism, and the media, in L.A. Wenner (ed.) *Mediasport.* London: Routledge.

Sabo, D. and Jansen, S.C. (1992) Images of men in sport media: the social reproduction of the gender order, in S. Craig (ed.) *Men, Masculinity and the Media.* Newbury Park, CA: Sage.

Said, E. (1978) *Orientalism.* London: Routledge and Kegan Paul.

Scannell, P. (ed.) (1991a) *Broadcast Talk.* London: Sage.

Scannell, P. (1991b) Introduction: the relevance of talk, in P. Scannell (ed.) *Broadcast Talk*. London: Sage.

Scannell, P. (1992) Public service broadcasting and modern public life, in P. Scannell, P. Schlesinger and C. Sparks (eds) *Culture and Power: A Media, Culture and Society Reader*. London: Sage.

Scannell, P. and Cardiff, D. (1991) *A Social History of British Broadcasting*, vol. 1: *Serving the Nation: 1922–39*. Oxford: Blackwell.

Schegloff, E.A. (1999) 'Schegloff's texts' as Billig's data: a critical reply, *Discourse and Society*, 10: 558–72.

Schegloff, E.A. and Sacks, H. (1973) Opening and closing, *Semiotica*, 8: 289–327.

Schirato, T. and Yell, S. (2000) *Communication and Cultural Literacy: An Introduction*. St Leonards, NSW: Allen and Unwin.

Schlesinger, P. (1987) *Putting 'Reality' Together: BBC News*. London: Methuen.

Schultz, T. (1999) Interactive options in online journalism: a content analysis of 100 US newspapers, *Journal of Computer-Mediated Communication*, 5(1). www.ascusc.org/jcmc/vol5/issue1/schultz.html.

Shaw, R.B. (1997) *Trust in the Balance: Building Successful Organizations on Results, Integrity, and Concern*. San Francisco: Jossey-Bass.

Shoemaker, P.J. and Reese, S.D. (1996) *Mediating the Message: Theories of Influence on Mass Media Content*. White Plains, NY: Longman.

Slembrouk, S. (2003) What is meant by 'discourse analysis?'. bank.rug.ac.be/da/da.htm#ca (accessed 22 Sept. 2004).

Slevin, J. (2000) *The Internet and Society*. Cambridge: Polity Press.

Sperber, D. and Wilson, D. (1986) *Relevance: Communication and Cognition*. Cambridge, MA: Harvard University Press.

Stubbs, M. (1983) *Discourse Analysis: The Sociolinguistic Analysis of Natural Language*. Oxford: Basil Blackwell.

Stubbs, M. (2001) *Words and Phrases: Corpus Studies of Lexical Semantics*. Cambridge: Blackwell.

Sunstein, C. (2002) *Republic.com*. Princeton, NJ: Princeton University Press.

Swales, J. (1990) *Genre Analysis: English in Academic and Research Settings*. Cambridge: Cambridge University Press.

Talbot, M. (1992) The construction of gender in a teenage magazine, in N. Fairclough (ed.) *Critical Language Awareness*. London: Longman.

Talbot, M. (1997) 'Randy fish boss branded a stinker': coherence and the construction of masculinities in a British tabloid newspaper, in S. Johnson and U.H. Meinhof (eds) *Language and Masculinity*. Oxford: Blackwell.

Tedder, R. (1999) A magazine's neat summation of the product, *Robert's Radio Pleasure*, 24 November. www.robert-tedder.org.uk/radio/saddest.htm (accessed 2 Nov. 2004).

Thomas, J. (1995) *Meaning in Interaction: An Introduction to Pragmatics*. New York: Longman.

Thompson, J.B. (1984) *Studies in the Theory of Ideology*. Cambridge: Polity Press.

Thompson, J.B. (1995) *Media and Modernity: A Social Theory of the Media*. Cambridge: Polity Press.

Thornborrow, J. (2001a) Authenticating talk: building public identities in audience participation broadcasting, *Discourse Studies*, 3(4): 459–79.

Thornborrow, J. (2001b) Questions, control and the organization of talk in calls to a radio phone-in, *Discourse Studies*, 3(1): 119–43.

Threadgold, T. and Kress, G. (1988) Towards a social theory of genre, *Southern Review*, 21: 215–43.

Thwaites, T., Davis, L. and Mules, W. (2002) *Introducing Media and Cultural Studies: A Semiotic Approach*. Houndsmills: Palgrave.

Tihanov, G. (2000) *The Master and the Slave: Lukács, Bakhtin, and the Ideas of their Time*. Oxford: Clarendon Press.

Tolson, A. (ed.) (2001) *Television Talk Shows: Discourse, Performance, Spectacle*. Mahwah, NJ: Erlbaum.

Tracy, K. and Coupland, N. (1990) Multiple goals in discourse: an overview of issues, in K. Travy and N. Coupland (eds) *Multiple Goals in Discourse*. Clevedon: Multilingual Matters.

Trew, T. (1979) Theory and ideology at work, in R. Fowler, B. Hodge, G. Kress and T. Trew (eds) *Language and Control*. London: Routledge.

Turkle, S. (1995) *Life on the Screen: Identity in the Age of the Internet*. New York: Simon and Schuster.

Turner, G. (2004) *Understanding Celebrity*. London: Sage.

Tyers, S. (2003) Double Take. *Off the Telly*. www.offthetelly.co.uk/reviews/2003/doubletake.htm (accessed 30 Sept. 2004).

van Dijk, T. (1985) Structures of news in the press, in T. van Dijk (ed.) *Discourse and Communication: New Approaches to the Analysis of Mass Media Discourse and Communication*. Berlin: Walter de Gruyter.

van Dijk, T. (1988a) *News as Discourse*. Hillsdale, NJ: Lawrence Erlbaum.

van Dijk, T. (1988b) Semantics of a press panic: the Tamil invasion, *European Journal of Communication*, 3: 167–87.

van Dijk, T. (1991) *Racism and the Press*. London: Routledge.

van Dijk, T. (1993) *Elite Discourse and Racism*. London: Sage.

van Dijk, T. (1997) The study of discourse, in T. van Dijk (ed.) *Discourse as Structure and Process: Discourse Studies, A Multidisciplinary Introduction*. London: Sage.

van Dijk, T. (1998) *Ideology: A Multidisciplinary Study*. London: Sage.

van Dijk, T. (1999) Discourse and the denial of racism, in A. Jaworski and N. Coupland (eds) *The Discourse Reader*. London: Routledge.

Van Leeuwen, T. (1999) *Speech, Music, Sound*. London: Macmillan.

van Sterkenburg, J. and Knoppers, A. (2004) Dominant discourses about race and gender in sport practice and performance, *International Review for the Sociology of Sport*, 39(3): 301–21.

Vološinov, V.N. (1986) *Marxism and the Philosophy of Language*. Cambridge, MA: Harvard University Press.

Wang, Z. (2004) It's pride of Asia, Liu Xiang says, *Xinhuanet*. 28 August. news.xinhuanet.com/english/2004-08/28/content_1902300.htm (accessed 10 Oct. 2004).

Ward, M. (2002) *Journalism Online*. Oxford: Focal Press.

Wateridge, S. and Donaghey, B. (1999) Do not underestimate the power of the endline! Reviewing the value of endlines as branding tools, *The Research Business International*. www.trbi.com/papers.htm# (accessed 17 June 2004).

Watson, N. (1997) Why we argue about virtual community: a case study of the phish.net fan community, in S. Jones (ed.) *Virtual Culture: Identity and Communication in Cybersociety*. London: Sage.

Webb, J., Schirato, T. and Danaher, G. (2002) *Understanding Bourdieu*. Crows Nest, NSW: Allen and Unwin.

Welch, M. (2003) Emerging alternatives: blogworld: the new amateur journalists weigh in, *Columbia Journalism Review*, (5). www.cjr.org/issues/2003/5/blog-welch.asp.

Welch, P.D. (2003) Human diversity and race. www.siu.edu/~anthro/welch/Anth104/ Human diversity and race.pdf (accessed 6 Oct. 2004).

Wellman, B., Quan-Haase, A., Boase, J., Chen, W., Hampton, K., Isla de Diaz, I. and Miyata, K. (2003) The social affordances of the Internet for networked individualism, *Journal of Computer-Mediated Communication*, 8(3). www.ascusc.org/jcmc/ vol8/issue3/wellman.html.

Wetherell, M. and Potter, J. (1992) *Mapping the Language of Racism: Discourse and the Legitimation of Exploitation*. New York: Columbia University Press.

Wetherell, M., Taylor, S. and Yates, S.J. (eds) (2001) *Discourse Theory and Practice: A Reader*. London: Sage.

White, P.R. (1995) News and story telling: generic structure, Telling media tales: the news story as rhetoric, unpublished PhD thesis, University of Sydney.

Williams, K. (1998) *Get Me a Murder a Day: A History of Mass Communication in Britain*. London: Arnold.

Williams, R. (1961) *The Long Revolution*. London: Chatto and Windus.

Williams, R. (1974) *Television: Technology and Cultural Form*. London: Fontana.

Williamson, J. (1978) *Decoding Advertisements: Ideology and Meaning in Advertising*. London: Boyars.

Winship, J. (1987) *Inside Women's Magazines*. London: Pandora.

Wittgenstein, L. (1922) *Tractatus Logico-Philosophicus*. London: Routledge and Kegan Paul.

Wittgenstein, L. (1953) *Philosophical Investigations*. Oxford: Blackwell.

Wodak, R. (1996) *Disorders of Discourse*. London: Longman.

Wodak, R. (2001) What critical discourse analysis is all about, in R. Wodak and M. Meyer (eds) *Methods of Critical Discourse Analysis*. London: Sage.

Wright, W. (1995) Myth and meaning, in O. Boyd-Barrett and C. Newbold (eds) *Approaches to Media: A Reader*. London: Arnold.

Young, K. (1999) Narrative embodiments: enclaves of the self in the realm of medicine, in A. Jaworski and N. Coupland (eds) *The Discourse Reader*. London: Routledge.

INDEX

JOURNALISM
CRITICAL ISSUES

Stuart Allan (ed)

This new book explores essential themes in news and journalism studies. It brings together an exciting selection of original essays which engage with the most significant topics, debates and controversies in this fast-growing field. Topics include:

- Journalism's role in a democracy
- Source dynamics in news production
- Journalism ethics
- Sexism and racism in the news
- Tabloidization, scandals and celebrity
- Reporting conflict, terrorism and war
- The future of investigative journalism

The book is written in a lively manner designed to invite discussion by identifying key questions around a critical issue. Each chapter assesses where journalism is today, its strengths and its challenges, and highlights ways to improve upon it for tomorrow. Essential reading for students and researchers in the fields of news and journalism, media studies, cultural studies, sociology and communication studies.

Includes essays by

Stuart Allan, Alison Anderson, Olga Guedes Bailey, Steven Barnett, Oliver Boyd-Barrett, Michael Bromley, Cynthia Carter, Simon Cottle, Chas Critcher, Matthew David, Máire Messenger Davies, Bob Franklin, Robert A. Hackett, Ramaswami Harindranath, Ian Hutchby, Richard Keeble, Justin Lewis, Minelle Mahtani, P. David Marshall, Brian McNair, Martin Montgomery, Alan Petersen, Susanna Hornig Priest, Jane Rhodes, Karen Ross, David Rowe, Prasun Sonwalkar, Linda Steiner, Howard Tumber, Ingrid Volkmer, Karin Wahl-Jorgensen, Barbie Zelizer.

Contents

*Contributors – Introduction: Hidden in plain sight: journalism's critical issues – **PART I:** Journalism's histories – **PART II:** Journalism and democracy – **PART III:** Journalism's realities – **PART IV:** Journalism and the politics of othering – **PART V:** Journalism and the public interest*

408pp   0 335 21475 4 (Paperback)   0 335 21484 3 (Hardback)

MEDIATIZED CONFLICT

Simon Cottle

We live in increasingly conflict-ridden times. We also live in increasingly mediatized times. *Mediatized Conflict* explores the powered dynamics, contested representations and consequential impacts of media conflict reporting in the contemporary era. It examines how the media today do not simply 'report' or 'represent' diverse situations of conflict, but actively 'enact' and 'perform' them.

This important book brings together the latest research findings and theoretical discussions to develop an encompassing, multidimensional and sophisticated understanding of the social complexities, political dynamics and cultural forms of mediatized conflicts in the world today.

Case-studies discussed include anti-war protests; 'dissent events' and anti-globalization demonstrations; moral panics and mediatized public crises centring on issues of 'race' and racism; war journalism and peace journalism; risk society and the environment; the politics of outrage and terror spectacle post 9/11; identity politics and the politics of recognition and reconciliation; and humanitarian action and media interventions in traumatized societies.

Contents

Mediatized Conflict in the World Today – Mediatized Conflict: Getting a Theoretical Fix – Reporting Demonstrations and Protest: Public Sphere(s), Public Screens – Moving stories of 'Race' and Racism: Moral Panics to Mediatized Public Crises – War Journalism: Disembodied and Embedded – Peace Journalism: Media, Hopes and Prayers – Media, Risk Society and the Environment: A Different Story? – Journalism After 9/11: Terror Spectacle and the Politics of Outrage – Identity Politics: Media Recognition and Reconciliation – Humanitarian Action and Media in Traumatized Societies – Mediatized Conflicts: Conclusions

224pp   0 335 21452 5 (Paperback)   0 335 21453 3 (Hardback)

A CRITICAL AND CULTURAL THEORY READER

Antony Easthope and Kate McGowan (eds).

Praise for the first edition

"The selection is judicious and valuably supplemented by thorough commentaries that contextualise and clarify the debates and issues and the importance of each excerpt. Though today there may be many readers in and around cultural and media studies, Easthope and McGowan's remains vital . . . " *THES*

This Reader introduces the key readings in critical and cultural theory. It guides students through the tradition of thought, from Saussure's early writings on language to contemporary commentary on world events by theorists such as Baudrillard and Žižek. The readings are grouped according to six thematic sections: Semiology; Ideology; Subjectivity; Difference; Gender and Race; Postmodernism.

The second and expanded edition of this highly successful Reader reflects the growing diversity of the field.

* Features thirteen new essays, including writing by Homi Bhabha, Simone de Beauvoir, Franz Fanon and Judith Butler
* With a general introduction as well as useful introductions to each of the thematic sections
* Including summaries of each of the readings – invaluable for students and lecturers

Key reading for areas of study including cultural studies, critical theory, literature, linguistics, English, media studies, communication studies, cultural history, sociology, gender studies, visual arts, film and architecture.

Essays by

Louis Althusser, Roland Barthes, Jean Baudrillard, Homi K. Bhabha, Judith Butler, Hélène Cixous, Simone de Beauvoir, Ferdinand de Saussure, Jacques Derrida, Umberto Eco, Frederick Engels, Franz Fanon, Michel Foucault, Sigmund Freud, Julia Kristeva, Jacques Lacan, Jean-François Lyotard, Colin MacCabe, Pierre Macherey, Karl Marx, Kobena Mercer, Laura Mulvey, Rajeswari Sunder Rajan, Edward Said, Slavoj Žižek.

304pp   0 335 21355 3 (Paperback)   0 335 21356 1 (Hardback)
This edition not available in the USA and Canada

MEDIA TALK
CONVERSATION ANALYSIS AND THE STUDY OF BROADCASTING

Ian Hutchby

Media Talk provides an accessible introduction to the analysis of the spoken word by examining linguistic and discursive aspects of broadcast media.

Beginning with the observation that talk is central to all genres of radio and television, Ian Hutchby examines the forms of speech used by broadcasters as their primary means of communicating with audiences. He looks at a range of media forms and genres, including televised audience debates, confrontational TV talk shows such as Oprah Winfrey and Ricki Lake, open-line talk radio shows, advice-giving broadcasts, news interviews and political panel discussions.

Hutchby argues that the study of talk provides insights into the very nature of mass communication, and invites the reader into further consideration of a range of important issues, such as the relationship between broadcasters and audiences, and the public role of media output.

The book not only describes the role of media talk but also provides detailed examples of analytical tools. It is key reading for students on courses in language and the media, media discourse, communication and cultural studies.

Contents
Discovering Media Talk – Analysing Media Talk: Language, Discourse and Interaction – Audience Participation Television and Public Discourse – From Private to Public: Opinions and Arguments on Talk Radio – Talking – Politics in the Broadcast Agora: Orchestrating Opinions and Alignments – Media Talk, Authenticity and Controversy – Transcription Conventions – References – Index

192pp   0 335 20995 5 Paperback   0 335 20996 3 Hardback

CITIZENS OR CONSUMERS?
WHAT THE MEDIA TELL US ABOUT POLITICAL PARTICIPATION

Justin Lewis, Sanna Inthorn and Karin Wahl-Jorgensen

"Written with great verve, passion and unswerving clarity, *Citizens or Consumers?* promises to become an instant classic in the study of the failings – and the still untapped promise – of the news media to further democracy."
Susan J. Douglas, Catherine Neafie Kellogg Professor and Chair, Department of Communication Studies, The University of Michigan

"The two great duelists for our attention – citizens and consumers – are locked in a struggle for the future of democracy. *Citizens or Consumers?* offers its readers a sharp lesson in how the media highlight and distort that struggle. It's the kind of lesson we all need."
Toby Miller, University of California at Riverside, author of *Cultural Citizenship*.

Most of us learn what we know about politics and politicians from the news media – so what do the media tell us about our role as citizens in a democracy? Are we encouraged to be active, informed citizens, contributing to public discussion and debate? Or is politics presented as something that is irrelevant to our daily lives?

In recent years there has been much concern about the decline in civic participation, especially among young people, in both Britain and the United States. At the same time we have seen decreasing budgets for serious domestic and international news and current affairs, amidst widespread accusations of a "dumbing down" in the coverage of public affairs. This book enters the debate by asking whether the news media have played a role in producing a passive citizenry, and, if so, what might be done about it?

Based on the largest study to date of media coverage of public opinion and citizenship in Britain and the United States, this book advocates a notion of democracy that values and depends upon active and engaged forms of citizenship.

Contents
Introduction: Public opinion, political participation and the news media – Meet the public: an overview of the ways citizenship is represented in British and US news – How engaged is public opinion in news coverage? – The news media and opinion polls – The vox populi: out of the mouths of babes and citizens – Speaking off the cuff: what journalists say about us – The representation of citizenship in the coverage of September 11th and its aftermath – The citizen as consumer: how the media might promote active citizenship – Index

224pp   0 335 21555 6 (Paperback)   0 335 21556 4 (Hardback)